See Page 102

OREGON STATE PARKS

A Complete Recreation Guide

OREGON STATE PARKS

A Complete Recreation Guide

JAN BANNAN

THE
MOUNTAINEERS

 Published by
The Mountaineers
1011 SW Klickitat Way
Seattle, Washington 98134

Published simultaneously in Canada by Douglas & McIntyre, Ltd., 1615 Venables Street, Vancouver, B.C. V5L 2H1

Published simultaneously in Great Britain by Cordee, 3a DeMontfort Street, Leicester, England, LE1 7HD

5 4 3
5 4 3 2 1

Manufactured in the United States of America

Edited by Meredith Waring
Maps by Word Graphics
All photographs by the author
Cover design by Watson Graphics
Book design, typesetting and layout by The Mountaineers Books

Cover photographs: *top left,* Smith Rock State Park; *top right,* beach strollers and Haystack Rock from Ecola State Park; *bottom left,* Wizard Island and Crater Lake, Crater Lake National Park; *bottom right,* Multnomah Falls, Bridal Veil Falls State Park
Frontispiece: View south from Cape Sebastian State Park

Library of Congress Cataloging-in-Publication Data
Bannan, Jan Gumprecht.
    Oregon State parks : a complete recreation guide / Jan Bannan.
        p.   cm.
    Includes index.
    ISBN 0-89886-380-5
    1. Parks--Oregon--Recreational use. 2. Parks--Oregon--Directories. I. Title.
    GV191.42.O7B36   1993
    796.5'09795--dc20   93-41780
                                                              CIP

CONTENTS

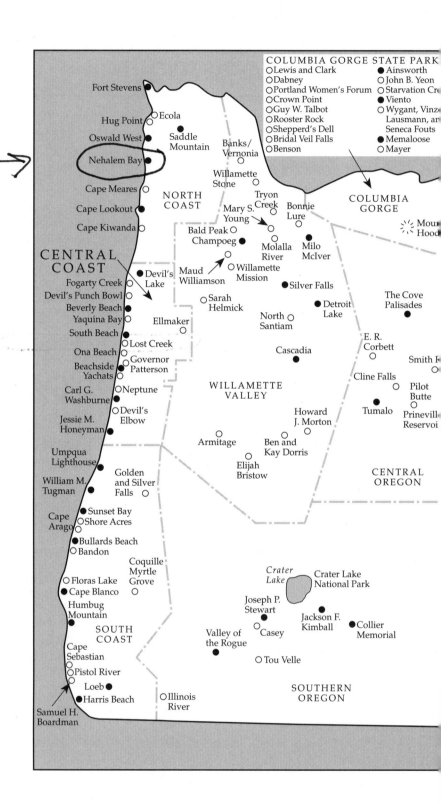

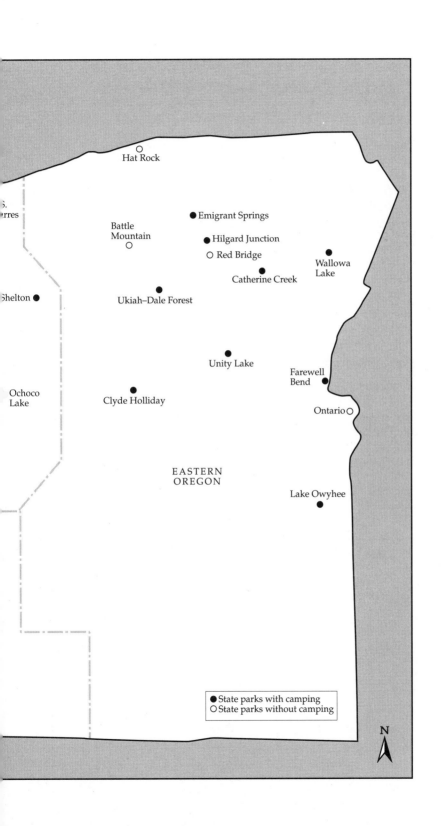

Hat Rock ○

○ ·rres

Battle
Mountain ○

● Emigrant Springs

● Hilgard Junction

○ Red Bridge

● Wallowa
Lake

● Catherine Creek

●
Ukiah–Dale Forest

Shelton ●

●
Unity Lake

Farewell ●
Bend

Ochoco
Lake

●
Clyde Holliday

Ontario ○

EASTERN
OREGON

Lake Owyhee
●

● State parks with camping
○ State parks without camping

N

Picnic area 🪧	Scenic attraction/viewpoint 📷	Boat launch
Campground ▲	Forested area/reserve	Building ■
Hiker/biker camp	Hiking 𝕏	Parking area
Horse camp	Horseback riding	Cemetery †
Lighthouse	Bicycling	Bridge

Trail (hiking, equestrian
or bicycling) - - - - - - - - - - - - - - - -
Unpaved road - - - - - - - - - - - - - - -
Paved road ————
Highway ═══════
Cliffs/bluffs
Mountain peak ▲

River/stream
Waterfall
Body of water
Dock or pier
Sand/sand dunes
Marsh

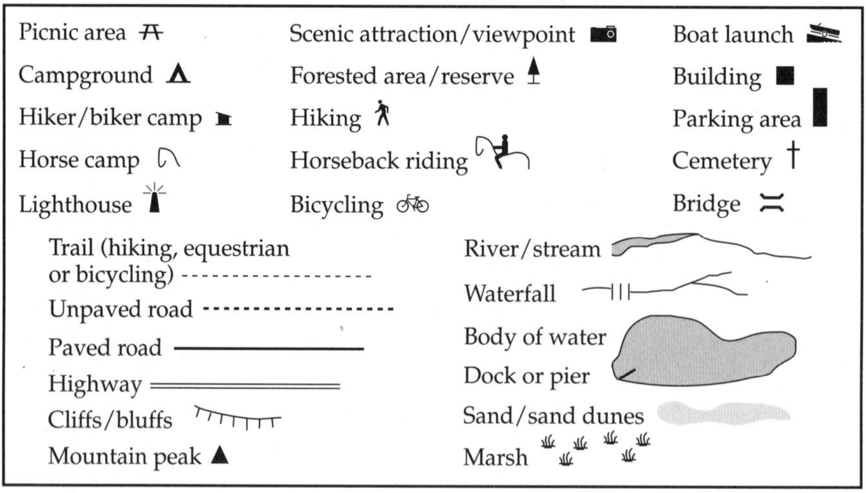

INTRODUCTION

A The landscapes of Oregon are diverse and scenic. They surpass imagi-
I nation; they are the essence of nature at its most creative. One can see
and encounter mountain ranges that pierce the clouds, a magnificent gorge
carved by the Columbia River, the Willamette Valley that lured pioneers,
renowned forests, the solitude of the high desert, a profusion of rivers and
lakes, and the wondrous edge of its coast. The recreational, aesthetic, and
educational resources are unending.

When I moved to Oregon fourteen years ago, I began exploring the territory as a photographer/writer. I was soon impressed with the more than
two hundred state parks that since 1929 have preserved some of the best
land for public use.

As I traveled throughout the West, I often heard the comment, "Oh,
you're from Oregon where they have such wonderful state parks." It's true.
Over forty million people—local, national and foreign—used the day-use
facilities in the year from June 1991 to June 1992. Over two million used the
overnight areas.

Scattered throughout the state, these parks are not just for picnicking and
camping. They have trails, waterfalls, lighthouses, mountains, lakes, rivers,
beaches, sand dunes, boating, fishing, wildlife, wildflowers, and geological
formations that will tug at you to linger, to ask questions, to learn, to nur-

Oregon Trail history abounds

9

ture your sense of wonder. And many parks impart a spiritual contact with the past in exhibits and memorials.

Some parks are located where pioneers stopped on the Oregon Trail, or on the path of Lewis and Clark. Certain parks attract quiet encounters. Others seem to lure large reunions or exuberant boating. Some are on main routes, some in isolated areas.

Oregon's weather is an eclectic affair, as if someone had programmed a computer to provide variations on a theme and put locations to the music, instead of words. Travelers can choose summers of hot, dry deserts; temperate, breezy beaches; or fresh, cool mountain slopes; and winters of often pleasant, warm coastal days or invigorating inland ski country.

Specific write-ups in this book will concentrate on the 110 parks that are named state parks and will not cover the waysides, recreation areas, and so forth. A few waysides (and one recreation area) of special interest that are near state parks are included under that park write-up. To avoid conflict with information put out by the State Parks and Recreation Department, the same eight areas are used for classification.

Because the state parks are stepping stones to discovering Oregon, a preamble at the beginning of each regional section presents an overview of the scope of that area. Following this, you will learn about the special features of each park: facilities and campground information, natural and human history, recreation possibilities, and nearby excursions. The many photos hint at what you will see and will help photographers select new locations.

HISTORY OF THE PARKS

Though Oregon officials early recognized the value of preserving and maintaining the natural scenery along its state highways and providing stopping places for travelers, the impetus for the development of a state park system was the increased mobility of wanderers.

In the late 1910s and early 1920s, motorized vehicles opened a new era in exploration, a way to get to a trailhead or waterway for self-propelled recreation. Tourists could purchase a Model T Ford for $500, equip it with food, cooking utensils, bedding, tents, etc., and take to the open road. They stopped to camp where they could find water. With few commercial places available for camping, and speeds of only about thirty miles per hour, it was an economical way to travel. With the benefits of pleasure, health, and education, this mode of traveling became an antidote to ignorance.

The problem was that increased numbers of camping enthusiasts brought on more fenced private property and "no trespassing" signs. The demands for public camping grew. Governor Olcott made the comment in 1921 that "We are expending thousands of dollars in urging the tourist to come here. It is necessary that we care for him when he comes."

The need for land acquisition for parks—by donations, eminent domain, and purchase—was already underway. Various committees and commissions had met to further the formation of state parks, and some highway parks had been provided. Official sanction for the park program, however, occurred with the newly appointed State Park Commission on July 24, 1929. A policy statement was written and adopted:

> *To create and develop for the people of the state of Oregon a state park system, to acquire and protect timbered strips on the borders of state highways, rivers, and streams, to secure in public ownership typical stands of the trees native to Oregon, to maintain the public right to the use of the sea beaches of the state, to seek the protection of our native shrubs and flowers and to preserve the natural beauty of the state.*

The need for both recreational facilities and overnight camping by tourists escalated the development of more state parks. Fortunately, earlier legislation urged by Governor Oswald West had reserved Oregon's beaches for the public for a highway in 1915. The days of horses and buggies using the beach as a road soon passed with the advent of travel by car. Today, many beaches are closed to motorized use. The result was that the public beaches became a playground strung with parks. One fine inland park arose early as a result of a historical meeting at Champoeg in 1843, site of the official birth of Oregon.

The original notion of parks involving beautification and extensive tree-planting at highway stops expanded to include the need to preserve special natural features of the state, not just easily accessible ones. Enthusiasm in-

Storm waves and sea gulls

Windsurfers enjoy easy ocean access

creased after several Oregonians attended the 1928 National Conference on State Parks in San Francisco.

Samuel H. Boardman served as Parks Engineer, or Superintendent, from 1929 to 1950. He has been called the "Father of Oregon State Parks" because of his furtherance of land acquisitions. During this period, 495 transactions secured 50,842 acres for parks, and in retrospect have saved many acres of old-growth forest.

Other agencies worked to develop these state parks. The Civilian Conservation Corps (CCC) in particular, under the technical supervision of the National Park Service and cooperating with other park agencies, employed youths who couldn't find work during the Depression. They constructed trails and bridges, rustic buildings, picnic areas, roads, parking areas, viewpoint shelters, and did property line surveys and marked corners. Seventeen of their camps were in Oregon State Parks, though improvements were made in forty-five parks. Many fine stone and wooden structures standing today attest to their good work.

A VARIETY OF PARKS

Oregon has organized its parklands into eight areas—South Coast, Central Coast, North Coast, Willamette Valley, Columbia Gorge, Central Oregon, Southern Oregon, and Eastern Oregon.

Within these recreation areas, parks are classified into waysides, state parks with day-use only, state park campgrounds only (just one at Ukiah-Dale Forest), state park campgrounds with day-use facilities, a few recreation areas (these have camping also; located at Minam, Deschutes River, Succor Creek, and Goose Lake), two other accommodations (Frenchglen Hotel and Wolf Creek Tavern), and one museum (Kam Wah Chung Wayside).

Nearly eighty of the parks are located along the coast. Many have expansive vistas, trails leading to beaches, and are access points for sections of the Oregon Coast Trail—which is complete along 60 percent of the coast. Activities include beachcombing and clamming, exploring tidepools, whale watching, building sand castles, flying kites, birdwatching, surfing, and enjoying seductive trances focused on dynamic waves and incredible sunsets. Several parks feature historic, often active lighthouses.

Rivers dominate the parks in the Willamette Valley—the McKenzie, the Clackamas, the North and South Santiam, and especially the Willamette. Most parks have access to lakes, rivers, and streams for paddling, boating, and fishing.

The parklands of the Columbia Gorge are places of waterfalls, hiking in the forested Cascade Mountains, and water sports on the mighty Columbia River. Geology and nature study are eye-openers in this river-carved gorge through the Cascade Mountains.

Those who like the high desert plateau will want to head for Central Oregon where there are several reservoir lakes—Lake Billy Chinook, Prineville Reservoir, and Ochoco Lake. Parks are also adjacent to two scenic waterways—the John Day and the Deschutes Rivers. For spectacular rock formations, with hiking and a premier rock-climbing spot, Smith Rock along the Crooked River is a magnet.

Several parks in Southern Oregon feature the Rogue River's changing character as it flows from Crater Lake National Park to the coast. Miles and miles of hiking on the Upper Rogue River Trail are accessed from Joseph P. Stewart State Park.

The parks of Eastern Oregon are situated in the rugged Blue and Wallowa Mountains and the pine forests of this high plateau. Lake Wallowa State Park is in a lovely environment called "Little Switzerland."

Each of the parks throughout the state has its own beauty, along with its recreational and educational aspects. Quite a few parks have exhibits of historical interest.

AMENITIES

Day-Use Areas. Most of the day-use parks provide picnic sites and drinking water. Many have group picnicking facilities (see Appendix) that include covered shelters with electrical outlets. Most parks have restroom facilities. Exceptions are E. R. Corbett (*no water*), Floras Lake (*no water*), John B. Yeon (*no water*), Pilot Butte (*no water*), Portland Women's Forum, Shepperd's Dell (*no water*), and Willamette Stone (*no water*). Some day-use parks have pit toilets but no water. These are Bald Peak, Bonnie Lure, Cape Sebastian, Coquille Myrtle Grove, Golden and Silver Falls, Howard J. Morton, J. S. Burres, Lone Ranch, Neptune, Pistol River, Seneca Fouts, Vinzenz Lausmann, Whalehead, and Wygant. Availability of restrooms and water is not written in stone, however. Sometimes the water becomes unpotable and certain restrooms may be closed for repairs.

Several day-use areas have special facilities. Shore Acres has oceanside botanical gardens and a garden house. Cape Blanco, Bullards Beach, Champoeg, Collier Memorial, Crown Point, Fort Stevens, and Yaquina Bay have historic museums. Boat docks and marinas are found at popular boating parks. Silver Falls and Tryon Creek have nature visitor centers. Several parks have facilities for equestrians. A couple are popular with RC airplane flyers. Rooster Rock has information on wind and weather conditions for windsurfing on the Columbia River.

Starting in 1993, a day-use fee for vehicle parking at twenty-six of the more popular state parks is in effect from May 8 through September 26. Hikers and cyclists are exempt from this charge. An annual, nontransferable parking permit can be purchased at park offices. Boat moorage fees are charged at Detroit Lake, Wallowa Lake, Prineville Reservoir, and Devil's Lake. Group picnicking reservations are a good idea at some of the parks—these can be made through the specific state park.

Campgrounds. Three major types of sites are found in developed campgrounds. Full hookups have sewer, water, and electrical hookups at the site. Electrical hookups have only electricity and water. Improved tent sites have water nearby. All three of these have paved parking areas, tables, and campstoves. Site lengths indicate the largest sites in each park, not all the sites. Most campgrounds have restrooms with flush toilets and showers located nearby. Limited facilities are found in the few primitive campgrounds, usually a table and campstove, flush toilets, but no shower. Primitive campgrounds at Shelton and Jackson F. Kimball, however, have pit toilets and Kimball has no drinking water. Some listed telephone numbers are located in registration booths that are not always staffed.

All fifty state park campgrounds are open from mid-April to late October. Sixteen of these are open year-round. Most of the winter campgrounds are on the temperate coast, where recreation and hiking can be pursued all year. Five are inland parks. (See the Appendix for a list of these.)

Except for thirteen parks that offer reservations, campsites are available on a first-come, first-served basis. The other thirty-seven parks have 2,600 sites. During July and August, it is best to check into popular parks early on a Friday to avoid the weekend rush, although many campgrounds have space available even on summer holiday weekends. Daily checkout time is 2:30 P.M.

Camping fees cover a range from lowest for primitive to highest for a full hookup. A two-tiered fee system was recently introduced with higher fees at busier parks. A few parks have only sites with full or electric hookups and every camper pays the same fee. Most campgrounds, however, have both tent and hookup sites. Additional fees are often charged for extra vehicles. Gift certificates purchased from the state park offices are redeemable at all fifty campgrounds and have no expiration dates.

Campsites may be reserved at thirteen of the campgrounds from Memorial Day weekend through Labor Day weekend. These thirteen parks have 3,100 sites available. (See Appendix for list, addresses, and phone numbers.) Reservation applications may be made from the second Monday in January until Labor Day of that year. They must be made directly at the park or by mail (best during the off season as staff may not be in the offices), not by telephone. An advance deposit (which includes a reservation fee) must accompany the application. Application forms may be obtained from state park, state police, most motor vehicle division offices, and from many chamber of commerce visitor information centers. Reservations will hold the site until 10:00 A.M. the next day.

Group Camps. Tent camping areas, designed to accommodate twenty-five people, are available in fourteen parks (see Appendix for list and contacts). Special arrangements for groups can sometimes be made at other parks by contacting the park manager. During the reservation season, groups can reserve adjacent sites in the main campground.

Meeting halls with kitchen facilities for group use are located at Cape Lookout, Nehalem Bay, Champoeg, Silver Falls, and Emigrant Springs. A conference center is available at Silver Falls.

Fee information is available at parks with these facilities or at state park offices.

Hiker/Biker Camps. A number of campsites are designated for use

Signs point to horse trails

15

for both hikers and bikers, mostly along the coast but a few inland. Usually in separate areas, these sites have tables, fire ring, water, and use of restrooms and showers in the main campground. A nominal fee is charged. (See Appendix for list.)

Equestrian Camps. Four of the campgrounds feature separate sites adjacent to corrals and/or hitching rails for horseback riders: Silver Falls, Nehalem Bay, Bullards Beach, and Cape Blanco. Check with these parks for fees and reservations.

Campsite Information Center. For both up-to-the-minute information on campsite availability and recreational information at specific parks, call the Oregon State Park Campsite Information Center at 1-800-452-5687. Portland and out-of-state callers should phone (503) 238-7488.

The Center is staffed from 8:00 A.M. to 4:30 P.M. Monday through Friday. It is open from the first Monday in March until Labor Day weekend. Reservations cannot be made through the Center, but reservation cancellations are accepted.

PARK RULES

Rated in the nation's top ten in attendance in the country, Oregon's state parks need the cooperation of users to maintain their attractive, clean appearance. Read the list of regulations posted in each park and become familiar with your responsibilities while visiting. It's not difficult to see that all litter is pitched into disposal containers, even if it's not yours. Also check to see whether paths are used for walking, bicycling, or both.

Pets are allowed, if on a leash up to six feet long, and if the owner is in control at all times. Walk pets in designated or isolated areas and clean up any messes that land in other places. If a pet creates a health hazard, a public disturbance, or is out of control, the owners will be asked to leave the park. Only seeing-eye dogs are allowed in buildings.

Quiet hours for campers are from 10:00 P.M. to 7:00 A.M. Your neighbor may want to get up early to photograph a sunrise and not appreciate noisy late-evening entertaining. Respect the rights of those around you. Don't leave your vehicle idling unnecessarily, and park only in designated areas. At some sites, only one vehicle is allowed.

If noisy visitors threaten your enjoyment of the park, report them to park personnel—friendly, efficient professionals. It's best to avoid confrontations with unreasonable offenders. If a park ranger is unavailable, a list of local law enforcement telephone numbers is posted at campground registration booths.

Don't bring unneeded valuables along. If you do, keep them with you. And if you have firearms, you can't use them in the parks. In fact, any noisy, explosive substances (such as fireworks) are prohibited.

With the recent drought years in Oregon and the resource value of its forests—and of lives that might be threatened—careful control of campfires is required.

Observe any special regulations of the season posted in each park. For instance, ocean beach recreation areas have additional rules. Motor vehicles and horses are prohibited on certain beaches. No fires are allowed in driftwood piles. Firepits can be used for that beach party, but be sure to douse them later with wet sand or water. No trespassing or digging on sand cliffs is allowed. Permits are required for log and sand removal and any commercial activities.

CONCERNS FOR SAFETY

In case of emergency, contact a park ranger or call 911. If you are prepared and use caution, however, the chances are that your park visits will be safe—and enjoyable—ones.

The Beach. For those visiting parks along the ocean, the beauty of the scene sometimes overpowers a sense of caution. Keep back from the edges of the many unstable cliffs. Giant sand dunes look like places for digging and tunneling, but this is hazardous and can cause avalanches that trap people.

The surf is powerful and can lift huge logs up on the beach and roll them around. Stay clear so you don't suffer from this power landing on you. Children, especially, should be warned not to walk on logs or play on them. Be aware of incoming tides and don't become stranded on offshore rocks or rounding headlands. Keep an eye on waves as they vary and occasionally send a sneaker wave ashore that could sweep you out to sea. It is better to grab onto some object, rocks or whatever, even if you get soaked, than be carried away. If you go into the ocean, be alert for outgoing currents. Very few Oregon beaches have lifeguards.

Shellfish Poisoning. At certain times, there is a public alert against harvesting bivalves—clams, oysters, mussels, and scallops—because of a profusion of growth in a certain red algae in the ocean called *Gonyaulax catanella.* This is a toxic single-celled organism that is always present in small numbers. Certain environmental conditions cause rapid multiplication of this microorganism. Since bivalve shellfish feed by filtering water, they take in enough toxic organisms to threaten our health when numbers are high. Though called a "red tide," toxic conditions for us occur before growth is enough to cause this coloring.

Paralytic shellfish poisoning (PSP) can cause serious illness and even death. Shellfish are carefully monitored by state authorities and notice is given to the public if any danger is present in eating shellfish.

Another potentially life-threatening chemical ingested by eating shellfish is *domoic acid—"amnesic shellfish poisoning."* It appears that certain marine phytoplankton are responsible for this neurotoxin, possibly one not native to the West Coast. In addition to causing problems in bivalves,

17

Be aware of shellfish poisoning alerts

domoic acid is also found in Dungeness crab. It is carefully monitored, so be aware of any alerts. These are usually posted in the collecting area, but you can check with the Oregon Department of Fish and Wildlife.

Boating and Water Sports. Whether canoeing, kayaking, rafting, swimming, water-skiing, or any way you choose to enter the water, make it a fun experience. If it's to be a safe undertaking, match your skills to the local conditions and consider the weather. In Oregon it often changes quickly. Ask locally about specific water routes. Wear life jackets and don't drink alcoholic beverages while enjoying this activity.

Hiking Cautions. Certain regions in Oregon have rattlesnakes, so be alert. If it's a hike of any length or difficulty, it's best to be prepared for the unexpected, whether it's a change in weather, getting lost, or whatever. Take along drinking water, map, walking stick, suntan lotion, sweater, insect repellent, sunglasses and/or sun hat, dry matches, compass, pocket knife, flashlight, a snack (add an extra high-energy bar just in case), and mini-first-aid kit (include forceps for tick removal and aspirins). Either know how to start a fire with wet wood or carry one of the commercial fire starters and cubes. New disposable gear that takes little room includes toe and hand heaters (flat 3-inch squares), ponchos (a flat 3 x 5 inches), and insulating blankets (2 x 4 inches). One of the pleasures of outdoor recreation is a picnic at the foot of a waterfall or some other scenic spot. These items are easily carried, with hands free, in a knapsack on your back. Throw in an extra roll of film.

CONCERNS FOR NATURE

Fishing. All persons fourteen years of age or older (except for certain disabled persons) require a valid angling license in their possession to take any fish except smelt for personal use. Special tags are necessary for salmon, steelhead, and sturgeon. The Oregon Department of Fish & Wildlife recommends the practice of releasing wild game fish—handled carefully—and only before a limit of fish is taken. Check with the state for limits and other restrictions.

Shellfish and Marine Invertebrates. No license is required to take smelt, shellfish, or other marine invertebrates. There are limits, however, and certain locations are closed to any taking. Check with Oregon Fish & Wildlife, or local authorities, for daily catch limits, harvest method, locations, and special regulations. Some of the popular tidepool areas would soon lose their appeal if people indiscriminately took organisms. Some marine gardens are protected. Anyone enjoying the tidepool areas should also remember to treat the animals with respect. Please turn rocks back the way you found them after you look underneath.

Trails. There is nothing quite like the joy of hiking a trail in solitude or quiet company, watching for wildlife, and seeing what nature is doing at the moment. This joy is easily destroyed by the loud noises of other hikers and/or their radios, or an unexpected, uncontrolled approach of a pet, just when you have discovered a fawn near the path. Please respect the enjoyment of others.

The beauty of the surroundings is marred by litter left behind. "Leave nothing but footsteps," as they say, and they should not be heavy jogging ones on a muddy trail that can't recover. Even though orange and banana peels are organic, they are slow to decompose and unsightly. Pack out any garbage.

Don't shortcut on switchbacks. It causes erosion and can send rocks down below and cause injury to others. Enjoy the vegetation; don't destroy or remove it. Instead, take a photo of that exquisite wildflower.

Wildlife. Oregon has good wildlife viewing, from marine animals to inland species. It's amazing how often travelers fail to respect the wildness of the animals they see, and want to approach them closely. Besides the possible danger, most animals don't want you to approach them closely, particularly when they have young. Survival in the wild is not easy and your close approach may lower the odds of that happening. And please don't feed them. If you want to watch tame animals, go to the zoo.

Coastal Wildlife Refuges. Hundreds of thousands of sea birds return to the Oregon coast each spring to nest. This is only successful on isolated islands and headlands. Protected as part of the National Wildlife Refuge System, all public entry on Oregon's offshore rocks, islands, and reefs is strictly prohibited. In the past, boaters used to collect gull and other sea bird eggs for human use. Don't even think of doing it today.

VOLUNTEERS

The state parks often have volunteers that are key members of the staff team. Some are park hosts in campgrounds. Some assist at visitor centers, do maintenance chores, and help with special events. Several parks have affiliated support groups called "Friends of the Park" that focus on educational and informative projects.

Nine "Friends" groups are now assisting the state parks through fundraising and volunteer work. The first of these was at Tryon Creek in 1969, followed by Fort Stevens in 1979, Champoeg in 1980, Crown Point in 1982, Shore Acres and Silver Falls in 1986, Collier Memorial in 1987, and Cape Blanco and Yaquina Bay in 1988.

HOW TO USE THIS BOOK

To use this book as a guide to visiting Oregon's state parks, I would suggest the following approach:

1. Read the introduction for general information.
2. Decide which of the eight areas to visit.
3. Read the introductory material to those regions.
4. Scan the vital statistics at the beginning of specific park write-ups to choose attractions and facilities that interest you.
5. Read specific state park write-ups for more detailed information.
6. Check Appendix and Index for additional information.
7. Plan routes and schedule time to do the recreation you have selected, choose appropriate gear to take, and make reservations if necessary.

Campers can easily travel throughout the state using campgrounds as base camps. Maps will help you plan your trip.

I have tried to make this a useful and beautiful guidebook for both tourists and local residents, and a good read even for armchair travelers. My thanks to an enchanting state, and to those who have guided me to enlighten you.

A NOTE ABOUT SAFETY

Safety is an important concern in all outdoor activities. No guidebook can alert you to every hazard or anticipate the limitations of every reader. Therefore, the descriptions of roads, trails, routes, and natural features in this book are not representations that a particular place or excursion will be safe for your party. When you follow any of the routes described in this book, you assume responsibility for your own safety. Under normal conditions, such excursions require the usual attention to traffic, road and trail conditions, weather, terrain, the capabilities of your party, and other factors. Keeping informed on current conditions and exercising common sense are the keys to a safe, enjoyable outing.

The Mountaineers

SOUTH COAST

Rugged and often pristine, the uncrowded nature of the South Coast lures those who want to avoid crowds. Many of the self-reliant people who choose to live there, as well as visitors, believe this region embraces the most spectacular scenery of the coast, with its many rocky headlands, sea stacks, and natural bridges. One might also hazard the comment that the best sportfishing is in this area of the coast.

This is the "banana belt" of Oregon and its climate is good, being temperate all year round. Most of this area rarely sees freezing conditions near the ocean and it is not unusual to experience some warm, sunny days sandwiched between winter storms, which are themselves popular enough to bring visitors to the coast to watch their wild artistry. Summer days are sometimes windy, particularly in the afternoon, but they are dry for the most part, with unpolluted blue skies.

Except for traveling on the backside of Humbug Mountain, US 101 is smack on the edge of the coast from the California border to Port Orford where it swings inland a few miles, so even the drive is a high.

Many long-distance bikers travel the length of this highway during the summer. The smart ones go with the wind, heading north during spring and south as the wind shifts to the northwest in the warmer months. This mode of transportation lets travelers savor natural history.

Bushy yellow-flowered lupine grows in thick carpets along coastal edges, a plant introduced from California to control shifting sand. Fireweed offers contrast with its bright magenta. Queen Anne's lace pops up from its umbrella-shaped brackets. Tall dried stalks of Fuller's teasel form silhouettes against the sunsets, and masses of Oregon iris cover sloping hillsides.

Opposite: *Port at Charleston near Sunset Bay State Park*

One of the best wildflower hiking trails is inland from Gold Beach on the Illinois River Trail. Try it in spring before it gets baking hot.

No major roads go inland south of Bandon, so access is limited, though forest roads weave through the Siskiyou National Forest. In this area are found the "Wild and Scenic" sections of the legendary Rogue River, as well as both the Wild Rogue and the Kalmiopsis Wilderness. Both wilderness areas have extensive trail systems.

The twin cities of Coos Bay and North Bend are the largest population center (and shipping port) along the entire coast, though their size does not compare to major cities of the state. Just north of them is the beginning point of the Oregon Dunes National Recreation Area (ODNRA), where the coastline switches from jagged cliffs and coves to flat terrain where wind can deposit sand from the ocean's reservoir.

The Visitor Center for ODNRA is located in Reedsport on US 101. The Umpqua River—the largest river between the Columbia River and San Francisco—empties into the sea just north of this city. Only a little over a century ago, schooners sailed up this river with supplies for mining camps.

Because of the low human population of this region, animal life is rich in its natural habitat. Black bears are often seen in wilder parts inland, particularly around berry patches, and are usually not dangerous if caution is used. Black-tailed deer are abundant, and drivers should keep a wary eye out for them, especially at night when the deer are often blinded by lights while crossing the highway.

Viewpoints on coastal headlands are the best places to scan for passing whales, since you can see much farther out to sea. (See Appendix for specific sites.) The grays move south to Baja in the winter and then return with their young in spring, on their way to summer in the Arctic, but other whales are also seen infrequently throughout the year. Humpbacks, in particular, are sometimes seen along the South Coast, but rarely further north.

These high points are also great places for surf watching, where waves grind away at the rocks. Wave refraction—the bending and turning of waves as they strike the coast—focuses its energy on the projecting points of rocky promontories and eventually straightens out segments of the coast.

This southern tip is the oldest part of the Oregon coast. Once inundated by the sea, older rocks along the coast began as sediment laid on the floor of the Pacific Ocean, but were then scraped onto the edge of the continent during tectonic plate movements. The result is enchanting scenery.

LOEB STATE PARK

Hours/Season: Overnight; year-round
Area: 320 acres
Facilities: Picnic tables, campground with 53 electrical sites (maximum site is 50 feet), wheelchair-accessible restrooms with showers, hiker/biker camp, firewood

Attractions: Myrtlewood grove, redwoods, hiking, swimming, fishing, rafting and driftboating, photography
Nearby: Kalmiopsis Wilderness; Vulcan Lake Trail
Access: From US 101 at the south end of Brookings, follow North Bank Chetco River Road 10 miles northeast

Coastal residents know that summer warmth is only a few miles upriver where swimming will be the ticket. Loeb State Park is Oregon's only state park with camping in such a location. The river is the Chetco, which flows out of the Klamath Mountains.

Campsites are nestled in an outstanding grove of old-growth myrtlewood trees, with some sites fronting on the river. It is unusual today to find such a grove of these trees, and the park was purchased to preserve them. A later purchase added a parcel with redwood trees, at the northern edge of their habitat.

The picnic area fronts the gravel bar of the river, where driftboats can be launched. Across the water is rugged forest land, where Emily Creek, the most important salmon-spawning tributary of the Chetco River, enters the river.

Trailhead parking is along the entry road to the day-use area. Brochures

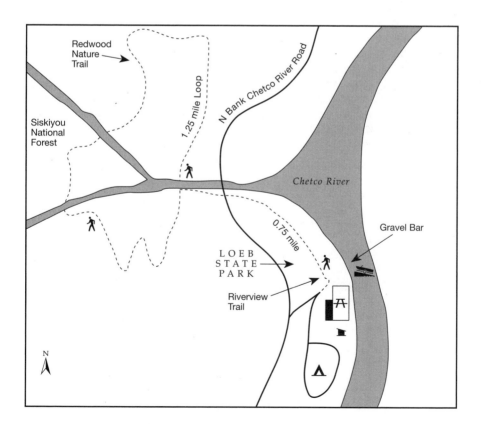

with a hiking map and interpretive information are available. The 0.75-mile Riverview Trail is the connecting path to the Redwood Nature Trail in the Siskiyou National Forest. It climbs up along a ledge from the river and weaves around through a forest where a creek flows down a hillside.

A short distance after crossing the road, the Redwood Nature Loop is reached. It can be traveled in either direction, a moderately steep up-and-down traverse of 1.25 miles. Along the trail, you will see various ages of redwoods, from young ones growing out of old stumps to some large ones between three hundred and eight hundred years old—one is over 33 feet in circumference and 286 feet tall. This forest also has myrtle, rhododendrons, evergreen huckleberry, several species of ferns, salal, red alder, Douglas fir, bigleaf maple, tanoak, a carpet of wood sorrel, and the hanging lichen called Grandfather's Beard. Bridges cross a creek that runs through a deep gash in the land.

For a different hike in this vicinity, wilderness enthusiasts seeking the unusual might want to continue on the North Bank Chetco River Road another 5.7 miles to Forest Road 1909. Paved at first, this road becomes gravel and ends in 14.7 miles, where the 1.4-mile Vulcan Lake Trail begins. *Trailers are not recommended.*

This is the Kalmiopsis Wilderness, a region of unusual plant species that developed during the fifty million years that the Siskiyou Mountains were an island in the Pacific. Pre–Ice Age specimens that survived include the rare *Kalmiopsis leachiana*, carnivorous species, and Brewer (or weeping) spruce. The topography is rugged and water is hard to find in summer.

The trail switchbacks to a ridge and then drops down to four-acre Vulcan Lake, which fills a dramatic rock basin. In summer, this wilderness is very hot, dry, and home to poison oak, rattlesnakes, and yellowjackets. Go in late spring, however, and see beargrass blossoms and smell the wild azaleas flowering along the path.

HARRIS BEACH STATE PARK

Hours/Season: Overnight; year-round
Area: 172.8 acres
Facilities: Picnic tables, campground with 34 full hookups, 53 electrical, and 69 tent sites (maximum site is 50 feet), hiker/biker camp, wheel-chair-accessible site and restrooms with showers, dumping station, firewood, slide program, playground, summer reservations available; (503) 469-2021
Attractions: Beachcombing, hiking, rockhounding, surf-fishing, tidepools, photography
Access: Off US 101, 2 miles north of Brookings

▲ Huge rock sculptures of many shapes and shades rise from the sandy
⊥ beach of this park and attract visitors like magnets. Some climb them;

Beach walkers at Harris Beach State Park

some graffiti and paint them; some photograph their enhancement of the beach landscape. It is a mystical sight to watch sunsets atop these natural stone pieces of art as a full moon rises and sea gulls swirl in the lift of twilight.

Paths weave about picnic tables that sit on stone terraces overlooking the ocean with its tangle of offshore rocks and wildlife refuges. Ground squirrels scamper about and gulls seem particularly argumentative. One large bird rookery is named "Goat Island" and a massive stone is called "Hunch Back." A fine sandy beach invites walkers and collectors. Storms have tossed ashore huge driftwood trees and the dynamic sea often pushes a large pool up on the beach at high tide, deep enough for children and dogs to swim in.

The campground is a little uphill and inland from the day-use area, in a wooded tract that contains azaleas. Unfortunately, only a couple of sites have an ocean view.

The name of the park honors George Scott Harris, a native of Scotland, who obtained the property in 1871. His journey to this land was a long route, involving a stint in the British Army in India, trips to Africa and New Zealand, arrival in San Francisco, and work in railroad construction and mining before coming to Curry County. There he settled down to raise sheep and cattle.

Several trails access different areas of the park. A short hiking trail across

27

from the entrance to the campground switchbacks up Harris Butte to a vista point that looks north. Enroute to the top, there are good views south.

A nature trail begins near site C 6 at the upper end of the campground, weaves through a wetland area, crosses the road, and connects with the South Beach Trail, paved downhill to good beach walking in front of ocean-front homes and access to a good intertidal marine garden. Collecting in the park is by permit only.

Adjacent to site A 12, the Rock Beach Trail crosses the road and heads toward the beach and day-use area, with several interesting side paths for getting the right camera angle for sunset shots. Beach-walk north of the picnic area to the tidepools of North Harris Beach.

Nearby Brookings Harbor is a major recreational ocean-fishing center, with access to the sea from the Chetco River. The area produces about 75 percent of the Easter lilies grown in the United States, and one can see vast fields of these flowers south of town in early July. The bulbs are shipped all over the world. Daffodils are also raised commercially.

SAMUEL H. BOARDMAN STATE PARK

Hours/Season: Day use; year-round
Area: 1,471 acres
Facilities: Picnic tables, wheelchair-accessible restrooms (certain areas)
Attractions: Hiking, photography, surf-fishing, tidepools, beachcombing, wildlife viewing
Access: Off US 101, starts 4 miles north of Brookings

For 11 miles of coastline south of Burnt Hill Creek, this park encompasses the grinding edge of jagged, forested cliffs meeting the ceaseless energy of surf surging past the many offshore rocks. Every mile is a different scene, an unexpected bounty of geology, of random creativity where small sandy beaches hide at the bottom of steep canyons. It is not exaggeration to call this one of the world's finest coastline stretches.

It is easy to see why Samuel H. Boardman, first State Parks Superintendent from 1929–1950, conceived the idea of a great coastal park in Curry County, which many think is the choicest real estate on the Oregon coast. He worked tirelessly to acquire the land. One gift of land was the first park grant by a foreign owner, Borax Consolidated, Ltd., of London, England. Boardman approached U.S. Department of the Interior Secretary Harold L. Ickes to propose that it should be a national park. Though federal officials toured the region, that idea did not take hold. Instead, it became a state park honoring Boardman.

This unusual treasury of seascapes has a succession of developed areas that suggest using the overnight facilities of nearby Harris Beach State Park to give one time to explore the terrain and natural history.

Heading north, the first area is Lone Ranch, a picnic area with restrooms

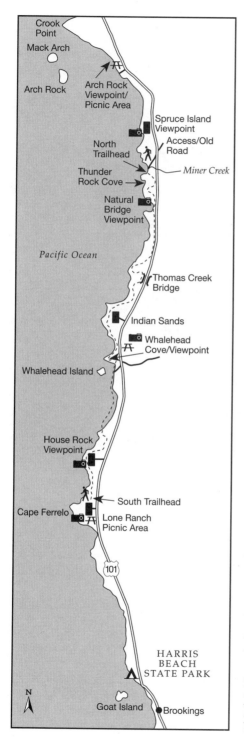

at beach level in a rocky cove south of Cape Ferrelo. An extensive intertidal region of fascinating organisms among overhangs, caves and rocks is found here, with easy access via good trails.

The southern trailhead for the 7 miles of Oregon Coast Trail in the park is next, atop Cape Ferrelo, where there is good off-road parking. Pick up the trail at the northwest corner of the parking area and follow it over open, rolling grasslands overlooking the sea. After crossing a wooded area and small stream, and coming out into the open again, House Rock Viewpoint is reached in 1.5 miles. Watch for peregrine falcons, offshore whales, and sea birds. Also reached by a road spur, this viewpoint has a commemorative monument honoring Boardman.

The next highway stop is at Whalehead Viewpoint, with beach and Oregon Coast Trail access. Though the trail is more difficult between House Rock and this area, it's worth the effort. From the northwest corner of the parking at House Rock, enter a spruce-lined corridor where you might look for chanterelle mushrooms if the season is right. The open trail then crosses a sharp ridge and drops steeply to a grassy bench before taking to the beach. It's an easy 1.5-mile beach walk from there to the next developed area at Whalehead Cove, which is accessed by a steep road down from the highway.

Whalehead Cove has picnicking and restrooms. A huge rock just offshore is aptly named Whalehead Island, as it looks like a beached whale frozen in stone.

Cove below Crook Point, Samuel H. Boardman State Park

To find the trail north, follow the spur road toward the highway where you'll see the usual Oregon Coast Trail marker at the start of the path up to an awesome headland view. A mile of hiking leads to Indian Sands, where a connecting trail descends from the viewpoint parking. If it's spring, watch for a waterfall on the backside of a headland.

Indian Sands is totally unique; shore pines edge sand dunes in the process of turning into sandstone high above the sea. An Indian midden—*it is a federal offense to disturb this*—is seen on the south edge of the area, where seafood feasts left a huge pile of shells and bones. Watch for showy rose iceplant blossoms in summer among the loose sand.

The path continues north through a saddle overlooking a small cove, then twists and climbs around headlands with great views, and follows the shoulder of the highway for a short distance before entering the woods again. The trail ends for roughly a mile at 345-foot-high Thomas Creek

Bridge—you can follow the road, however. Just north of Spruce Creek, the path enters an alder wood before arriving soon at Natural Bridge Viewpoint.

The last 2 miles to the north trailhead at Miner Creek is an exciting area of wave sculpturing of rocks and grassy points projecting into the ocean. Some curiosity about paths off the main route in this area will lead you to incredible spots that you will hug into your memory. Bring a picnic lunch and linger. From Natural Bridge Viewpoint, the path re-enters the woods, proceeds to parking at Thunder Rock Cove, and then continues on to a waterfall and beach access at Miner Creek, an idyllic spot. The route back to the highway is up a steep, abandoned roadway where there is a small parking area behind a highway guard rail.

This Oregon Coast Trail section is not a sedate, windy beach walk, but an up-and-down excursion among geological happenings and natural history.

The park has more vehicle stops, the next at Spruce Island Viewpoint, followed by a lush seascape at Arch Rock Picnic Area, where there are trails to view Arch Rock and Mack Arch. A different view is seen at Arch Rock Viewpoint, where surf curves onto the beach below Crook Point.

If you've taken the time to sample much of this park, you'll probably agree with Boardman. It is mighty fine scenery, but many drive by and miss the added wonders of the trail.

PISTOL RIVER STATE PARK

Hours/Season: Day use; year-round
Area: 440 acres
Facilities: Chemical toilet, *no water*
Attractions: Beachcombing, windsurfing, birdwatching, exhibit information, fishing, photography
Access: Off US 101, travel 11 miles south of Gold Beach

Few can resist stopping at this park once they've caught a glimpse of it while coming down the hill south from Cape Sebastian. The north parking area, Myers Beach, has beach access and lures one to walk the sandy edge of this spectacular seascape, where it looks like a giant has hurled massive boulders into the sea. You might want to stay for some sunset photography.

The south parking area is a pocket of sandy land with European beach grass, bordered on the south side by the curving arm of Pistol River as it empties into the Pacific. It has no beach access, but bring your binoculars and check the birds in the estuary. The park actually goes all the way south to Crook Point and includes rolling sand dunes with some vegetation, but there is no development in that protected area.

In the last Rogue River Indian War, the Battle of Pistol River was fought here in March of 1856. Thirty-four Minutemen under the command of

Sea stacks at Myers Beach, Pistol River State Park

George H. Abbott were attacked in an improvised fortification of logs by a large number of Indians. After several days of hand-to-hand fighting, regular troops under Captains Ord and Jones drove away the Indians.

The name of the park was adopted because James Mace lost his pistol in the river in 1853.

CAPE SEBASTIAN STATE PARK

Hours/Season: Day use; year-round
Area: 1,104 acres
Facilities: Chemical toilets, *no water*
Attractions: Hiking, beach access, fishing, photography
Access: Off US 101, 7 miles south of Gold Beach *(entry road is steep and not recommended for trailers or motorhomes)*

▲ Most people come to see the superb views from this park atop Cape Sebastian, but some include a hike on the section of the Oregon Coast Trail found here. The entry road branches to give two viewpoint parking areas. The north view encompasses the seemingly endless scallops of surf hitting the 43-mile stretch of coastline which includes the town of Gold Beach and on to Humbug Mountain and Cape Blanco. From the south viewpoint, the many rocky sea sentinels off the beach at Pistol River State Park dominate the 50-mile seascape that is visible to Point St. George in California. The coast highway winds south like a tiny ribbon carrying toy cars.

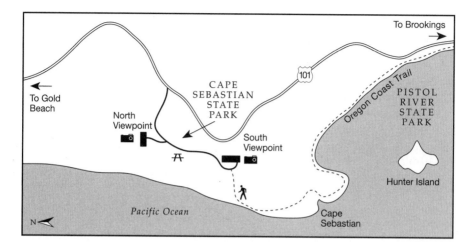

Some days, fog lies below the cape and the place seems like an island in a sea of frothy egg white.

The first navigators to explore the Northwest coast were the Spanish, only fifty years after Columbus discovered the Americas, and it was Sebastian Vizciano who named this cape after the patron saint of the day of his discovery in 1603.

A more recent tidbit of history occurred in 1942, when fog obstructed the view. A caretaker was checking the trail when he heard a foreign tongue being spoken below the cliffs. When a break in the fog layer opened up, he saw a Japanese submarine that had surfaced to recharge its batteries. He was soon on his way to tell the Coast Guard.

From the south viewpoint parking area, a paved path leads west through open meadows where summer wildflowers bloom, to the cliff's edge, where a portion of the Oregon Coast Trail begins. The beginning of the path edges the headland which drops off almost vertically to the water below. Trees lean from the force of the wind which often roars here.

Soon, however, the path descends through old-growth forest of Douglas fir, grand fir, and shore pine, and reaches the beach in 2 miles. One can continue hiking along the beach to Pistol River.

HUMBUG MOUNTAIN STATE PARK

Hours/Season: Overnight; *campground closed in winter*
Area: 1,842 acres
Facilities: Picnic tables, campground with 30 full hookup (maximum site of 55 feet) and 78 tent sites, hiker/biker camp, wheelchair-accessible restrooms with showers, firewood, dump station, phone: (503) 332-6774

Attractions: Hiking trails, beach access, beachcombing, fishing, photography
Nearby: A unique port, Port Orford Heads
Access: Off US 101, 6 miles south of Port Orford

Mountain, beach, and forest landscapes meet in a wonderful trilogy at Humbug Mountain State Park—explore one or all of these scenic feasts. The campground is a long, flat peninsula bordered by the beach, the mountain, and Brush Creek, and backed by steep forest. A walkway runs through the campground, the west end passing under a highway bridge to the 4-mile stretch of beach included in the park. This is a great place for beachcombing or watching sunsets with the Redfish Rocks and Island Rock in the foreground.

South of the campground, US 101 threads its way in sharp curves between Brush Creek and the back side of the mountain, through Humbug Canyon, to the separate day-use area located a mile south. Picnic on spacious meadows surrounded by tall trees. The town of Port Orford hides Easter eggs for its children in the lush grass.

Rising at the edge of the sea, Humbug Mountain is a landmark on the south coast of Oregon, the highest coastal point at 1,748 feet. Originally called Sugar Loaf Mountain, it became known as Humbug Mountain after a scouting party sent by Captain Tichenor, founder of Port Orford, became disoriented in the area and dubbed it Tichenor's Humbug.

A fairly strenuous 3-mile trail built by the Civilian Conservation Corps in 1934 weaves up switchbacks to the summit. It passes through a pocket of temperate rain forest lush with vegetation. The temperate climate makes this an interesting and varied all-season hike. It is a rare day in a rare winter when there is snow, even on the summit.

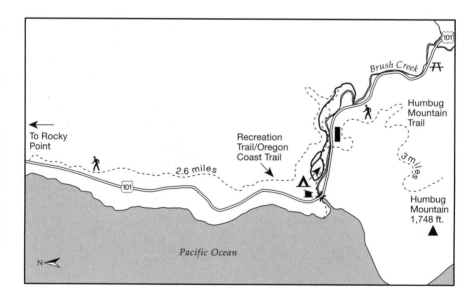

The trail is accessed either from a signed parking space off US 101, just before it swings north of the mountain to follow the coast, or from the campground. In the middle of the campground, near the road, a walkway crosses Brush Creek and then passes beneath the highway to connect with the trail.

Hiking begins by a creek bordered by enormous bigleaf maples and thick ferns. On a spring ascent, look for the blossoms of trilliums, bleeding hearts, fairy lanterns, vanilla leaf, rhododendrons, and myrtlewood trees among the huge Douglas firs, hemlocks, and Port Orford cedar. Port Orford cedar—a much-valued wood—is found only on the southern coast of Oregon and a short distance into California, not more than 40 miles inland. This hike is through the last uncut old-growth grove along the coast between Redwood National Park and the Cummins Creek Wilderness north of Florence.

About a third of the way up, you cross a small creek and round a curve into hanging mosses on trees, with a waterfall in the distance. The forest is mostly quiet, but be alert for wildlife and you may hear a chickaree scold you, or see a varied thrush. Edwin Way Teale called this bird "the true voice of the rain forest."

Sun flirts with the forests, sending shafts of light through the trees. A few openings in the trees reveal views north up the coast past Cape Blanco. One can imagine the scene in the early 1800s when there were Tututni Indian tepees on the beach and hand-crafted canoes of cedar were launched into the sea.

The habitat changes with madrone and tanoak trees near the top. The summit is a small grassy slope, a perfect spot to sit with a picnic lunch and scan the wide-open view of the coast south, which includes the Sisters Rocks, Cape Sebastian, ridges of the Siskiyou Mountains, and on into California.

This park offers another, less well-known hike—both are sections of the Oregon Coast Trail. Take the campground walkway east, just past the fee booth, to a signed 2.6-mile Recreation Trail that follows the route of the old highway. The dirt path soon crosses a creek and then turns west and uphill on broken slabs of concrete (the old highway), with the steep forest up on one side and down on the other.

View of Humbug Mountain from Port Orford

35

Truckers didn't look forward to traveling this narrow, high road in the old days. Continue high above the campground and then north with good views of the ocean until the trail ends at the highway just south of Rocky Point, which is included in the park and has an excellent intertidal area, including the sessile jellyfish, *Haliclystrus*, and a small population of native littleneck clams.

Don't miss a visit to Port Orford, the oldest townsite on the Oregon coast. Stop at the Battle Rock Viewpoint and climb the rocky island that projects into the water, a natural fortress where the settlers fought the Indians and won. The town has a unique port, the only natural ocean harbor of the state (the other ports are on rivers with bar crossings). Commercial fishing boats are hoisted in and out of the water daily during the storm season to avoid being capsized at anchor—which still seems to happen occasionally.

For a look at what's still underwater, including the marine life, the town of Port Orford is a favorite with both recreational and commercial scuba divers. A new industry, harvesting sea urchins, has sprung up recently. The gonads are considered a delicacy by the Japanese and are flown overseas to them.

The Port Orford Heads Wayside is reached by turning west on Ninth Street in Port Orford and then taking the Coast Guard road to its terminus at the abandoned Coast Guard installation. A path leads to a spectacular viewpoint on the heads both south to Humbug Mountain and north to Cape Blanco—good reason for the Coast Guard lookout that was once here.

CAPE BLANCO STATE PARK

Hours/Season: Overnight; horse camp open year-round; *campground closed in winter*
Area: 1,880 acres
Facilities: Picnic tables, campground with 58 electrical sites (maximum site is 70 feet) including one wheelchair-accessible site, dumping station, wheelchair-accessible restrooms with showers, firewood, hiker/biker camp, horse camp with corrals, boat ramp on Sixes River, phone: (503) 332-6774
Attractions: Horse and hiking trails, wildlife viewing, beachcombing, clamming, tidepools, boating, photography, surf-fishing, pioneer cemetery, historic Hughes House
Nearby: Cape Blanco Lighthouse
Access: Take signed road 4 miles north of Port Orford on US 101 and travel 5 miles west to park

The most westerly point in Oregon, Cape Blanco State Park includes beaches and bluffs both north and south. The campground and horse camp were carved out of a Sitka spruce forest with an undercover of huckleberry, salmonberry, salal, and thimbleberry left to provide seclusion for the sites. These sites are great places to look for mushrooms in autumn. The toxic red and white amanitas are photogenic; others like the puffballs are edible. *Be sure of your identification if you plan to indulge.* The picnic and boating area is reached by the spur road to the historic Hughes House by the Sixes River.

Patrick Hughes, born in Ireland, came to the cape in 1860 and originally bought "Sullivan's Mine" to take advantage of the gold on the black sand beach to the south. Eventually, the family's land expanded to almost 2,000 acres and became a prosperous dairy ranch. In 1898, P. J. Lindberg built them a two-story, eleven-room Eastlake Victorian house, framed with Port Orford cedar, which had a chapel on the second floor. This home is all that remains of the ranch complex, occupied by the family for 111 years. It was restored by the "Friends of Cape Blanco" and is now on the National Register of Historic Places. It is open to the public from May through September, Thursday through Monday, with volunteers of the Friends available for tours and information. Visit the pioneer cemetery located along the main road to the campground.

Hikers will delight in the Oregon Coast Trail accessed from the south end of the campground. After a short walk on the road south, it reaches the beach and officially continues to Paradise Point Wayside, just north of Port Orford. This requires crossing the Elk River, which is only possible in summer at low tide, and not easily then. One can, however, easily hike about 2 miles to a side channel of the river.

The coast trail also takes off north from the campground, and skirts the

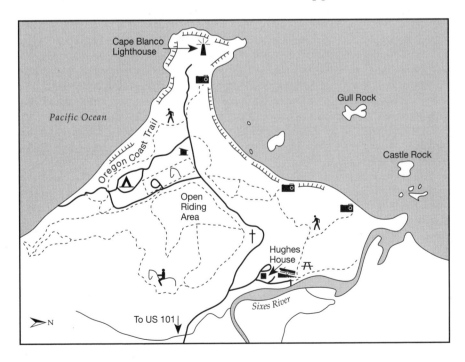

Cape Blanco lighthouse, on westernmost point of Oregon

edge of the bluff for magnificent views south which include the Blanco Reef, the Orford Reef, and Humbug Mountain. Fishing boats hug the mouth of the Elk River during salmon spawning. Cross the road to a view of the lighthouse or jog east on the road to connect with a trail that reaches the mouth of the Sixes River on the north side of the Cape in about 2 miles. This route passes hillsides of wildflowers and descends to a good tidepool area and favorite beach for razor clam digging. Surf booms on the ocean rocks and brown pelicans skim the waves. Gull Rock and Castle Rock are offshore bird-nesting refuges and Blacklock Point is across from the river. A trail follows the Sixes River estuary to connect with the day-use picnic area. Take time to look for migratory ducks in the pastured area by the water.

East and south of the horse camp, 3.5 miles of riding trails wander through open areas and woods, with beach access at the south end for a gallop to the Elk River.

If you do any beachcombing, particularly in winter and spring, be alert for glass floats tossed ashore. Coming from lands across the sea, the prettiest of these floats are a clear aquamarine. Quick discovery—which is necessary—will find the indentation left from blowing them filled with wiggling gooseneck barnacles. These foreign treasures come ashore from their ocean floating in the same strong southerly or westerly winds that spin windrows of *Velella velella* ("by-the-wind sailors") onto the beach. These small marine organisms of the open sea have round, bluish, cellophane-like floats and erect triangular sails which allow them to tack with the wind. Pretty when fresh, by-the-wind sailors soon become a mass of slippery, smelly debris on the beach.

Though closed now to the public, the Cape Blanco Lighthouse is a photogenic landmark easily viewed from the park. The oldest active lighthouse on the Oregon coast, it was built in 1870 on chalky cliffs named in 1603 by a Spanish explorer, Martin d'Anguilar. The original Fresnel lens and apparatus, imported from France and costing $20,000, still flashes every twenty seconds from an elevation of 245 feet above the Pacific Ocean. Winter winds on this exposed point are often the most violent along the coast, with velocities of one hundred miles per hour or more not unusual. These conditions, combined with dangerous offshore reefs, can prove a nightmare for ships at sea.

FLORAS LAKE STATE PARK

Hours/Season: Day use; year-round
Area: 1,371 acres
Facilities: Undeveloped
Attractions: Orienteering, geology, beach, waterfall, photography
Access: Off US 101, 4 miles south of Langlois, go west on Airport Road to end of road

Expect no sign for this park. It was originally called Newbergh, a name still on the old maps of the area. Floras Lake State Park is for the adventurous, the wilderness explorer who doesn't get lost. For that person, it offers many wonders. Development of this park is planned for the future.

The northeast corner borders the west side of Floras Lake and the area runs 2.5 miles along the ocean to include Blacklock Point to the south. It contains the Blacklock Point Preserve Forest with its dwarfed trees, Sitka and shore pine, growing on acid-leached soils. Its forest also supports Port Orford cedar and hemlock. The undergrowth consists of huckleberry, rhododendron, Labrador tea, salal, and myrtle.

Although one would not notice it now, Blacklock Sandstone Company quarried sandstone in this area, starting in the 1880s. Gone are the sawmill and the tram cars with rails that were used to carry the heavy rock to the shore where it was shipped by sea to San Francisco. Rock was extracted for some years but eventually proved uneconomical, leaving behind only the company's name on the basalt rock of the point.

When the U.S. Navy needed an airstrip in Curry Country during World War II, some of the park's land was leased to the county and the Navy built a road and airport. In 1971, the airport land was transferred to the State Board of Aeronautics for the Curry County Airport. Though it has a long runway to serve bigger planes, only an occasional private plane wings in to land next to the sea.

A look at a Cape Blanco quadrangle map reveals two jeep trails branching off from the northern end of the airport runway. One runs northwest to Blacklock Point and the other goes straight north to a series of limestone cliffs. The latter is easier to follow. The trail to Blacklock Point is confusing,

View from Blacklock Point, Floras Lake State Park

but try your hand at it. It can be done, as I have gone that way.

In winter and spring, this land frequently has huge areas of standing water (often full of tadpoles) which require boots. Spring brings a variety of wildflowers. The surrounding private area has cranberry bogs.

The north trail is not so ambiguous. Follow your nose and you'll arrive at the coast in slightly over 1 mile of hiking. Viewed while standing on top of a bluff, the landscape to the north is a long strip of scalloped limestone cliffs carved by the wave action of the encroaching sea, a postcard view different from any other place on the Oregon coast. Use caution on the cliffs; they are fragile. Immediately south, a creek exits the bluff in a waterfall to the beach below.

The way north is breaking up, hazardous for walking, but one can orient south to Blacklock. There is no trail, but it is easy at first to weave along the edge of the cliffs among flower-anchored sand, step across the small creek and continue until forest closes in. I have negotiated myself to the point, so it is possible.

It is easy to walk around the top of Blacklock Point where the view is of the Sixes River and the Cape Blanco Lighthouse to the south. You can easily descend rocks down to this beach, where the sea is a stew of stacks splattered with guano droppings from the myriad of common murres that live on them. Only the barrier of the river prevents many from discovering this headland via Cape Blanco Park.

One wonders at the name of this park, since Floras Lake is not accessible from this area. Perhaps Blacklock might have been a more appropriate name, unless access will later be from the Floras Lake corner.

BANDON STATE PARK

Hours/Season: Day use; year-round
Area: 893 acres
Facilities: Picnic tables, wheelchair-accessible restrooms, *no water*
Attractions: Hiking, beachcombing, photography, wildlife viewing, tide-pools, surf-fishing, storm watching
Access: Off Beach Loop Road, just south of Bandon

Several entrances to Bandon State Park are strung out along the coast from 1 to 5 miles south of Bandon. They provide access to several areas of this extremely photogenic beach area, walkable for several miles.

Nearest to downtown Bandon is the circular parking area overlooking Face Rock, a distinctive landmark of the town. The "face" is said to be that of a beautiful Indian maiden named Ewauna, daughter of Chief Siskiyou,

Viewpoint overlooking Face Rock and the Kittens to the north, Bandon State Park

who swam alone in the sea and was caught by Seatka, the evil spirit of the ocean. After Seatka tossed her cat and kittens into the sea, they and Ewauna were all turned to stone.

The Face Rock area has picnic tables, wheelchair-accessible restrooms, and a trail leading down stairs and onto the beach.

This viewpoint has a scope for birdwatching, with more than 300 species seen locally. Several species nest on the multitude of scenic sea stacks in this area, which are part of the National Wildlife Refuge system—public entry is prohibited. Watch for common murres, Brandt's cormorant, fork-tailed storm-petrel, Leach's storm-petrel, Cassin's auklet, and rhinoceros auklet. Tufted puffins return to the coast each April and are magnificent in their full breeding plumage.

Going south from Face Rock, the next area is called Devil's Kitchen, with restrooms, benches on a hill overlooking the sea, and two paths to the beach. The south path leads to picnic tables in a wind-sheltered area and a creek.

The third area has beach access up a steep dune, but no facilities. The last area also has access to a gorgeous beach, but no facilities.

The town of Bandon was twice, in 1914 and again in 1926, almost completely destroyed by fire. The extremely flammable yellow-flowered and sharp-thorned gorse imported from Ireland, which covers much of the undeveloped land in the area, did not help the situation.

In a more positive vein, Bandon organized a group called the Bandon Storm Watchers in 1983 for the many locals and visitors who find the winter season exhilarating. Free talks and slide shows are given on Saturdays at 3:00 P.M. each week from mid-January through mid-April by experts on history, flowers, wildlife, tidepools, the cranberry industry, and other related subjects. Bandon is often called the "Cranberry Capital of Oregon."

BULLARDS BEACH STATE PARK

Hours/Season: Overnight; year-round
Area: 1,289 acres
Facilities: Picnic tables, campground with 92 full hookup and 100 electrical sites (maximum length is 64 feet), wheelchair-accessible restrooms with showers, dumping station, firewood, slide program, playground, hiker/biker camp, boat ramp, horse camp, phone: (503) 347-2209
Attractions: Coquille River Lighthouse, Bandon Marsh, exhibit information, hiking, bike trails, equestrian trails, boating, surf- and river-fishing, crabbing, clamming, kite flying, beach access, wildlife viewing, photography
Access: Off US 101, 2 miles north of Bandon

⊥ Just before the Coquille River empties into the Pacific, it takes a jog south and then turns sharply at the north edge of Bandon to join the sea.

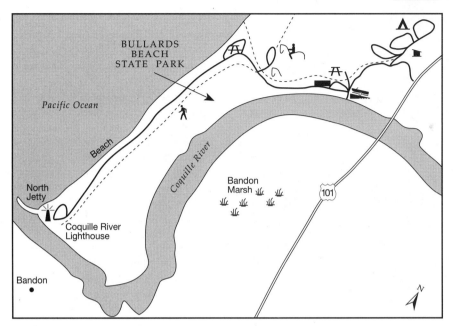

Bullards Beach State Park is situated in this pocket bounded by river and ocean, and extends some distance north over level terrain to Cut Creek. Campsites are sheltered by forest from the windy weather of the area.

There are picnic tables southwest of the campground along the river, where driftwood edges the water. Only a sandy foredune separates the horse camp and corrals from sunset rides on the beach, which stretches unhindered miles to the north.

The park was named for the Bullard family, who were early settlers in the Bandon area. Robert Bullard established a store and post office at the mouth of the river, and a ferry was operated at the location of the present bridge.

Several trails are open to various recreation uses. Equestrians can travel the 7-mile horse trail. Hikers and bikers can access the beach by a 1.5-mile trail. A 3-mile path wanders through woods and then open fields to the historic Coquille River Lighthouse, located on the North Jetty where surf collides with the breakwater.

Built in 1896, the lighthouse was designed to serve as both a harbor and a seacoast light. Its fog trumpet sounded frequently. In those days, a large number of steam schooners and sailing vessels crossed the treacherous river bar to go upriver where timber and coal deposits were plentiful. In 1903, during a winter storm, an abandoned schooner rammed the lighthouse.

The lighthouse was abandoned in 1939. Vandals streaked red paint on its exterior and graffiti collected on its walls until it was restored and

listed on the National Park Service's Register of Historic Places in 1976. Today, as a museum, it is a much visited and photographed landmark, open daily to the public. The interior walls are decorated with dramatic photographs of old ships that have navigated the river (and some that have wrecked there). It is a great winter storm-watching spot. Hundreds of Christmas lights decorate the exterior during the holiday season.

One can walk out on the rock jetty and see views of the town of Bandon across the water. The power of the surf has lifted huge trees onto the end of the jetty.

Bandon lighthouse at the mouth of Coquille River, Bullards Beach State Park

Though it can be quite windy at the lighthouse, the picnic area along the river is protected and boaters launch there. There is good fishing for steelhead, coho, and Chinook, and crabs can be caught using pots in the lower tidal section of the river. Clams are found on the flats at low tide.

This wide estuary at the mouth of the Coquille River is a National Wildlife Refuge, Bandon Marsh, with 289 acres of salt marsh. There are 115 species of migratory birds, 8 species of mammals, 45 species of fish, and many invertebrate organisms.

CAPE ARAGO STATE PARK

Hours/Season: Day use; year-round
Area: 134 acres
Facilities: Picnic tables, restrooms
Attractions: Trails, tidepools, fishing, wildlife viewing, beach access, photography, exhibit information
Access: From US 101 in Coos Bay, follow signs southwest for 14 miles

Located at road's end, Cape Arago State Park is backed by high cliffs, forest, and a roadless area to the south. If you look that direction in the spring, you'll be rewarded with ribbons of seasonal waterfalls cascading down notches in the limestone bluffs.

Whale watching at Cape Arago State Park

Cape Arago is a 200-foot-high, partly forested promontory that juts out into wild ocean surf. Simpson Reef is offshore, a stretch of rocks that often break the water surface and are home to seals and sea lions. Picnic tables are scattered around the edges of the cliff for vista viewing while lunching.

This headland was first called Cape Gregory by English navigator James Cook, in honor of the saint of the day of sighting, March 12, 1778. After the 1850 U.S. survey, the cape was renamed to honor French physicist and geographer Dominique F. J. Arago (1786–1853).

It is believed that Sir Francis Drake anchored in the South Cove in June of 1579. It seems he mistook the sand dunes north of Coos Bay for snow-covered hills, abandoned his search for the Northwest Passage, and headed back south to California.

The park was originally part of the Simpson Estate (see Shore Acres State Park) and was given to the state in 1932. The CCC did improvements in the park; a few of these remain. After the Coast Guard and the U.S. Army used the location as a radio station and lookout during World War II, it was reopened for public use in 1945.

Three coves—North, Middle, and South—provide beach access, although Middle Cove is more for mountain goats. A paved path easily takes you to North Cove for a short stretch of beachcombing and grand views along the way. North Cove is closed between March 1 and July 1 each year to protect seal and sea lion pups. South Cove, however, is the destination for serious tidepooling. Guided walks are available in summer, down a steep path and over a curve of sandy beach which meets a rocky shoreline surrounded by sheer cliffs. At a good minus tide, negotiation over an expanse of slippery rocks will take you horizontally through the various zones of intertidal organisms. Each of the numerous small pools in the rocks is exuberant with life of intricate design and adaptive mechanisms. Besides the ubiquitous sea stars and anemones, notice the black turban snails and tiny porcelain crabs, and try to find three species of chitons. The seaweeds will certainly challenge your identification attempts as you travel west. Near the treacherous surf, notice the sea urchin homes, circular holes carved out of rock. Great blue herons and seals are often seen near the beach during the tidal drainages of water in the cove. Permits are required for collecting in this park.

A 3-mile section of the Oregon Coast Trail can be accessed by following the road for a short distance to the north. The final portion to this park has been eroded by wave action and is now unsafe. The trail to Shore Acres is not traveled often, though it has grand views, and provides a nice measure of quiet introspection. (See Sunset Bay State Park for a map of trail and park.)

Few except the locals know of the other trail that starts at Cape Arago. Accessed near the south end of the park, it leads east up a forested hillside. After an ocean view at a higher elevation, it drops down into lovely coastal rain forest and crosses a creek before ascending again and curving back downhill to the road. One can easily return via the road to Cape Arago in about an hour.

SHORE ACRES STATE PARK

Hours/Season: Day use; year-round
Area: 743 acres
Facilities: Picnicking, observation shelter, gift shop, wheelchair-accessible restrooms, summer day-use fee for vehicles
Attractions: 7-acre botanical garden, exhibit information, hiking trail, wildlife viewing, storm watching, photography, beach access
Special events: July concert, annual holiday lights display
Access: From US 101 in Coos Bay, take signed road 13 miles southwest

It is hard to imagine that this stretch of spectacular coastline was once the family estate of California shipping magnate and founder of the city of North Bend, Louis J. Simpson. Although his impressive home is gone, much of the magic remains.

Crawling through dense brush, Simpson discovered this rocky headland while on a timber cruise in 1905 and thought it a wonderful place for a country home. He purchased 320 acres for $4,000 of inherited cash from Jake Evans, a "squaw-man" who lived alone there in a cabin after his Indian wife died.

In 1906, Simpson began to build a Christmas present for his wife, Cassie

Superb waves at Shore Acres State Park

Hendricks—a mansion, located in what is now known as Shore Acres State Park.

Much of the land was cleared and 200 acres were cultivated. The sprawl of coastal acreage that Simpson owned included a dairy and farm to the south for his cattle and chickens. North of the house, beyond the stables and carriage house, were concrete tennis courts, now being eroded by wave action.

A glass-enclosed observation building occupies the homesite now. In it, and at the entrance to the garden, are exhibits showing the history of this place. The procession of spruce-topped sandstone cliffs weaving among wild coves is the same view that was seen from the windows of the Simpson mansion.

The rich peat soil found by the logging crews (once an oceanside bog)

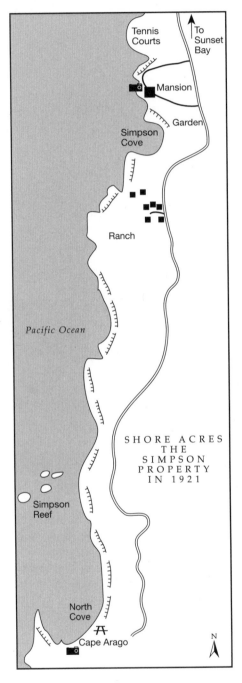

Tennis Courts
To Sunset Bay
Mansion
Garden
Simpson Cove
Ranch
Pacific Ocean
SHORE ACRES
THE
SIMPSON
PROPERTY
IN 1921
Simpson Reef
North Cove
Cape Arago
N

was good reason for planting extensive gardens. Hydrangeas were the first specialty; then roses, rhododendrons, wisteria, and exotic trees and shrubs began arriving by Simpson ships from faraway lands. The meadow in front of the house was bordered by red and white hawthorns.

The gardens have been kept in beautiful condition by Oregon's state park system. They are open to the public during daytime hours.

Except for a short period in winter, the geometrical flower beds splash lavish colors against the connecting carpets of green grass that stretch between giant spruce trees thriving in the salty sea air. Hummingbirds nest here to be near their nectar supply. Walk among the multitude of rose hybrids and choose your favorite, if you can select just one.

Linger in the sunken Oriental garden where Simpson placed ocean-washed rocks from the cove below. Cherry trees blossom near a lily pond where two sculptured bronze herons make shadows on the water. Stone lanterns and bamboo stands add to the quiet, refined atmosphere, called *Shibusa*, that is a goal of the Japanese garden.

A 3-mile section of the Oregon Coast Trail connects Shore Acres to both Sunset Bay State Park and Cape Arago State Park, occasionally taking to the road for a few feet where the cliffs become too precipitous. At Shore Acres, you can access it easily by walking north along the cliffs, or walk behind the Japanese garden to Simpson Cove to hike south to Cape Arago. The year-round trail meanders up from the beach, where the Simpsons once sunbathed and swam, along secluded cliff tops. Be alert for the unexpected.

One winter day I spotted a bald eagle less than 50 feet away, and you may hear the boisterous barking of seals below on Simpson Reef. (See Sunset Bay State Park for a map of the entire trail.)

Geology buffs will want to take time to explore the sandstone cliffs and varied formations north of the observation building. Layers of rock are exposed, some tilted sideways, some thrown flat with long creases. Punched groups of holes and rounded knobs add patterns and textures. Take care, though; there are many places to explore without accessing steep, slippery, and eroding limestone cliffs.

Wave-watching is a good reason to visit in winter. Shore Acres is one of the premier spots to see the fury of a winter storm. A 75-foot seawall is not high enough to contain the surf splash during a stormy period, but the observation building will let you stay dry and see 180-degree views.

In July, as part of the Oregon Coast Music Festival, a garden concert is held on the lawn of Shore Acres. People spread blankets and unload picnic baskets as music fills the outdoor space. Music, flowers, and the coastal environment—what luncheon ambiance!

A beautiful annual custom was started in 1986 by the newly formed nonprofit Friends of Shore Acres, Inc. During the last three weeks of December, colored lights decorate trees and outline plantings all over the botanical garden, and it becomes a fairyland. Arrive before dusk (and perhaps a good ocean sunset) to photograph the luminous colors and the garden when a hint of light in the sky shows both these subjects at their best.

The festively lit garden house, with its antique furnishings and old photographs on the walls, is open to visitors. Volunteers answer questions about the park and its history while refreshments are served. Thousands of people from all over the world see this impressive display.

SUNSET BAY STATE PARK

Hours/Season: Overnight; year-round
Area: 395 acres
Facilities: Picnic tables, bathhouse, campground with 29 full hookup, 34 electrical, and 75 tent sites (maximum site is 47 feet), hiker/biker camp, wheelchair-accessible restrooms with showers, fish-cleaning station, playground, firewood, summer day-use fee for vehicles, summer reservations available, phone: (503) 888-4902 *541-888-4902*
Attractions: Hiking, swimming, skin diving, fishing, surfing, beachcombing, boating, photography, wildlife viewing
Nearby: Cape Arago Lighthouse, South Slough National Estuarine Sanctuary
Access: Off US 101, follow signs from Coos Bay 12 miles

⚓ The day-use area of Sunset Bay State Park is an unusual, wind-protected cove just south of the inlet to enormous Coos Bay. Its charm is that steep sandstone bluffs on the north and south of the sandy beach leave only a

Great blue heron in bay

narrow passageway to open sea, mellowing the shallow water of the cove into a quieter area that warms in the summer sun and permits some ocean swimming.

The Sitka spruce-covered cliff to the north is not difficult to access and people venture out on it for its fine views, though caution is needed as its edges are unstable and accidents happen.

The protective nature of the cove was discovered long ago—it is rumored that it was once a haven for pirate ships. Since those days, fishing boats and shallow draft vessels have entered this tiny harbor as a refuge from violent ocean storms.

The forested campground is on the east side of the road, with the waters of Big Creek weaving through its campsite loops. A path goes under the road just south of the Big Creek highway crossing for access to the picnic area.

The park was once part of the Simpson Estate. After their home was built at Shore Acres, the Sunset Bay Inn was constructed at the edge of this cove in 1913.

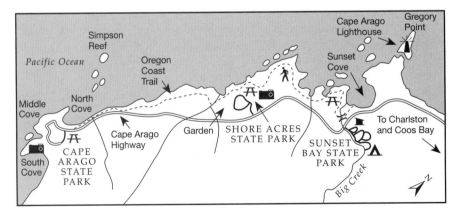

Today, one of the reasons for visiting Sunset Bay—besides the good sunset vistas—is the 3-mile Oregon Coast Trail section. Walk across the footbridge over Big Creek to the south of the beach and continue along the forested cliffs and through meadows until the path edges the paved road. As it re-enters a wooded area, the trail splits. The left spur roughly follows the path of the old entry road to the Simpson Mansion. Take the right spur to continue along the coast trail, which is now in Shore Acres State Park.

The geology is fascinating along this stretch of the trail, with steep-walled coves of striated rock and massive stone slabs gouged, flipped sideways, and stood on end. Some which had protruding knobs have left shattered rock balls strewn about the beach. Swirled patterns in gray, beige, and gold form steep-sloped rock perches for oystercatcher birds with their red bills and black bodies. The surf booms on the many rocky interruptions to the shoreline. This wonderful landscape is backed by good views of the Cape Arago Lighthouse in the distance.

The lighthouse is situated on a small islet called Gregory Point, just north of the park. It perches on a section of sandstone cliffs eroded by tremendous surf action. The light guards a dangerous section of the coast near the shipping center of North Bend/Coos Bay. The first lighthouse here was built in 1866, but what with encroachments on the land, the third structure, 44 feet high, now sits 100 feet above the water. The public is denied access via the footbridge to the islet.

While in the area, visit the South Slough National Estuarine Sanctuary by traveling south from Charleston for four miles on Seven Devils Road. The 4,400 acres of the reserve is located in the southern half of South Slough and includes a visitor center, hiking trails, fishing, educational workshops, and canoeing, which is one of the best ways to see this estuary ecosystem with its varied wetlands. The canoe launch is just east of the Charleston Bridge, but the trip is tricky, so it needs some planning. Go with the tide: south and up the slough at, or shortly after, low tide, with your return at, or shortly after, high tide.

COQUILLE MYRTLE GROVE STATE PARK

Hours/Season: Day use; year-round
Area: 7 acres
Facilities: Picnic tables, vault toilets, *no water*
Attractions: Myrtlewood trees, fishing
Access: From Myrtle Point, proceed 3 miles east on Oregon Highway 42, then 11 miles south on the road to Powers

▲ This lovely stand of old myrtlewood trees along the banks of the Coquille River was given to the state by Save the Myrtlewoods, Inc. in 1950. An old rutted dirt road winds down to the river for access by fishermen.

A carpet of myrtlewood tree fruits

Also called California laurel or Pacific myrtle—*Umbellularia californica*—these trees are prized for their hardwood, which is a rich, light brown that is hard, strong, and heavy. The cut wood is textured with varying shades of color and patterns that finish to a high polish and mellow wonderfully with age. Commercially, the wood is used for many items that are turned on a lathe—bowls, candlesticks, plates, and other specialty products—but it also makes excellent furniture and cabinets, as long-time residents of the growing area know. Many of the larger stands of myrtlewood have been cut, so there is only a limited quantity of large logs available for use.

These slow-growing trees are found from lower California to as far north as Coos Bay, usually close to the coast at lower altitudes. Although they tolerate many soil types and conditions, the largest trees are found in deep, rich soils like that of valley bottoms. A couple of natural history guides gave their maximum height as around 80 feet, but you will find that they exceed this height in some of these old protected stands. The Oregon coast with its rain and rivers seems to produce the giant ones. In poorer soil, they are often multi-trunked. The shape is often a rounded one; sometimes old ones have a gnarled appearance.

The deep-green evergreen leaves are lance-shaped and about ten centimeters long, with a strong pungent odor when torn. Small yellow flowers are produced in clusters from December to early spring, followed by an abundant crop of spherical fruit of up to 2.5 centimeters that are yellowish green to purplish green, with a fleshy layer around one large seed. If you visit this park in autumn you will walk on a carpet of myrtlewood fruit. Squirrels, other rodents, and some birds feed on the fruit and seeds.

GOLDEN AND SILVER FALLS STATE PARK

Hours/Season: Day use; year-round
Area: 157 acres
Facilities: Picnic tables, pit toilets, *no water*

Attractions: Hiking trails, waterfalls, old-growth forest, fishing, photography

Access: From US 101, at the south end of Coos Bay, follow signs to Allegany and then 10 more miles to the park, 24 miles northeast of Coos Bay

For a taste of dramatic waterfalls and old-growth wilderness habitat at the end of the road, Golden and Silver Falls State Park will serve nicely. Be warned, however, that the last 5 miles are on a gravel road and the last 2 miles of that are quite narrow, so please don't attempt the drive with an RV. Logging trucks use this road, so one is advised to visit on weekends or holidays.

On a weekend or holiday, the drive from Coos Bay is a pleasant one, first along the Coos River, where boaters and fishermen are out in numbers, then skirting the Millicoma River and passing a series of farms before reaching a scattering of homes for those who want to live a more isolated life. The final miles of the road follow Glenn Creek, a feeder stream into the Millicoma just past the southern boundary of the Siuslaw National Forest.

The road ends at the picnic area of the park, a shaded piece of flat bottomland along Silver Creek and Glenn Creek. Great blue herons feed along the water as it flows over boulders and through small pools. Beyond the creeks lies a lovely forest canyon.

As you hike, consider the road that once continued through the park

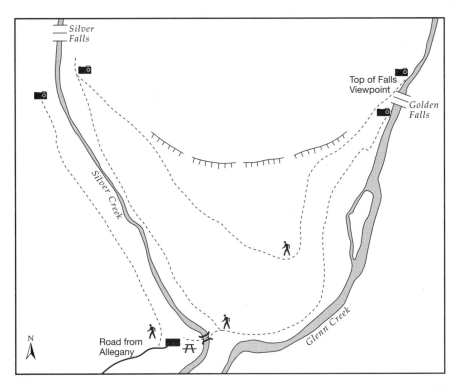

View of Silver Falls, Golden and Silver Falls State Park

area, skirting the falls. One information source said that a "tortuous road crossed the base of Silver Falls and followed a narrow ledge to leave the park above Golden Falls." Another source said that the bridge across Silver Creek collapsed and it was decided not to rebuild the steep, narrow portion of the road around the falls. Even in the mind's eye, it is difficult to envision this road. Is that the remains of a bridge in the creek at the bottom of Golden Falls?

Three hiking trails let you choose, or you can easily hike all three. Taking off to your left is the 1,550-foot path to Silver Falls. It climbs gently to a view of this more than 100-foot-high waterfall. In the past, a narrow path descended through vegetation to let one approach closer to the water, but a slide of several trees has blocked the path and this is no longer possible. In open sunshine, the water falls like silver strands of hair from a round "head" of dark basalt rock. The water catches on another notch lower down before cascading onto rocks. To the side, another ledge of rock forms another small fall. All in all, it's an unusual waterfall in appearance, not fitting into any one type.

Golden Falls can be viewed from two trails accessed via a bridge over Silver Creek. A level 1,375-foot walk through old-growth forest of Douglas fir, myrtlewood, alder, and bigleaf maple takes you to the bottom of the falls. This wood is all that remains of the ancient forest that covered this 25-mile valley, saved because it is a state park. This is in the midst of what was once the "Timber Capital of the World," but most of the forest was logged in less than a human lifetime.

To reach the top of the falls, and a grand overview of the old forest and the landscape to the west, take the 1-mile trail to the left after you cross the bridge. This climbs moderately to a close view of Silver Falls and then switchbacks up to the top of Golden Falls. The last portion of the trail is a ledge midway between huge rocky cliffs topped with a few trees overhead, and a straight drop to the forest below. *Please use caution.* The waterfall cascades down from Glenn Creek into a wedge of rock, sliding over more ridges of rock before it hits bottom. The forest is lush with mossy trees and dew-sprinkled ferns, and mushrooms pop up in spring and fall. Huge fallen leaves of bigleaf maples soften the path in autumn.

WILLIAM M. TUGMAN STATE PARK

Hours/Season: Overnight; *campground closed in winter*
Area: 560 acres
Facilities: Picnic tables, group picnic shelter, campground with 115 electrical sites (maximum site is 50 feet), hiker/biker camp, dumping station, wheelchair-accessible restrooms with showers, firewood, boat ramp and wheelchair-accessible fishing pier, playground
Attractions: Fishing, boating, swimming, coho fish trap, photography
Nearby: Oregon Dunes Recreation Area (ODNRA)—Umpqua Dunes Trail
Access: Off US 101, 8 miles south of Reedsport

Resident geese at edge of Eel Lake, William M. Tugman State Park

▲ Tugman State Park offers a good base to explore the recreational opportunities in the area. Picnic tables are scattered along the waterfront and throughout the spacious lawn of the day-use area, where you can choose sunny or shady locations. Mallards and geese are lakeside residents. A walkway connects this area with the campground, with sites among the forest of pines, Sitka spruce, cedar, salal, and evergreen huckleberry. Explorers will head for the nearby dunes.

Fishermen launch boats to enjoy the good fishing in freshwater Eel Lake (eel-shaped, of course) on the east side of the highway. The lake was formerly used by the Oregon State Game Commission as a brood lake for coastal cutthroat trout, but over many years it became partially filled with logging debris. After the Game Commission cleaned out the lake, the west half of it and the surrounding land was given to the state for park protection to insure public access and use. This is one of a series of lakes formed long ago when sand dunes blocked the flow of inland waterways.

Coho go upstream from Eel Lake to spawn in fall and winter. A fish trap to collect coho eggs for hatcheries was established in the park in 1978. When

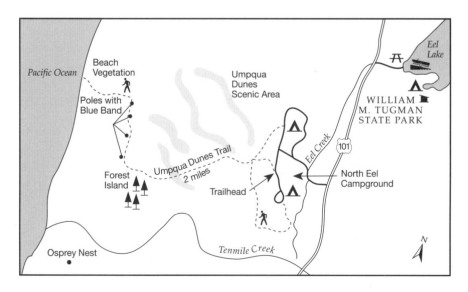

these needs are met, coho are allowed upstream to spawn. It is encouraging to see that 1991–1992 was the best year so far. Visitors can view coho in the trap.

The park was named after a prominent newspaperman of Eugene and Reedsport, William M. Tugman (1894–1961), who headed Governor Paul Patterson's State Park Advisory Committee. That committee made the important 1956 citizens' report and recommendations on state parks. Tugman became the first Chairman of the State Parks and Recreation Advisory Committee, formed in 1957, and was known as a "rugged character" who championed wise use of Oregon's natural resources.

One of the best hiking trails in the Oregon dunes—the Umpqua Dunes Trail—is just across the highway and a short distance south of this campground. Accessed from Eel Creek campground, ORVs are restricted in this area, making it a safe and quiet experience among dunes that rise to 400 feet in elevation.

After a 0.25-mile hike through coastal forest, a 2-mile-wide expanse of sand dunes can be traversed to the beach. The trail is unmarked in these shifting dunes. Climb the nearest tall dune and head west, aiming for the north end of the distant "forest island." Route markers are visible near the vegetated deflation plain and lead to the beach.

This trail is the quickest route to the beach, but perhaps the uniqueness of the dune environment might entice you to meander around to more discoveries. Angling south and west from the tall dune will route you past deflation plains with sparkling ovals of water, and eventually to the mouth of Tenmile Creek, if you persist long enough. If the season is right, watch for a pair of ospreys feeding young in a nest on the south side of the creek. Rushes, twisted orchids, and monkeyflowers grow in the wetlands adjacent to the creek. Explorers should be careful to orient themselves by landmarks along the route. People do get lost in the dunes, but it's a high to find your own way in this open landscape. You might imagine yourself in the Sahara Desert, but for the temperate climate.

UMPQUA LIGHTHOUSE STATE PARK

Hours/Season: Overnight; *campground closed in winter*
Area: 450 acres
Facilities: Picnic tables, campground with 22 full hookup (maximum site is 45 feet) and 42 tent sites, restrooms with showers, boat ramp, firewood
Attractions: Hiking, boating, photography, fishing, sand dunes, adjacent lighthouse
Nearby: Dean Creek Elk Viewing Area
Access: Follow Discovery Drive from US 101 to park, about 1 mile south of Winchester Bay

▲ In a wooded basin between the highway and the ocean, Umpqua Light-
⊥ house State Park is centered on small Lake Marie and bounded by sand

dunes thrown ashore by the wind and wave action of the Pacific Ocean. Located on the southern shore of the mouth of an important river named after the local Umpqua Indians, the park and adjacent lighthouse have also taken that name. This was once an even larger park meant to include the preservation of the adjoining sand dunes, but 2,265 acres in the dunes were exchanged with ODNRA in 1981 for potential park land in other areas.

In summer, Lake Marie is a favorite water playground for youngsters, who float around kicking on small rafts. It is a good place to canoe. Just north of the lake, on a bluff overlooking the sea, is a whale viewing area with good exhibit information on behavior, migration, birthing, and different species. An enclosed triangular area at the mouth of the river offers birdwatching and canoeing. A local oyster and mussel farm is located within this triangle.

Steep, paved paths lead downhill to the lake from the three loops of the campground. These connect to the 1.3-mile hiking trail which circles Lake Marie. By turning north and going counterclockwise on this path, one soon reaches a series of picnic spots on the lake shore. Continuing, hikers pass through a tunnel of huckleberry and rhododendron until a spur branches off that climbs to a dune overlook and access point. A huge expanse of dunes called the Punch Bowl is found here, though these get heavy ORV traffic at times. This is a good area, however, to watch the annual Oregon Dunes Mushers Mail Run in March when dog sleds on wheels traverse the dune hills from Coos Bay to Florence. To get to the beach, it is a walk over dunes, then through vegetation, to the sand by the ocean.

The lake loop continues to the south past this dune spur, where multiple springs feed the lake and water the lush vegetation of fir, Sitka spruce, hemlock, lodgepole pine, and cedar.

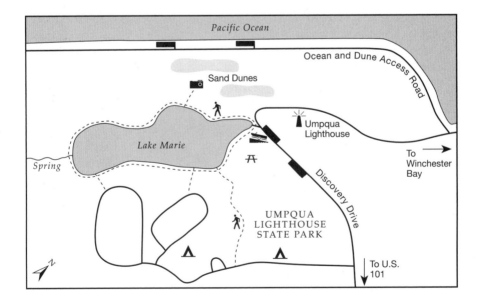

The Umpqua Lighthouse is seen from the day-use area by the lake and can be reached by an easy walk. It is fenced, however, and visitors are not allowed in the structure without special arrangements.

This is not the original Umpqua River Lighthouse, which was completed in 1857. That one stood as a sentinel on its sand foundation at the mouth of the river for only four years before erosion toppled it.

In 1894, a light again flashed from a new lighthouse wisely built up and away from the river entrance to the sea. The light at the top of the 65-foot tower is now at an elevation of 165 feet and is visible for 19 nautical miles.

It's a short drive from the park to the Dean Creek Elk Viewing Area, located a few miles east of Reedsport, on the south side of Oregon Highway 38. A scenic overlook has been constructed recently for travelers.

Roosevelt elk move down from the higher elevations in the winter and are frequently seen in herds on the bottomlands of the Umpqua River. At this particular spot, chances to see them are good in early morning or evening.

Lighthouse at Umpqua Lighthouse State Park

CENTRAL COAST

▲ Sand dunes continue north along the ocean to Florence. Visitors might at first be intimidated by all that sand and the conflict with beach access, but those who take time to explore the dunes, especially on foot, will find they offer a rare kind of open-space orienteering.

The dunes vanish abruptly where Heceta Head rises high above the sea. One of the coast's most photographed lighthouses is perched here, and a famous sea lion cave occupies a huge cavity in the ocean side of the headland.

One of the attractions of the Oregon coast is its alternation of headlands with stretches of sandy beaches and coves. It causes one to ponder the geological explanation of what happened here. One has another shot at beach walking before Cape Perpetua lifts up the coastline to a height of 800 feet.

The town of Yachats (pronounced *YAH-hots*) lies on the downslope of Perpetua and is known for its smelt catches. Many of the names on the coast are legacies of the Indians and the rich life they lived in this land of plenty, before they were moved to reservations.

The Siletz Indian reservation once occupied 125 miles and 1,300,000 acres along the central coast, but after forty years their land had shrunk to 47,000 acres and the reservation held only a few hundred Indians. Some still live on their land in the town of Siletz, inland a few miles, and they still perform wonderful pow-wows in Indian dress.

In 1991, an exciting event occurred at Waldport's Alsea Bay: a new bridge was completed, and the old one was dynamited into oblivion, an awesome sight. The bay offers good crabbing and windsurfing.

The Central Coast is replete with state parks, waysides, and resorts. Both Newport (the coast's second largest city with a comfortable 8,700 residents) and Lincoln City draw large numbers of tourists to the natural opulence of

Opposite: *View of punch bowl area and marine gardens of Devil's Punch Bowl State Park from Cape Foulweather*

their surroundings. Yet there is much elbow room for recreation in the great outdoors.

Newport's new Performing Arts Center, the Visual Arts Center, and the many galleries along the entire coast attest to the magnetism the coast exerts on artists. The city's bayfront area is a good place for a stroll.

North of Newport, the short Otter Crest Loop, atop Cape Foulweather, makes an interesting detour. This cape was named by Captain Cook as he explored the coast. It is not difficult to guess what the day was like, but rain along the coast does have pluses. Trees and vegetation are lush and green. Mushrooms abound. Groups get together to learn safe species and commercial pickers have their secret chanterelle patches.

Depoe Bay is billed as the world's smallest navigable harbor—just six square miles—but that doesn't seem to inhibit the many charter boats that often go to sea to fish or whale watch.

In Lincoln City, another superlative attaches to the "D" River, which connects Devil's Lake to the ocean. Is it really the world's shortest river? This city is a composite of five smaller towns that ran together, with the influx of regulars from Portland, and were consolidated into one. On fair days, its skies are often filled with kites.

JESSIE M. HONEYMAN STATE PARK

Hours/Season: Overnight; year-round
Area: 522 acres
Facilities: Picnic tables, campground with 66 full hookup (maximum site is 60 feet) and 240 tent sites, hiker/biker camp, group camping, wheelchair-accessible restrooms with showers, playground, slide program, firewood, dumping station, boat ramp and dock, swimmers' float, store, restaurant, summer day-use fee for vehicles, summer reservations available, phone: (503) 997-3641
Attractions: Hiking trails, sand dunes, three lakes, boating, water-skiing, fishing, swimming, photography, birdwatching
Nearby: Darlingtonia Wayside
Access: Off both sides of US 101, 3 miles south of Florence

▲ Jessie M. Honeyman State Park has long been one of Oregon's most popular parks. In the late 1950s, *Life Magazine* listed it as one of the outstanding state parks in the United States. Besides having a campground and picnic area nestled against dramatic sand dune formations, the park has lovely lakes for water sports, trails for exploring, and nature for observing.

Woahink Lake, on the east side of the highway, has a group camp, a vast lawn sprinkled with picnic tables, boat ramps, and a roped-off area for swimming. In autumn, a flock of tagged Canada geese takes over the waterfront lawn and wild ducks land on the lake.

Lake Cleawox, the campground, and the dune environment are west of the highway. This lake, though considerably smaller than Woahink, also has swimming, fishing, and boating, but in a totally different environment, with tall dunes sliding into the lake on one side. Picnic tables edge the dune parking area and are placed along the shore of the lake in several areas.

The CCC was busy here in 1935–1940, designing and constructing improvements adapted to their surroundings. The concessions building on the north shore of Lake Cleawox—originally a bathhouse—is listed in the National Register of Historic Places, the stone and log caretaker's house and garage is now the park office, and there are several rustic kitchen shelters. Stone curbings edge landscaped roadways.

The park name honors Jessie M. Honeyman of Portland (1852–1948), a leading advocate for roadside beautification, scenic preservation, and Oregon parks. She was a staunch supporter and guide for Sam Boardman.

The various areas of Honeyman State Park can be accessed by several paths. One trail connects the dune parking area with the campground as it follows a wetland area along the third park lake, Lily, which is indeed topped with many water lilies. Another lakeside trail leads from this dune parking area around the edge of Cleawox to the north day-use and concession area. A trail branches off from this one near the entry road and leads across the highway to Woahink Lake. These trails are mostly through wooded areas of fir, spruce, hemlock, salal, and thimbleberry. Outstanding areas of old rhododendrons border the lakes and dunes, blooming in early summer.

Explore the huge sand hills by accessing them from the dune parking

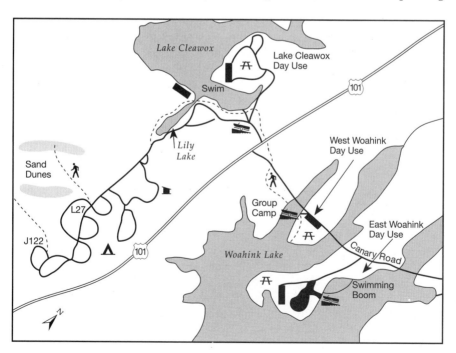

Walker on trail fronting Lake Cleawox, Jessie M. Honeyman State Park

area, or from sites L 27 or J 122 in the campground. Be alert for ORVs in certain areas of these dunes, although they are restricted on vegetated dunes. Most of the dunes west of Cleawox are now part of the ODNRA.

The huge long dune formations that waddle toward the beach are called *oblique dunes*, a unique type found in the ODNRA. Take a long walk on top of one of these dunes where the sand is packed for easy hiking and the views are great. Look for the succession of small transverse ridges that form at right angles to the summer northwest winds, with steep slip faces where the sand blows over the edge. If it's windy, hike the still valleys between sand hills.

It's interesting that the dunes are also a great place to study plant succession, from pioneer plants that grow on open sand, to intermediate vegetation, and eventually to forest. Some orienteering in the dunes will reveal all of these stages. This 32,000-acre recreation area has 426 species of wildlife. Some animals are difficult to spot, but it is easy to find their tracks in the patterned sand. Birds are the most numerous species. The number and density of songbirds is greater here than in the coastal mountain forests.

For a look at some fascinating and rare plants, visit the Darlingtonia Wayside 3 miles north of Florence. Paths lead to an observation platform that overlooks a swampy wetland with a thick growth of *Darlingtonia californica* plants. Also known as cobra-lily and pitcher-plant, this species traps and digests insects with its enzymes.

DEVIL'S ELBOW STATE PARK

Hours/Season: Day use; year-round
Area: 546 acres
Facilities: Picnic tables, wheelchair-accessible restrooms, summer day-
use fee for vehicles
Attractions: Heceta Head Lighthouse, hiking, wildlife viewing, fishing,
beach access, photography
Nearby: Sea Lion Caves
Access: Off US 101, travel 13 miles north of Florence

Devil's Elbow State Park embraces spectacular Cape Cove and is bounded by Heceta Head on the north and a steep, craggy cape to the south that contains Sea Lion Point. Cape Creek flows under the high, reinforced concrete deck arch bridge—another of Conde McCullough's artistic constructions—that connects these headlands as its waters join the Pacific in the midst of this sandy ocean cove. Picnic tables are scattered around the edge of the sea in terraces and give great visual pleasure while lunching.

At the tip of the north headland is the active Heceta Head Lighthouse, one of the most photographed features of the Oregon coast. Its name honors

View of Heceta Lighthouse and Keeper's House, Devil's Elbow State Park

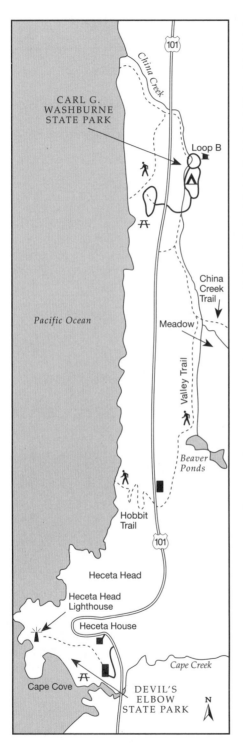

the Spanish navigator Bruno Heceta. Built in 1894, the lighthouse has a rotating Fresnel lens with 640 glass prisms, mounted in a 49-foot tower that is visible 20 miles to sea. The lighthouse is not visible from the picnic area, but the renovated assistant lighthouse keeper's residence is part of the day-use view. The best place to photograph the lighthouse is from turnouts on the south cape, where Ocean Cove adds a wonderful foreground to photo compositions.

Although the main keeper's house is no longer here, the remaining residence is in good shape. It is maintained in part by Lane Community College since the Coast Guard transferred the property to the U.S. Forest Service, who restored the building. Called Heceta House, it is an 1893 Queen Anne–style residence that is now a Historic Landmark. In the past, rumors were circulated that it was haunted. In fact, one commentator rated it as one of the ten most haunted structures in the country. The television movie *Cry for a Stranger* was filmed here.

A good trail of approximately 0.5 mile lets visitors view both of these structures and the spectacular scenery. A side trail near the beginning leads down to the rocky shore, where one can maneuver back to the beach at low tide. Although an offshore island would be easy to access at low tide, it is a national wildlife refuge and access is prohibited. It is too bad that the necessity of the keep-off sign mars photographs.

Back on the main trail, several places reveal excellent seascapes south which include the bridge, park, and rocks. One can walk around Heceta House before continuing on to the lighthouse. Sea birds are abundant and include cormorants, surf scoters, and tufted puffins.

A visit to nearby Sea Lion Caves, on a headland to the south, reveals some of the aspects of the lives of wild Steller's sea lions. One can view them inside their huge cave, where they spend most of the winter months, and on outside rock ledges during spring and summer when they are breeding and birthing.

CARL G. WASHBURNE STATE PARK

Hours/Season: Overnight; year-round
Area: 1,089 acres
Facilities: Picnic tables, campground with 58 full hookup (maximum site is 45 feet), 2 tent, and 6 primitive sites, hiker/biker camp, dumping station, firewood, restrooms with showers
Attractions: Hiking, beachcombing, clamming, tidepools, fishing, elk viewing
Nearby: Audubon Tenmile Creek Preserve
Access: Off US 101, 14 miles north of Florence

Step out onto the sand at the day-use area of Washburne and you will often see at least one of the capes that bracket the beach wreathed in ribbons of fog. One can walk as far south as Heceta Head—where there are tidepools—and north to Big Creek and its scenic bridge. In the distance is Cape Perpetua. Those who search the sands of the beach may find agates and other colorful rocks. Though the day-use area is on the ocean side, most of the picnic tables don't have views of the ocean, since they are set among the thick dune vegetation.

This vast park is gently rolling hills—really ancient sand dunes—that are now covered with Sitka spruce, shore pine, and much coast huckleberry, particularly near the windy ocean frontage. This area has often been called "the Persian Carpet" because of the bright bronze-colored new growth on the huckleberry in springtime.

The campground is east of the highway with two loops bordering China Creek. A trail leads from the north end of Loop "B" along the creek to the beach, or visitors can cross the highway and follow a trail through the day-use area.

Carl G. Washburne State Park is a memorial to a Eugene businessman who was Oregon Highway Commissioner from 1932 to 1935. The original tract for the park was a gift from the estate of his wife, Narcissa. Their modest home was once in the northeast corner of the property.

A good 4-mile loop trail, through several habitats, can be hiked in the park by combining two specific trails with a beach walk. The northern trailhead begins by the creek at the entry to the campground. (Park your car

Beaver pond along Valley Trail, Carl G. Washburne State Park

in the day-use area and cautiously cross the highway.) This Valley Trail climbs gently for 1.5 miles to the highway. A dirt path branches off to the west at about 0.25 mile, but stay left and you'll soon come to a meadow and wetland area where China Creek comes in from the east. A bridge at this location accesses the China Creek Trail, a pleasant 0.5-mile dead-end walk through the more typical inland forest of firs, maple, and hemlock. The main trail continues on what was once a wagon road constructed in 1895 between Yachats and Florence, now being partially reclaimed by new growth and mossy green forest floor. A short path branches off to the left to access a beaver pond, with water lilies, great blue herons, and lush tall grasses, or you can continue to the right and come to an observation platform overlooking the wide pond. Though it is shallow at its edge, one can see deeper moving water in its center. The park staff initially fought the efforts of the beaver construction along the creek, but eventually rerouted the trail and let the beaver get on with its livelihood. These beaver ponds have recently been shown to improve salmon habitat. The park also is home to at least two elk herds and an occasional black bear.

A parking area is seen upon reaching the highway. Walk across the highway to the signed Hobbit Trail. A path was first blazed to the beach by those going to the good clam-digging and mussel-collecting beach on the north side of Heceta Head. It plunged steeply downhill in a tunnel-like affair that suggested its name to someone in the 1970s, when J. R. R. Tolkien's fantasy books about underground-dwelling Hobbits were so popular. The park staff upgraded the trail and eased the sharp descent into switchbacks that weave through the thick growth of rhododendrons, salal, stunted shore pines and Sitka spruce. Mushrooms, especially studded puffballs, are numerous on the trail in mid-September. The loop continues by walking north on the beach for 1.5 miles to the day-use area, where you have probably parked your car. If the tide is out, take time to explore the rocky crevices that house marine creatures near the beginning of the beach walk. One can, alternately, park at the southern trailhead and hike north on the Valley Trail first. It depends whether you prefer to end or begin with your uphill section.

Travelers interested in seeing good forest habitat might want to visit the Audubon Tenmile Creek Preserve. This is reached by taking the next inland road north from Washburne and following Tenmile Creek into the Siskiyou National Forest for 5 miles. A small neighborhood group, the Tenmile Creek Association, realized the uniqueness of the mostly undisturbed forest of 65,000 acres between Cape Perpetua and Heceta Head. The corridor strip along Tenmile Creek lies between two designated wilderness areas, Cummins Creek and Rock Creek, and offered the possibility of a large unfragmented wilderness tract that would preserve both forest and the wildlife that needs this habitat. The first success at preservation was convincing Audubon to buy this 116-acre tract.

A sign for the preserve is seen at the beginning of a walk across the large grassy lowland meadow that fronts the creek. A huge maple tree stands majestically in the midst of the sanctuary. The land around the meadow rises steeply and is heavily forested, with many old-growth trees. This is good habitat for marbled murrelets, which like the mossy bends in the old branches of trees for nests. Continue to follow the meadow to the creek with its rich vegetation, mushrooms, beaver signs, dippers, and clear spawning habitat for salmon. Tenmile Creek Association continues efforts to save more of this acreage from logging.

NEPTUNE STATE PARK

Hours/Season: Day use; year-round
Area: 302 acres
Facilities: Picnic tables, wheelchair-accessible vault toilets, *no water*
Attractions: Tidepools, hiking trails, photography, beach access, wildlife
viewing, saltwater fishing, spouting horn
Nearby: Cape Perpetua Scenic Area
Access: Off US 101, 3 miles south of Yachats

▲ Two of the developed areas of Neptune State Park straddle Cummins
⊥ Creek as it flows into the sea after its descent from the steep rain forests

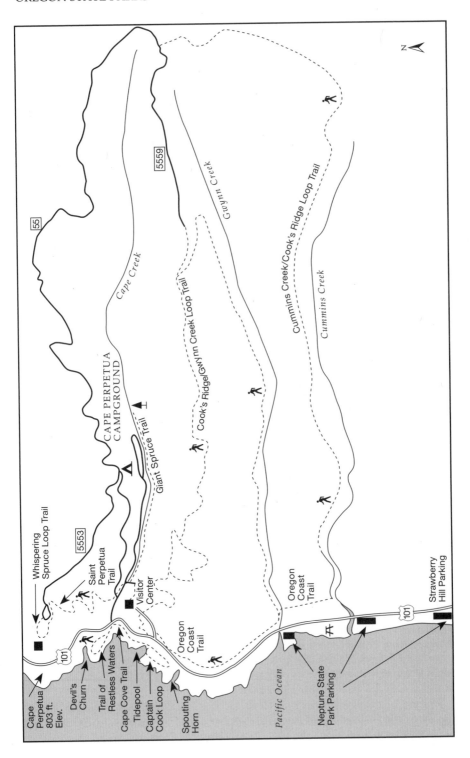

of the Cummins Creek Wilderness, just east of the park. Split by the highway, about 2.5 miles of ocean frontage in Neptune State Park extend from Captain Cook Point almost to Bob Creek. The violent merging of wave action with the spill of basalt rock along the shore suggested the name of the Roman god of the sea for this park.

The beach is a mixture of cobble rock below the low terrace with sand closer to the edge of the sea. Short trails access the beach from both sides of the creek for wandering among the rocky shore and exploring the tidepools at low tide.

A third developed area is Strawberry Hill to the south. The best tidepools of the park are found here, where a good trail leads south to the beach from the parking lot. This rocky, sometimes sandy area has most of the common species of intertidal animals, plus abundant algae and surf grass.

Though Alsea Indians came to camp in this area in the summer for the bounty of the shellfish beds and left behind shell middens, the first white visitor to view this coast was Captain James Cook. When he sighted the nearby cape on Saint Perpetua's Day on March 7, 1778, he named the cape after this saint.

Where Neptune State Park ends to the north, the 2,700-acre Cape Perpetua Scenic Area begins, a great recreation area to visit. The rock of the cape is old bedrock sea floor (which extends into Neptune) formed from lava flows that erupted underwater some fifty million years ago, during Eocene time. Among the solid lava flows are several zones of broken and fragmented rock. The restless sea has sought out any weaknesses in the rock and made coves and fissures, leaving the more resistant basalt as headlands and sea stacks.

A visitor center staffed by the U.S. Forest Service has information about Cape Perpetua and its history, along with good trail maps for the many hiking possibilities that interconnect between Neptune and the scenic area.

A section of the Oregon Coast Trail begins just across the highway in Neptune State Park. This 1.3-mile trail with ocean views goes between this park and the visitor center and is part of the 7-mile loop made by the Gwynn Creek Trail and the Captain Cook Ridge Trail.

Short trails along the rugged coastline begin across from the visitor center. The first to the south is the 0.6-mile Captain Cook Loop. A shell midden and a spectacular closeup view of a spouting horn is seen from this trail. The surf roars into Cook's Chasm—a fissure in a rocky headland—and finds a cave that traps the water momentarily and ejects it violently after mixing it with air. The Cape Cove Trail continues from that trail for 0.3 mile to the north along the shelf above the craggy rocks to the next trail. The 0.4-mile Trail of Restless Waters loops around at the edge of the sea to give visitors a view of Devil's Churn, a deep gash eroded along a fracture. All of these oceanside paths provide access to tidepooling and saltwater fishing, but do use caution among these rocks and the pounding wave action.

The 1.3-mile Saint Perpetua Trail climbs from the visitor center, or the nearby Cape Perpetua Campground, up the south face of the 803-foot cape. Climbing through coastal forest, the trail switchbacks to great views of the

Spouting horn in Cook's Chasm at Cape Perpetua near Neptune State Park

coast and ends with an incredible seascape that motorists see after driving to the top and taking the 0.3-mile Whispering Spruce Loop. On a clear day, headlands to the south stack up behind one another, sometimes as far as Cape Blanco, and to Cape Foulweather to the north—a seascape that measures 150 miles. With a view of 37 miles out to sea, it's a good place (and an official site) to whale watch. Along this loop, a wonderful old shelter built by the CCC adds to photo compositions. The shelter was used as a lookout for ships during World War II.

For an inland hike through forest, walk the 1-mile (one-way) Giant Spruce Trail as it gently climbs above Cape Creek to a 500-year-old specimen of Sitka spruce that grew from a nurse log, now rotted away. Once 225 feet tall, it is now about 190 feet high after losing its top, with a diameter of 15 feet—a splendid tree. Other nurse trees are seen along the trail, some with several trees growing from them. Skunk cabbage blooms early and there is abundant wildlife and lush hillsides of ferns. This trail begins by the visitor center, or it can be accessed from the Cape Perpetua Campground in two places, making a loop trail possible with the campground road. This campground has spacious creekfront sites and is a good base for exploring in the area.

For a longer, more strenuous hike from Neptune, cross the highway and go 0.25 mile east to the Cummins Creek trailhead. A loop is made by connecting to the Cook's Ridge Trail to the visitor center and back to Neptune via the Oregon Coast Trail.

YACHATS STATE PARK

Hours/Season: Day use; year-round
Area: 93.6 acres
Facilities: Picnic tables, restrooms
Attractions: Fishing, birdwatching, photography, wave watching
Nearby: Smelt Sands Trailhead
Access: Off US 101, turn west at sign in Yachats on north side of river

Within the town of Yachats, this park preserves the rocky junction of the Pacific Ocean and the north side of the Yachats River, letting public use prevail over private development. It is enjoyed by mothers walking strollers, fishermen, and those who simply enjoy the wildness of the dynamic sea. Sea birds are plentiful in the booming surf area. Between aerial maneuvers, sea gulls line up in rows along a fence. Ruddy turnstones are not very skittish in the noisy background of surf booming off the rocks, yet their harlequin dark-and-light patterning is a flash of beauty as they take flight. Concrete steps lead downhill and end abruptly in the midst of surf and basalt rock.

Both salmon and steelhead migrate up the river from the sea and many fishing spots are found along the high banks and rocky bluffs. The beach in this area is good spawning ground for grunion (called smelts here) when they come ashore to lay their eggs in the sand during the summer months.

The Indian name *Yachats* means "at the foot of the mountain," appropriate since it is below Cape Perpetua.

Also in the town of Yachats, just to the north along the oceanfront, Smelts Sands Wayside is a good destination for hikers and wave watchers. A long swatch of cliff scallops and offshore rocks interact to maximize wave action at certain times. It is fascinating how different wind and current conditions, along with tidal effects, produce variations in surf along the rocky shore. Some places are more spectacular than others, and it is not always the same place.

But the wonderful thing about this wayside is the fact that a county road right-of-way platted on maps became a wheelchair-accessible 0.75-mile trail along the ocean. This happened because local citizens pursued saving this right-of-way for public use for fifteen years until the Oregon Supreme Court granted access for trail use in 1986. It was dedicated as the Yachats 804 Trail in 1990 after the State Parks Agency completed the path. When the

View south from Yachats State Park

coast was first settled, towns often platted roads right up to—and sometimes into—the edge of the ocean, not being very realistic about erosion at
the coast or simply not checking where the squares on paper really were.
For a long time, a path for fishermen took advantage of this publicly owned
strip of land.

The trail meanders atop an ancient, rocky beach that was formed by
wave erosion before the last Ice Age and is again being eroded, though the
resistance of the basalt rocks and old lava flows is slow. The sandstone ele-
ments, however, are less resistant. Short, sandy pocket beaches are intermittent. The rocks are part of the Yaquina Formation, which is about
twenty-five million years old.

The trail is a fine nature walk, vibrant with demonstrations of the tenacity of nature. Salal roots hold soil from falling off banks. Other vegetation includes bog anemone, leathery grape fern, ladies' tresses, and golden-eyed grass.

BEACHSIDE STATE PARK

Hours/Season: Overnight; year-round
Area: 16.7 acres
Facilities: Picnic tables, campground with 31 electrical and 50 tent sites (maximum site is 30 feet), hiker/biker camp, wheelchair-accessible restrooms with showers, horseshoes, summer reservations available, phone: (503) 563-3220
Attractions: Beach access, hiking, surf-fishing
Access: Off US 101, 4 miles south of Waldport

▲ Except for a few summer sites at Cape Lookout, the campground at ⊥ Beachside has the only state park oceanfront view sites along the Oregon coast where you can walk right out onto the beach. These are available all year, though there are not many of them. This is a small, cozy campground where choices are good in winter but reservations might be wise in summer. Campers are at the cutting edge of winter storms, but oceanfront sites do have some vegetation protection and sites in the shore pine and spruce woods offer even more. And sunny, calm days do sneak into the wild season.

A small creek separates the campground from the day-use area, with beach access on either side of the park. The hiker/biker camp is between the two facilities and adjacent to the day-use restroom.

The park is situated roughly midway along the approximately 8-mile section of Oregon Coast Trail between Yachats and Waldport, so round-trip day hikes could go to either destination. The level beach is smooth, hard sand and offers good walking.

GOVERNOR PATTERSON STATE PARK

Hours/Season: Day use; year-round
Area: 10 acres
Facilities: Picnic tables, restrooms
Attractions: Beach access, hiking, surf-fishing
Nearby: Alsea Bay Bridge Historical Interpretive Center
Access: Off US 101, 1 mile south of Waldport

▲ Since the Central Coast has longer stretches of beaches interspersed ⊥ among its headlands than the rest of the coast, a string of many state

75

View of new Alsea Bay bridge from Governor Patterson State Park

parks provide access to surf, sea birds, and scenery. Governor Patterson State Park is among these. The new Alsea Bay Bridge, however, is an unusual part of the vista seen from its beach.

Paths lead both north and south from the parking area to the ocean. At low tide, one can walk farther north near Yaquina John Point, at the edge of the bay. At this water level, several sandy shoals are seen in the bay and seals haul out on certain ones. A sand spit across the water serves as a resting spot for brown pelicans in summer. The view walking south is of Cape Perpetua.

Picnic tables overlook the beach on the low bluff of this wooded oceanfront tract that commemorates Governor Isaac L. Patterson, who was a strong believer in scenic area preservation and advocated park development. He appointed the first Park Commission in 1929 and died in office that same year.

Hikers of the Oregon Coast Trail can resume beach walking after crossing the Alsea Bay Bridge at this park. Except for small creek crossings, almost 8 miles can be hiked, to a headland just north of Yachats.

The Alsea Bay Bridge Historical Interpretive Center, on the south side of the bay in Waldport, is a new visitor center operated by the Oregon State Parks Agency and the Waldport Chamber of Commerce. It contains displays on the history of transportation along the central coast since the 1800s and information about the Alsi Native American Indians that once lived in the Waldport area.

ONA BEACH STATE PARK

Hours/Season: Day use; year-round
Area: 237 acres
Facilities: Picnic tables, boat ramp, restrooms
Attractions: Beachcombing, fishing, boating, paddling, birdwatching, photography
Access: Off US 101, 8 miles south of Newport

From inland pastoral wetlands, Beaver Creek empties into the Pacific at Ona Beach. As it flows beneath the low highway bridge, it edges a lawn fringed with picnic tables strung along the water and then turns back in an S-meander before it enters the ocean. From calm, deeper waters, the wide creek that approaches river status spreads out over a wide sandy estuary that ripples as it meets the tidewater of the sea. Shore pine and beach grass grow between the curves of the creek.

Ona is an Indian word for "razor clam" and doubtless they were successful at collecting these on the sandy beach here, as this once offered good clamming. In the days before the highway, this beach was used as an access road at low tide by motorists. The only barrier between Newport and Seal Rock is Beaver Creek, and following the mailman would show people the best place to cross its waters.

The park boat ramp for fishermen or paddlers is located east of the highway. Inexperienced paddlers can easily play in the creek. River otters are occasionally spotted.

Canoe paddlers on gentle Beaver Creek, Ona Beach State Park

Hiking paths lead through the picnic area and along the creek to a foot-bridge arching across the water to beach access. Many varieties of ducks are seen throughout the year. A wide beach stretches south for a couple of miles to Seal Rock. The walk is backed by tall, crumbling cliffs of pocked sandstone with precarious homes on top. Chunks of rock, some shaped like bowling balls, have been tossed onto the beach and cause sunlit pools to form where sea gulls float. Sanderlings rush ahead of you.

The Oregon Coast Trail is on the beach from Newport to Seal Rock, with a quick jog to the highway to cross the creek if one wants to do the entire piece. Sunday walkers can head south to the picturesque sea rocks below high Seal Rock, a photogenic area with some tidepools.

LOST CREEK STATE PARK

Hours/Season: Day use; year-round
Area: 34 acres
Facilities: Picnic tables, pit toilets, *no water*
Attractions: Beach access, hiking, surf-fishing
Access: Off US 101, 7 miles south of Newport

Lost Creek State Park capitalizes on having access to a long, straight stretch of sandy beach, part of the legacy of legislators saving Oregon's beaches for the public. From the large parking area situated on a low ocean bluff, a path drops downhill past oceanfront picnic sites to views of

Brown pelicans flying along the coast, Lost Creek State Park

Yaquina Head and Seal Rock in the distance. Though there are no sea stacks to enhance the view, fishing boats do dot the ocean, and surf is always enticing.

This narrow strip of park shoreland occupies both sides of the highway and includes a portion of the right-of-way of the abandoned Pacific Spruce Corporation Railway. The need for lightweight spruce timber in building aircraft during World War I precipitated the harvest of Sitka spruce along the Pacific Northwest coast. Several railroads were built to transport the logs. This particular railroad was in operation from 1918 to 1920 and ran from Yaquina Bay to south of Waldport.

Lost Creek State Park is along a beach section of the Oregon Coast Trail that can be hiked on the sand from Yaquina Bay to Beaver Creek in Ona Beach State Park. Those who want to hike the long distance as shorter day hikes will appreciate this access point.

SOUTH BEACH STATE PARK

Hours/Season: Overnight; year-round
Area: 434 acres
Facilities: Picnic tables, campground with 254 electrical sites (maximum site is 60 feet), hiker/biker camp, wheelchair-accessible restrooms with showers, dumping station, horseshoes, playground, slide program, summer reservations available, phone: (503) 867-4715
Attractions: Nature trail, beach access, fishing, clamming, crabbing
Nearby: Hatfield Marine Science Center, Oregon Coast Aquarium
Access: Off US 101, 2 miles south of Newport

South Beach State Park offers a camping base that is close to lots of action and recreation in its location on the southern edge of Yaquina Bay. The end of the south jetty and a long stretch of sandy beach form the north and west sides of the park. Between the beach foredune and campground are vast areas of marshes, wetland ponds, and grassy meadows that shelter campers from winds and provide sunny warmth. A few picnic tables are found at the day-use area, where it is only a few steps over the foredune to good walking on the beach.

Three level pathways lead from the campground to the beach, ranging from 0.25 to 0.5 miles. From the beach, the south jetty can be reached, where people watch the surf and throw out fishing lines. The most northerly, and longest, beach path has a grand panoramic view that includes the Yaquina Bay Bridge, Yaquina Bay Lighthouse, and Yaquina Head Lighthouse to the north, all framed by the waters of the bay and the ocean. A spur to the Cooper Ridge Nature Trail from this path takes you to a wooden bench on a forested hillside where you can savor this view. Each of these beach access trails is crisscrossed by another path for an alternate inland route to the south jetty.

Beach walkers and beached fishing vessel, South Beach State Park

The nature trail begins near the registration booth and winds through a young forest of shore pine and spruce, thickly packed with rhododendrons, salal, and evergreen huckleberry. The land along this trail is rolling country, constantly going up and down, so one gets some aerobic exercise. A couple of wetland ponds are glimpsed through the trees. Many side trails go to different loops of the campground and it gets a little confusing. The park staff put signs along the nature trail but they keep getting removed.

The beach below the south jetty was used as a life-saving station in the late 1800s. Visitors found it exciting to watch the lifesavers practice their maneuvers in the surf, but this dangerous sea coast also demanded some real rescue work. The unexpected has a way of happening on Oregon's coast. During the winter of 1993, a large commercial shrimp boat ran aground near the day-use area.

The bay offers good harvests of clams, Dungeness crabs, and salmon. Check with locals for the best spots. Sailboats are numerous and races are often held on summer weekends in the bay.

Just across the highway from the park is the Hatfield Marine Science Center (HMSC), an affiliate of Oregon State University, with research facilities and a public wing with an aquarium. This is your chance to touch a live octopus, watch it change color, and perhaps see it devour a crab. The touch pool is popular because of its hands-on aspect. Feel the surface of sea stars, watch giant green anemones contract at your touch, or pet one of the fish. Over 300 species of marine organisms in eighteen water-filled tanks are the main attraction, but there is more. The many exhibits will increase your knowledge of coastal environments and how to be a good steward of their resources.

On Memorial Day of 1992, a world-class interpretive center, the Oregon Coast Aquarium, opened next door to the HMSC. On 23 acres along the Yaquina Bay estuary, the aquarium theme or "storyline" allows visitors to follow the journey of a drop of rain from the coastal mountains to the ocean.

Inside the 40,000-square-foot building, four galleries are filled with the lives and sounds of sandy shores, rocky shores, coastal waters, and wetlands, plus the Whale Theater. Outdoor exhibits are set in forest, cliffs, bluffs, and beaches where you will find a trout-filled mountain stream, a sea otter pool, an octopus in its cave, seals and sea lions, a wave-raked tidepool, and a vast walk-through aviary of sea birds. This is a place of underwater camera views, of machine-generated waves, of feedings and movement, of lab demonstrations, and most certainly of education about coastal ecosystems.

YAQUINA BAY STATE PARK

Hours/Season: Day use; year-round
Area: 32 acres
Facilities: Picnic tables, restrooms, exhibit information
Attractions: Historic lighthouse museum, gift shop, beachcombing, fishing, kite flying, hiking trails, photography, wildlife viewing
Nearby: Newport Bayfront
Access: Off US 101 in Newport, go west at north end of Yaquina Bay Bridge

Several aspects of this park have made it Oregon's most visited state park, with over 1.5 million visitors in the year 1990–1991. One reason is the splendid location in a popular coastal city, where it occupies a 100-foot bluff overlooking the merging of the Yaquina River with the Pacific Ocean, so there is easy access to wave watching, beachcombing, and bay fishing. The restored lighthouse is the icing on the cake that pulls in even more people. Even a winter weekend finds the parking lot and the museum full.

The original lighthouse was not a success story. Erected in 1871, when carpenters were paid fifty cents an hour for its construction, it was soon realized that Yaquina Head, three miles to the north, blocked the light for ships past that point. After a lighthouse was built on that headland, the Yaquina Bay light was abandoned in 1874, only three years after its construction.

A story has circulated about the lighthouse being haunted in the late 1800s by a ghost named Muriel who was supposed to have vanished, leaving only bloodstains, while exploring the house. The story, published in the *Pacific Monthly*, reads like a piece of fiction, and appears to be just that.

Yaquina Bay Lighthouse, now a museum, at Yaquina Bay State Park

The first portion of the park, with the old lighthouse, was given to the state by the U.S. Lighthouse Service in 1934. Ignoring the building, a day-use state park evolved, with construction by the CCC. During the 1960s, removal of the lighthouse was considered, but a visit by park personnel made them realize that it should be preserved for its historical value. With the active participation of local historians, it became a Historic Landmark and was restored by the State Parks in the 1970s.

Rather than build a separate house for the lightkeeper's family, which was the usual plan, this light was perched atop the house structure. Many of the rooms on the first and second floors have been nicely done with furnishings that seem appropriate, not overdone. Notice the incredible views from most rooms. The narrow, winding stairs to the third floor access the watchroom, where the lightkeeper was on duty, climbing up the ladder to tend the light as needed from that small cubbyhole. The basement houses the gift shop. Volunteers are there to answer questions and show a video. Exhibits include actual Coast Guard apparel plus information, drawings, and photos about all coastal lighthouses, old ships and wrecks, wildlife, and Coast Guard drills. This is the oldest surviving building in Newport.

The lighthouse museum is open daily from 11:00 A.M. to 5:00 P.M. from Memorial Day through September, and from 12 noon to 4:00 P.M. on weekends during winter. It dons colored lights at Christmas.

Outdoors, picnic tables are scattered through the shore pine and spruce woods. Paths meander all about to private spots set amid a jungle of rhododendron and salal vegetation, and then disperse into the residential area of Newport. The steep bluff overlooking the sea is one of the official whale-watch sites manned by volunteers during migration times.

Two paved walkways lead down to an expanse of low windblown sand dunes, piled up by the obstruction of the north jetty. One can walk along the jetty and watch ships going to and fro between the bay and ocean. Besides sailboats and sport-fishing boats, the astute observer will pick out the commercial bottom trawlers, double-rigged shrimpers, longliners, and salmon trollers with their outstretched arms. What you see will depend on the weather and ocean conditions.

One can also walk the beach north all the way to Yaquina Head, with only a few creeks to cross or go around. Winds are often good for kite flying and agates are found at the north end of the beach. This beach is a good place to be alert for the spring sandering migration. The numbers of birds are immense and their flight is a spectacular flowing of motion. Other species are among this crowd, including dunlins and sandpipers. They stop to eat along the way north, leaving the beach riddled with tiny feeding holes.

It's an easy walk from the park east to Newport's working bayfront. No other port on Oregon's coast matches the ambiance of this stroll. The smells are of the sea and the fishing industry with boats unloading their catch. Sea lions dive for fish debris in the bay; brown pelicans join the action. Great blue herons, loons, ducks, and a variety of sea birds are often spotted. Crabbing is good in the bay, so you might want to try it, or go clamming on the south side of the bay. Upriver is oyster country, the marine resource that was responsible for the founding of this town.

Art galleries are numerous, with crafts and paintings of remarkable quality. The smell of fish and chips is in the air, and people stroll around with ice cream cones. Restaurant choices are many, with seafood naturally the specialty. Docks access the commercial fleet of boats along the walk and sportboat slips front the Embarcadero area with its sidewalk cafe, where our walk ends.

ELLMAKER STATE PARK

Hours/Season: Day use; year-round
Area: 77 acres
Facilities: Picnic tables, restrooms
Attractions: Rest stop on highway
Access: Off US 20, 31 miles east of Newport

On the highway between Newport and Corvallis, 1 mile west of Burnt Woods, this land gift of Harlan D. Ellmaker works well as a highway rest stop that protects trees. The donor, who had worked for the U.S. Forest Service, called it his "Garden of Eden."

Although the acreage is split by the highway and the Tumtum River, the developed area is on the north side, with a scattering of four picnic tables bordering a spacious grassy meadow. A small stream flows from the northeast through the fir forest to join the river.

Western skunk cabbage in wetland, Ellmaker State Park

BEVERLY BEACH STATE PARK

Hours/Season: Overnight; year-round
Area: 130 acres
Facilities: Picnic tables, campground with 52 full hookups, 75 electrical hookups, and 152 tent sites (maximum site is 65 feet), wheelchair-accessible restrooms with showers, hiker/biker camp, group camping, firewood, dumping station, playground, slide program, reservations available, phone: (503) 265-9278
Attractions: Beachcombing, hiking, fishing, kite flying, photography, surfing
Nearby: Yaquina Point Natural Area and lighthouse
Access: Off US 101, 7 miles north of Newport

With its proximity to lots of activities in the Newport area, Beverly Beach State Park has the third highest overnight use in the state. Located just east of the highway, a walkway goes under the highway to the long expanse of sandy beach that extends from Yaquina Head and a view of the lighthouse to the headlands of Otter Rock. On good days, kites color the air and whip in the wind, and sand castles are built. Surfers are often seen on the north beach. If you're a surfer, you might want to join them.

The picnic area is a grassy, treed spot with no views, but it is protected from summer northwest winds at the beginning of the beach access walk. The campground is several loops along Spencer Creek.

The day-use area was once a pond at the mouth of Spencer Creek. A fish hatchery was here and a farm was above the pond. The road in the park was once part of the Roosevelt Military Highway. During World War II, guard

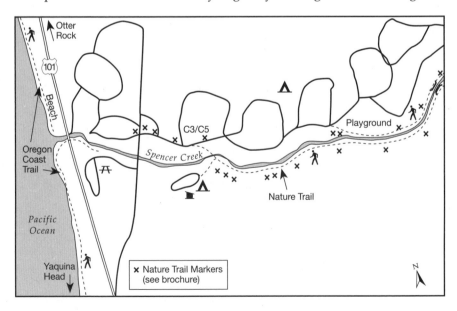

Surfing is popular at Beverly Beach State Park

dogs patrolled the beaches to secure it against Japanese attack.

The beach access joins a section of the Oregon Coast Trail. This 5 miles of beach is easily traversed, except for a promontory just north of Yaquina Head, and even this can be rounded easily at low tide. It is 1.2 miles to the north headlands, where the trail must revert to following the highway north. To the south, the OCT exit to the highway is via a primitive road to the north of Moolack Shores Motel.

A self-guided 0.75-mile nature trail—with an accompanying brochure—begins between campsites C3 and C5 and leads off towards the hiker/biker camp, with foot traffic only. Cross the bridge over Spencer Creek and follow the creek until another bridge recrosses the water at the end of the campground and follows the other side of the creek to just past the playground. Though logged in the past, the forest has grown back and this hike reveals an excellent example of rain forest shaped by coastal winter storms, as well as riparian wetland habitat. Huge old stumps, giant wind-sculptured trees, and nurse logs are seen. If you're not familiar with the various species of the temperate rain forest of this area, you will learn them here, as they are labeled and explained in the brochure. Western azalea, twinberry, giant horsetail, skunk cabbage, great hedge nettle, deer fern, and false lily-of-the-valley are some of the species. A few of the labeled vegetation spots are off the trail in other areas of the park.

Don't miss the side trip to Yaquina Head and the lighthouse there, which was built in 1873 and is still active. The original plan was to put the lighthouse on Cape Foulweather, but that proved too difficult for transport of materials. Even Yaquina Head was not an easy destination; supplies were transported up to the point with a windlass and derrick via a staircase hacked out of solid rock. In 1977, a *Nancy Drew* television production focused on ghost stories associated with the lighthouse.

Now managed by the BLM as the Yaquina Head Natural Area, a stairway leads to tidepools where many sea lions rest on the rocks, and exhibits line the end of the point, which overlooks Yaquina Head Rocks National Wildlife Refuge. These offshore nesting rocks are so close that it is easy to see young, nondescript sea gulls walking around in the spring. This is also an official whale-watch site.

A wheelchair-accessible tidepool area is in the process of being constructed on the side of the headland, and a visitor center will be added later.

DEVIL'S PUNCH BOWL STATE PARK

Hours/Season: Day use; year-round
Area: 4 acres
Facilities: Picnic tables, wheelchair-accessible restrooms, small playground
Attractions: Unusual geology, marine gardens, whale and storm watching, beachcombing, hiking, photography
Nearby: Cape Foulweather
Access: Off US 101, 8 miles north of Newport, on the Otter Crest Loop, a scenic alternate to US 101 on the Oregon Coast Bike Trail

During winter storms, water from the restless sea pours with a thundering roar into a hollow rock formation shaped like a huge punch bowl. The surf churns, foams, and swirls as if the Devil were mixing some violent brew. This natural landmark of intriguing geology, of sedimentary rock and basalt, juts out into the sea just west of the small community of Otter Rock and is the centerpiece of Devil's Punch Bowl State Park.

The punch bowl was probably created by the collapse of the roof over two sea caves, and shaped by wave action. The ocean enters the bowl from tunnels on opposite sides. It empties and fills with the tides.

This park is one of the whale watching sites staffed by volunteers from

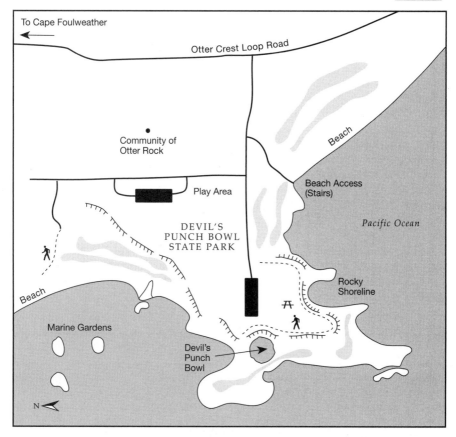

Hatfield Marine Science Center during whale migrations the last week in December and the week of college spring break.

Walkways circle and cross a scenic picnic area situated on the south side of the punch bowl, atop the undulating rocky shoreline that consists of soft sedimentary rock. These diverse formations make for varied wave watching as the surf bounces off the cliffs.

A wooden stairway, across from the restroom parking lot, descends to the long stretch of sand beach to the south. Notice the light-colored deposits of volcanic ash along the cliffs at the bottom of the stairs.

To visit the marine gardens, follow the street about two blocks north of the restrooms to a parking lot which accesses a recently rebuilt trail that descends to a nice area of tidepools. The last section is hazardous at high tide when the waves inundate the marine gardens, but during a minus tide it is a wonderland for exploring. A sandy beach edges a varied terrain of sandstone shelves and rock formations with channels and pools of water. You will see round holes carved out of underwater rocks where sea urchins live. Tiny sculpin fish dart around in pools. Sea anemones and sea stars hang onto rocks in the surge of waves. It takes time to see the diverse inhabitants of the pools, as they vary as you get closer to the sea, but there is a good collection of species here. The floor of the punch bowl can be entered from the south end of this beach, and you can see the tunnels where the water enters.

The best time to visit the tidepools is near the summer solstice in June when good minus tides occur. Check a tide book for times. Go an hour or so before the lowest tide and remember to watch for the incoming tide and leave the area before you're stranded by incoming water. No collecting of marine life is allowed in this much-visited area by anyone, even scientists and educators. Explorers should wear boots and proceed with caution, especially where slippery seaweeds flourish.

Travel another 1.25 miles north on Otter Crest Loop to see Cape Foulweather, a state park wayside. This picturesque promontory, which has a good view of the Devil's Punch Bowl environs, was sighted and named by Captain James Cook when he sailed back from his discovery of the Hawaiian Islands with two ships, the *Resolution* and the *Discovery*. It was a stormy March 7 of the year 1778; hence the name. The adjacent gift shop is privately owned, though the original owners donated land for the present park.

FOGARTY CREEK STATE PARK

Hours/Season: Day use; year-round
Area: 142 acres
Facilities: Picnic tables, restrooms, summer day-use fee for vehicles
Attractions: Beachcombing, fishing, hiking
Nearby: Boiler Bay Wayside
Access: Off US 101, 2 miles north of Depoe Bay

Fogarty Creek flows into the sea at an enchanting ocean cove in this park. In the afternoon sun, its waters are a fluid silver ribbon that curves often as it turns to the south, changing with the vagaries of the season. Many of the ingredients that make the spirit soar are found here. A jumble of rocks at the edge of the sea bounces the surf in all directions.

Beachcombers can access the beach by walkways on either side of the creek. The soft, golden bluff to the north—Fishing Rock—curves in and out in front of encroaching development.

Inland, under the highway bridge, the park fans out in a broad, level expanse of varied picnic choices. Arched foot-bridges cross the wide stream at several points as it flows lazily through the park, and paths offer considerable walking choices. A forest of shore pine, Sitka spruce, western hemlock, and alder have regrown after having been logged in the past. It is a pleasant stop along the highway. The creek and park are named for John Fogarty, a native of Ireland who became a Lincoln County judge.

Boiler Bay Wayside is a short distance south of this park, at Government

Meeting of creek, ocean, and shore, Fogarty Creek State Park

Point. It is a splendid place to watch wild surf action on the rocky spurs that project into the sea. The name derives from the boiler that is visible at low tide, reminder of the wreck of the freighter *J. Marhoffer* on these shores in 1910.

DEVIL'S LAKE STATE PARK

Hours/Season: Overnight; year-round
Area: 104 acres
Facilities: Picnic tables, campground with 32 full hookup and 68 tent sites (maximum site is 62 feet), hiker/biker camp, boat ramp, boat docks, restrooms with solar showers, phone: (503) 994-2002
Attractions: Fishing, boating, wildlife viewing
Nearby: Cascade Head Natural Area
Access: The park is in two separate units: the campground is off US 101 in Lincoln City; the day-use area is 0.75 mile east of the city on East Devil's Lake Road

▲ Devil's Lake State Park is the only campground on the Oregon coast located in the midst of a city, although Lincoln City is certainly not a metropolis. To balance that, the campground is on the west shore of Devil's

Boat moorage at Devil's Lake State Park

Lake, although no campsite has a view. A wide wetland area—with shore pine, alder and crabapple trees—separates the sites from the lake, but this is easily approached on foot, with boat docks available (*reservations only*). Wildlife is abundant with coots, cormorants, and ducks on the lake. A pair of great blue herons was startled from their treetop perch at the lake's edge by this visitor in winter.

The boat ramp, however, is at the East Devil's Lake day-use unit on the east side of the lake. Shallow water has lake tules, and bald eagles often perch on a tree to the north of the boat ramp. The name of the park appears to derive from the Indian feeling that spirits inhabited the lake.

An interesting piece of historical information ties Lincoln City with Willamette Mission State Park in the valley. Jason Lee, who set up that first Indian mission, came with his bride of one month, and another missionary couple and guide, over the Old Elk Trail to camp on the Oregon coast in 1837. It is believed they were the first to vacation on this scenic coast. A marker is located at 1333 NW 17th Street.

Any naturalist or hiker in the Lincoln City area should not miss the hike in the Cascade Head Natural Area to the north. The lower trailhead is accessed via Three Rocks Road, just north of the Salmon River. The upper trailhead is found by following Forest Service Road 1861, that goes west at the crest of Cascade Head on US 101. En route, if it's winter, be alert for

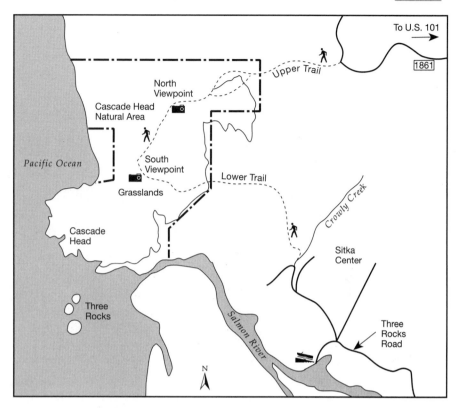

Roosevelt elk crossing the Salmon River or in the adjacent meadow. Although the trail has good forest and wetland habitat, much of it is an open walk on the sloping grassland of this sheer promontory that rises from the sea. This is a rare remnant of coastal prairie with native grasses, and a premier coastal seascape is seen to the south. Please follow the guidelines in this fragile area.

NORTH COAST

    Cascade Head is the scenic gateway to the north coast. The south slope of this 1,600-foot headland is owned and protected by the Nature Conservancy. It is a special place, with rare plants and butterflies, grassland, and forest.

As one travels north of the headland and past the salmon-rich Nestucca River, an alternate route to US 101—the 30-mile Three Capes Scenic Loop—offers an option to continue following the coastline. The first of the capes is Kiwanda, near Pacific City, the home of the dory fleet. In the summer wind shelter of this headland, fishermen launch their boats from the beach, through the surf, to farm the sea.

Patches of productive wetlands and another stretch of sand dunes (though unprotected) lie in the lowlands between Cape Kiwanda and Cape Lookout. The grand viewpoint south from Lookout is a layering of misty mountain ridges, forest, and surf scallops moving onto the beach. Do stop.

A long narrow spit projects north of Cape Lookout and encloses most of Netarts Bay, a favorite clamming area where multitudes come wearing high boots and carrying shovels. The scenic Three Arch Rocks National Wildlife Refuge is in the background. Many important nesting islands for birds are just offshore. From summer on into December, brown pelicans swoop low across the sea and then fly higher to dive and catch fish into their huge bills. Sea gulls are year-round entertainers as they use the wind to soar along the coastal edge.

An inland refuge is located at the third cape, Cape Meares. At the base of Cape Meares, another long sand spit, the Tillamook Spit, runs north. It once covered an even larger area. In 1907, a real estate developer from Kansas City decided to build a resort town called Bayocean Park—complete with a

Opposite: *Saddle Mountain State Park*

natatorium that housed a swimming pool, waterfall, and wave-making machine—and promoted it as the "Atlantic City of the West Coast." Alas, the sea has a great claim on the land that touches it and its dynamic actions swept away the transitory structures of man. Between the Pacific and wide Tillamook Bay, the spit is now a place for birdwatching.

Tillamook is surrounded by good dairy farms. The drive through town should include stops at the cheese-making plants, and a dip (or two) of excellent Tillamook ice cream is a good idea for the road. On the north side of Tillamook Bay, Garibaldi has good charter boat facilities and the fishing is good—salmon, halibut, rock fish, or longer trips for albacore tuna.

The north coast has its coastal mountain, Neahkahnie, though the elevated highway has room on the ocean side here. It passes the "Neahkahnie Punchbowl," an open meadow on the edge of cliffs where it is rumored that Spanish sailors buried treasure after their ship was wrecked. Many have searched for it without success.

East of the coastline, the ridge of mountains that make up the Coast Range is an integral part of Oregon's northern coastal scenery. It provides a backdrop of rugged wilderness sprinkled with climbing trails, wildlife, and few people.

Cannon Beach, along with Bandon on the south coast, has a beach with enough sea stacks, tidepools, wildlife, and walking length to rate as one of the finest on the Oregon coast. Photographers are drawn here and to Ecola Park, on its northern edge. Lewis and Clark traveled south over Tillamook Head to buy whale oil and three hundred pounds of blubber from the Indians. Along with Seaside, Cannon Beach is a busy resort center.

The north coast of Oregon ends at the mouth of the mighty Columbia River. This area was the terminus of the westward journey of Lewis and Clark, and the site of their wintering in 1805–1806 at the fort they built inland. Historic Astoria, the first permanent European-American settlement in the Oregon country, is a short distance upriver.

The climate changes somewhat as one travels north on the coast. Winters are colder; summer temperatures vary less. The air is not as fresh and clear. But the entire coast has exquisite weather in September and most of October. Winds diminish and the sun is warm. It is a magical time.

CAPE KIWANDA STATE PARK

Hours/Season: Day use; year-round
Area: 185 acres
Facilities: Restrooms
Attractions: Photography, hiking, boat launching from beach, ocean fishing, tidepools, wave-sculptured cliffs, wildlife viewing, sand dunes, hang gliding
Access: Off Three Capes Scenic Loop, 1 mile north of Pacific City *(no sign for the park, but there is one for the cape)*

Hang glider off north slope of Cape Kiwanda State Park

▲ The beach that hugs the southern side of Cape Kiwanda is the launch
⊥ pad of the dory fleet that calls Pacific City home. Getting their boats off
the sand and into—and through—the surf is no easy matter, requiring frequent pushes, jumps into boats, quick engine starts, and skilled maneuver-
ing to avoid capsizing. Sheltered from northwest winds by the cape in
summer, this is the place to watch fishermen in their struggle to ride the sea.

Why would fishermen—and women—want to go to sea where there is
no protective harbor or boat basin? Because the fish are there and it's a good
place to live. Nearby Nestucca River is a famous spawning region for
salmon. The double-ended design of the dory has been used for ocean fishing since the early 1900s, when horses and wagons and then Model As
hauled boats through the drifting sand. In the 1970s, about three hundred
boats fished for salmon. Fishing restrictions and fewer fish have reduced
the number of boats, but many still dory-fish at Cape Kiwanda. If you want
the thrill of this surf entry, charter boats will take you out.

Most summers, the Pacific City Dory Derby is held here in July, an exciting event to watch as they launch boats, circle Haystack Rock, and return
with a caught fish in almost the blink of an eye.

Cape Kiwanda is a photographer's paradise, particularly in winter after
a storm, but the geology is a wonder in any season. Although there are good
shots of dory boats, Haystack Rock with its jug handle, the tidepools at the

foot of the cape, and the cape itself, the awesome surf action photos demand a climb up the dune of the cape. This is accessed at the north end of the beach. Follow the footprints in the soft sand. At the top, explore—with caution—in several directions, except where signs forbid it. The succession of sculptured sandstone cliffs is truly impressive, as is the wave action that collides with them and continues to shape this soft rock. This is also a favorite resting spot for brown pelicans and other sea birds.

The park on the north side of the cape can be accessed from the sand dune at the back of the cape or, more easily, by driving north and parking by the road where the bluff ends. Then walk south on the beach for over a mile to the enormous sand dune that climbs the cape.

For some aerobic exercise, climb to the top of the dune. This is what hang glider pilots do, carrying heavy wings that weigh between fifty and eighty pounds. This dune is rated as one of the best for beginners in hang gliding, and lessons, which are important in this sport, are frequently given here. With winds deflected up cliffs, the coast often provides good lifts, or a simple glide from a high point.

The park goes north along the strip of beach to Sand Lake. The Oregon Coast Trail is on the beach between the lake and Cape Kiwanda, where it climbs over the dune to the parking lot and then takes to the road for a spell.

CAPE LOOKOUT STATE PARK

Hours/Season: Overnight; year-round
Area: 2,014 acres
Facilities: Picnic tables, campground with 53 full hookup (maximum site is 60 feet) and 197 tent sites, group camping, meeting hall, hiker/biker camp, wheelchair-accessible restrooms with showers, slide program, firewood, dumping station, summer day-use fee for vehicles, summer reservations available, phone: (503) 842-4981
Attractions: Hiking, wildlife viewing, kayaking, clamming, fishing, photography, beachcombing
Nearby: Netarts Bay
Access: Located 12 miles southwest of Tillamook, can be reached by driving south on US 101 to access spur, or by taking the Three Capes Scenic Loop west from Tillamook and continuing south of Netarts Bay

Cape Lookout is an outstanding example of the many coastal headlands preserved by the state park system that also contain fine examples of ancient forest. In the endeavor to create more designated wilderness areas, we sometimes forget how farsighted the state has been. When they lock up pristine coastline for recreation, it's a double blessing.

This vast park also extends to the tip of the Netarts sand spit that encloses Netarts Bay, so recreation opportunities are varied. European beach grass was planted over a period of several years to stabilize the dunes, some

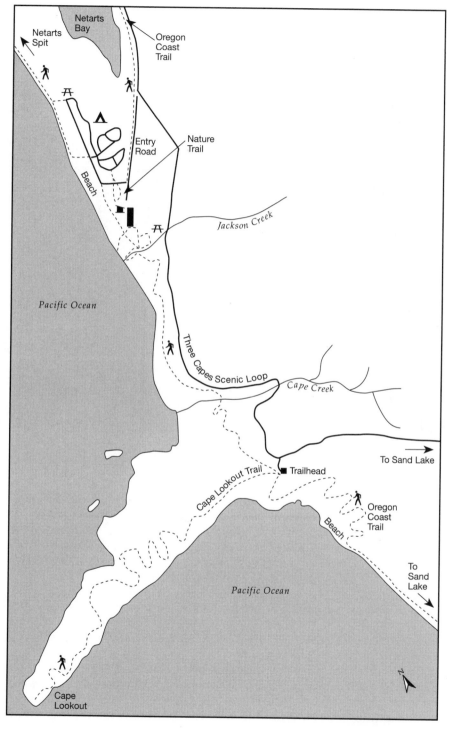

View of cape and ocean picnic area, Cape Lookout State Park

of which are 50 feet high. This grass is the introduced plant that has built our coastal foredune system.

Cape Lookout was named by John Meares, sea captain. He intended the name for what is now Cape Meares, but charts put it in the wrong place and it stuck. The original land for the park was a 1935 gift from the U.S. Lighthouse Service, since plans for a lighthouse also changed.

On a map, Cape Lookout resembles a dagger jabbed into the sea. The wave action on the cliffs has exposed a sequence of lava flows, some of which cooled on dry land and others that are pillow basalts which erupted under water. Gradually—but oh, so slowly—the surf is pounding this volcanic peninsula into sand and mud.

The facilities are along the ocean, reached by a road past gurgling creeks along a wetland habitat in winter. The campground has oceanfront sites but these are closed off in the stormy weather of winter, with more protected camping in the woods. Picnic tables to the south have good ocean views under the windblown spruce trees, near where Jackson Creek flows out to sea. Picnic tables are also situated north of the campground. At several points, trails access the beachcombing. Wildlife is easy to spot even in the developed area. Raccoons are almost tame, deer are seen, squirrels are numerous, Steller's jays make their presence known, and red-tailed hawks scout the cape.

Hike the nature trail between the campground and hiker/biker camp to learn the ways of the coastal rain forest. Cape Lookout averages over 100 inches of rain each year and the temperatures are moderate—ingredients for native plant success. Along the path, you can count tree rings, see ferns rooted to spruce trees, a springboard notch used by loggers, natural grafting of trees, and western red cedar—once the most useful tree to the North Coast Indians, which they used in canoes, nets, homes, and clothing.

For a longer trail, hike some of the Oregon Coast Trail that traverses the park. It enters from the north along the entry road and then borders the coast south of the campground, as it climbs in 2.5 miles through the forest to the top of the 800-foot ridge summit of the cape. It emerges here at the parking area for those hiking to the tip of the cape. Those parking here might be confused by the trails. Of the two trails, the south one goes to the tip of Cape Lookout, the north one comes from the campground. Another confusion might arise in a short distance when a trail branches off to the south. This trail is the continuation of the Oregon Coast Trail, which descends in 2 miles to the beach, where one proceeds to Sand Lake.

The popular trail is the 2.5-mile hike that drops down to the rocky terminus of the cape. It initially edges the southern portion of the cape, with views down steep cliffs to tree-framed azure water below. Level at first, the path is not difficult, with alternate down and up portions, and it then jogs into the ancient forest of Sitka spruce and western hemlock, with undercover of sword and maidenhair ferns, in the center of the cape. Along the trail is a plaque in memory of the crew of a B-17 bomber on coastal patrol that crashed on the cape on October 12, 1943, with only one survivor. A little past halfway, the trail reaches the north side of the cape, with a good view of Cape Meares, Three Arch Rocks, the spit, and Netarts Bay. After winding through the middle forest again, the path descends along the south edge to a tiny clearing on the rocky point. Though this is a year-round trail, it can have muddy sections in winter and caution is especially required on the last area where the dropoff is vertical.

This final view is to the south, and includes Cape Kiwanda with its huge sand dune. It is a good wildlife viewing area, with 154 species of birds being recorded. One can watch them fly from nesting and resting places. It is also an official whale watch site, staffed by volunteers, and must be fairly good since quite a few people make the hike out to watch whale migrations.

Netarts Bay draws crowds of people who wade in with hip boots for clamming and even pick up steamers on the mud flats without much effort. Others launch kayaks to paddle across the water to the end of the spit for some mostly solitary beach strolling. Humans, kingfishers, and great blue herons enjoy the fishing.

CAPE MEARES STATE PARK

Hours/Season: Day use; year-round
Area: 233 acres
Facilities: Picnic tables, exhibit information, restrooms
Attractions: Hiking trails, historic lighthouse, octopus tree, giant Sitka spruce, Cape Meares National Wildlife Refuge, paddling
Nearby: Three Arch Rocks National Wildlife Refuge, Tillamook Spit and Bay, hang gliding
Access: Off Three Capes Scenic Loop, 10 miles west of Tillamook

Most visitors are attracted to Cape Meares to see the lighthouse and the spectacular ocean views, perhaps having lunch on the lawn or at the few picnic tables. Others come with binoculars for the offshore wildlife refuge. Smart ones include some hiking on the trails. The boundaries of the park include the 138-acre mainland Cape Meares National Wildlife Refuge, which is managed jointly with the U.S. Fish and Wildlife Service.

The lighthouse was built in 1890 and its beacon of red and white alternating light shone until 1963, when it was replaced by an automatic light. The hand-ground French lens came around Cape Horn and was lifted onto the

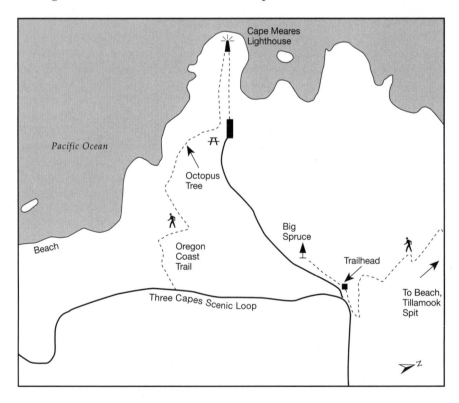

200-foot cliff and onto its tower by a hand-operated crane made from local spruce trees. From May through September and during the Christmas season, the gift shop and lighthouse, with its spiral staircase, are open to visitors.

It seems appropriate that this cape was named after John Meares, eighteenth-century British naval officer, fur trader, and explorer. He had named it Cape Lookout, but that name was misplaced on maps and this cape needed another name.

Hiking options are varied. From the ocean parking lot, a loop trail descends to the lighthouse on the tip of the headland via a wide paved path, with a spur going a few steps north at one point for a view that includes a steep-walled rocky cove with seasonal ribbon waterfalls. The return trail to the parking area hugs the southern edge of the headland where benches let one linger to view the seascape, which includes a broad wave-swept cove, the hillside town of Oceanside, and Three Arch Rocks National Wildlife Refuge, site of Oregon's largest sea bird colonies. Sea birds nesting there include about 75,000 common murres, tufted puffins, pigeon guillemots, storm-petrels, cormorants, and gulls. Sea lions share this habitat.

This trail continues past the restrooms and goes by the Octopus Tree, a large Sitka spruce tree on a point facing southwest that one assumes has been configured by the force of winter winds. Indian legend, however, holds that natives shaped the young tree for a sacred burial tree so that it

Viewpoint overlooking lighthouse, Cape Meares State Park

would hold the canoes of their deceased leaders. This portion of the Oregon Coast Trail continues to the highway in less than 1 mile through forest that skirts fine views south near its terminus.

In the past, these trails were contiguous with the Oregon Coast Trail north through the park, but storms and erosion plus a bald eagle nest have caused closure of the trailhead from the parking lot. If one parks near the beginning of the entry road where there is a trail map exhibit, however, the short segment west to a giant spruce tree is still open. This tree is truly impressive, a straight, majestic specimen that has a crown of gnarled limbs, a good example of this protected old-growth spruce and hemlock forest.

This entrance trailhead also goes north for 6 miles to the end of the Tillamook Spit. It gently descends through woods until it opens into sunlight and mind-elevating views of waves pounding the spit and Tillamook Bay beyond. Continue walking for good birding on the spit, but it is very worthwhile just to hike the first short distance, less than 0.5 mile, to the view.

The east end of Tillamook Bay offers good paddling combined with wildlife viewing. Several rivers empty into the bay, and traveling up these quiet river inlets allows the paddler to get close to many ducks and hawks that would normally be frightened away—a great experience.

When winds blow from the southwest, keep an eye out for hang gliders over the cape. Nearby 500-foot-high Maxwell Mountain, a promontory overlooking the town of Oceanside, offers good opportunities for hang gliders to lift their wings and glide north.

Inside Oregon
8Am - 4:30
1-800-452-5687

NEHALEM BAY STATE PARK ✷✷

Hours/Season: Overnight; year-round
Area: 890 acres
Facilities: Picnic tables, campground with 291 electrical sites (maximum site is 60 feet), horse camp has 17 sites with corrals, hiker/biker camp, wheelchair-accessible restrooms with showers, dumping station, firewood, meeting hall, playground, boat ramp, summer day-use fee for vehicles
Attractions: Hiking, biking, and equestrian trails, boating, paddling, fishing, clamming, crabbing, beachcombing, windsurfing, airport
Access: Follow signed spur road for 2.5 miles from US 101, 3 miles south of Manzanita Junction

▲ With a 2,400-foot airstrip, this park offers the unique opportunity of a fly-in camp. Located between Nehalem Bay and the ocean shore, Nehalem Bay State Park includes the long sand spit that edges the estuary to the south. Step off the plane or out of your vehicle, or arrive by bicycle or on foot, and recreation is just a few steps away. You can have wild surf at your feet or travel upriver to calm canoeing. The bay has excellent crabbing

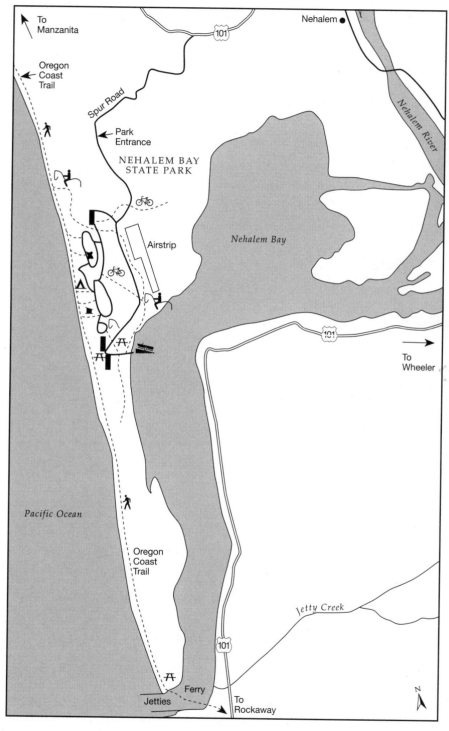

To Manzanita

Oregon Coast Trail

Spur Road

Park Entrance

NEHALEM BAY STATE PARK

Airstrip

Nehalem

Nehalem River

Nehalem Bay

101

To Wheeler

Pacific Ocean

Oregon Coast Trail

Jetty Creek

101

Ferry

Jetties

To Rockaway

N

Canoe race on Nehalem River, Nehalem Bay State Park

and a good supply of bay clams. In the past, Indians used "weirs," or fish traps, to catch salmon going upriver.

A foredune with European beach grass separates the campground from the beach, but many paths lead over this to the ocean. The horse camp is reached via the southern end of the campground. Picnic choices include three day-use areas: near the boat ramp on the bay, near the overnight camp and overlooking the boating activity on the bay with a backdrop of coastal mountains, and at the end of the spit (reached by foot or boat—*no potable water*).

The spit is formed by the continued dumping of sand where the outward flow of the Nehalem River meets incoming waves. The growth of the spit is to the south because it is influenced more by the southward longshore currents of the summer winds.

The park has a curious history of people finding chunks of beeswax, marked with shipping markings and religious Latin symbols, in fields about a mile south of the entrance. The theory is that a ship (perhaps the Spanish ship *San Francisco Xavier*) wrecked on the spit in 1705. The remains were visible at extreme low tide in 1930, but are now gone. At least six galleons left the Philippines for Acapulco, Mexico, and were lost at sea. Besides finding several uses for the beeswax, the Indians and early settlers also appropriated the teak planks of the ship and used them for furniture.

Today's arrivals at this spit are usually by air or land transportation, best left parked to take advantage of slower methods of getting around and getting closer to nature.

An equestrian trail weaves through the open area of the park for 7.5 miles, and riders will want to enjoy some excursions on the beach, where photographers should be alert for good silhouettes at sunset. Bicyclers can get their exercise on the 1.5 miles of bike paths.

The Oregon Coast Trail can be followed along the beach from Manzanita for 1.1 miles to the park. Continue along the beach for another 3.7 miles around the spit to a ferry landing. The Indians used to ferry pioneers across here in cedar canoes with the horses swimming behind. Advance arrangements will let you cross the bay by boat to continue hiking south on the beach past Rockaway to Tillamook Bay.

The stretch of beach at the foot of Neahkahnie Mountain from Manzanita to Nehalem Bay is a popular windsurfing region. Beach walkers might want to walk north to watch surfers leap on their boards as they turn back through the waves.

OSWALD WEST STATE PARK

Hours/Season: Overnight; *campground closed in winter*
Area: 2,474 acres
Facilities: Picnic tables, campground with 36 primitive sites (*foot access only*) with wheelbarrows available for campers, restrooms
Attractions: Hiking, ancient forest, photography, fishing, surfing, wildlife viewing
Access: Off US 101, 10 miles south of Cannon Beach

Oswald West State Park preserves a spur of the Coast Range that sits on the coastline and encompasses Arch Cape, Neahkahnie Mountain, Cape Falcon, and Smuggler's Cove—an incomparable 4 miles of shoreline geology, ancient forest, and majestic views.

The campground is a 0.25-mile walk-in affair for tenters, wheelbarrows provided for transport down the paved path. In a lush setting among red

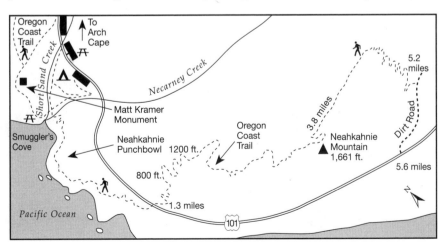

huckleberry, salmonberry, and salal bushes, the sites are located between Short Sand Creek and Necarney Creek, just before these two waterways merge at the tideline of the ocean in the middle of Smuggler's Cove, an unusual phenomenon. The name "Necarney" comes from the Spanish name for meat, *carne* (which the Indians thought synonymous with elk), to which the Indians added *ne*, which means "the place of," since this is the place to find Roosevelt elk. Steller's jays and chickarees are notorious camp robbers, so don't leave food out. Kingfishers catch their own fish; hairy woodpeckers peck into trees, and dippers go underwater in the streams for food.

Along the east side of the highway is a day-use area, with trails leading under the road along Short Sand Creek to an ocean picnic area and driftwood-lined Smuggler's Cove. Surfers put boards into the Pacific here and sea lions are curious about human activities. Fishing boats sometimes anchor in the cove in bad weather. The cove is edged by Cape Falcon to the north and Point Illga, named for a Tillamook Indian woman, to the south.

It is appropriate that this park honors Governor Oswald West, in office from 1911 to 1915, since Oregon's beaches were preserved for public use under his leadership.

It is thought that Cape Falcon was discovered and named by Captain Bruno Heceta in 1775. Rumors have long circulated that Neahkahnie Mountain has buried treasure, and stones with curious letters have been found, but no treasure as yet. One positive historical fact, however, is that three bronze handles of Norse origin were found in a swamp below the mountain, which adds strength to other evidence that Norsemen landed in the area in A.D. 1010.

Sea gulls along coast, Oswald West State Park

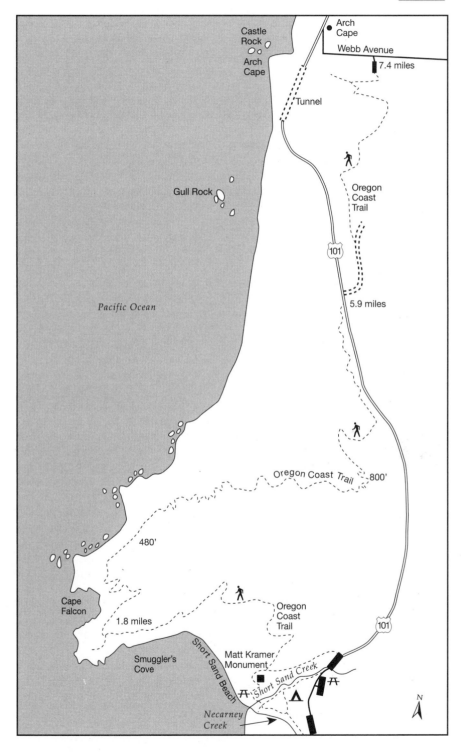

North Coast

Castle
Rock

Arch
Cape

Arch
Cape

Webb Avenue

7.4 miles

Tunnel

Gull Rock

Oregon
Coast
Trail

101

5.9 miles

Pacific Ocean

Oregon Coast Trail

800'

480'

Cape
Falcon

1.8 miles

Oregon
Coast
Trail

101

Short Sand Beach

Matt Kramer
Monument

Short Sand Creek

Smuggler's
Cove

Necarney
Creek

N

With 13 miles of the Oregon Coast Trail in the park (mostly constructed by the CCC), visitors might want to sample some of the varied hiking, or it makes a good backpacking trip, using the campground for overnighting. One should consider hiking through the ancient forest during the rainy season, when a drizzle is hardly felt under the giant trees and the wind is subdued, with the overflowing creeks and their sounds, and the green leaves forming small cups of water. You will see winter storm damage and the windswept litter that nourishes throughout the year. Summer is not the best time to feel the mystique of the rain forest.

Cape Falcon (prime example of ancient forest) and Neahkahnie Mountain (lots of wildflowers in season) are the most popular trail destinations, but information on the entire 13 miles of trail in the park will be given.

The 1.8-mile trail to 750-foot-high Cape Falcon begins just west of the picnic grounds by the cove. Near the start is a split in the trail that goes to a memorial to Matt Kramer, an Associated Press journalist whose articles were important to the passage of the 1967 beach bill. You will soon be in the midst of an ancient green forest of ferns and Sitka spruce, western hemlock, cedar, and fir. At one point, you'll pass a broken old-growth tree that split a few feet above the ground. Its remaining trunk looks like a mammoth shell rooted to earth, yet the unmistakable artistry of wood grains edges curves in the break. At the tip of the cape, take the west fork to a vegetated knoll beside the sea with south views of the cove and mountain, both often strung with fog ribbons. Listen to the sounds of surf against the steep slice of cliff as black sand beach is slowly formed. Wander the paths to see the scallops of cliff to the north, with views of the columnar basalt joints where lava cooled in straight lines. Watch for seals, sea lions, and whales below. (The official whale watch site, however, is south along the highway.)

To continue north on the coast trail, return to the main trail and continue north and east for 4.1 miles through dense forest, where little light reaches the forest floor, to a highway crossing. (The first segment of this edges more ocean coves.) East of the highway, the trail follows the mail route of the late 1880s to early 1900s as it descends Arch Cape through the only ancient forest left in Clatsop County on the east side of US 101. In 1.5 miles, the trail leaves the state park just south of the town of Arch Cape, soon crosses a small suspension bridge, and reaches Webb Avenue.

To begin the hike to the summit of Neahkahnie Mountain, cross Necarney Creek and travel through woods to the Neahkahnie Punchbowl, a broad meadow at the edge of sheer cliffs. In 1.3 miles the highway is reached, and the 2.5-mile climb up 1,661-foot-high Neahkahnie Mountain begins in switchbacks, a moderate grade of 7.5 percent. To the Indians, Neahkahnie was a special place. It is for hikers, too, with the soaring vista of the coast and Nehalem Bay, and sea views that span 50 miles.

From the top of the mountain, the trail continues south for 1.8 miles, through forest and many good views of mountain ridges, to a dirt road that leads to the highway. One can make a loop hike by returning north along the highway.

HUG POINT STATE PARK

Hours/Season: Day use; year-round
Area: 43.3 acres
Facilities: Picnic tables, restrooms
Attractions: Beachcombing, hiking, photography, fishing, waterfall, historic road around point
Nearby: Haystack Rock "Marine Garden"
Access: Off US 101, 5 miles south of Cannon Beach

This park gets its name from the fact that pioneers used the beach as a highway in the late 1800s and they had to "hug" this particular point at low tide to get around it. This was possible only after a wagon road was blasted out of the rock. Patience and planning were required in those days, as it is today for those taking this route on the Oregon Coast Trail. Hikers walking around this point on the rock road will feel some of the emotion that the incoming surf evokes on this narrow ledge.

The beach access from the parking lot emerges midway between Austin Point on the south and Hug Point to the north, reached past a lesser headland. The sandy cove south of Hug Point is a beautiful private place with a waterfall in its corner and caves eroded into the golden layered walls of sandstone. Jellyfish and sand dollars are often seen on the sand. Austin Point has more of this tilted sedimentary rock. This area is one of those special locales that appeals to the emotions and is also particularly photogenic when the inundations of curving headlands are backlit by a sparkling sea or washed by a setting sun.

This section of the Oregon Coast Trail is a scenic one and can be hiked on the beach between Third Street in Cannon Beach to the inland route over Arch Cape, a distance of 6.8 miles. Day hikes could go in either direction from Hug Point State Park. It is 10.4 miles round-trip north to Third Street and 3.2 miles round-trip south to Arch Cape. It is 4.1 miles one way north to Haystack Rock (yes, there are two of these on the north coast) which is an excellent destination if you can be picked up there. Whether you hike to

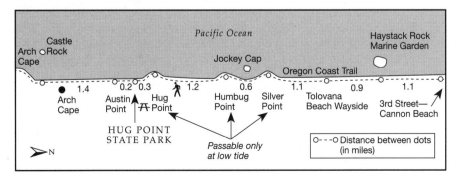

Inland caves and point where pioneer wagons "hugged," Hug Point State Park

Haystack or drive, it's worth some exploring in that area. *Please remember* that this hike must be done at low tide to round several of the points.

This hike is part of the continuous 64 miles of the Oregon Coast Trail that ends at the Columbia River to the north and Tillamook Bay to the south. From the park, it is 0.3 mile to Hug Point, and then 1.2 miles more to Humbug Point, where pioneers were "humbugged" to discover that they had another mile to go to Hug Point. In another 0.6 mile, past a rock called Jockey Cap and a slide area to the east, Silver Point is reached, so named because of the color of the weathered Sitka spruce trees on top.

The hike between Arch Cape and Silver Point is a good place to see hardened sediments in cut-away places of bluffs. These sandstone bluffs were once under water and only recently uplifted. The pressures exerted on them can be observed in the tilted and twisted patterns of layered rock. In addition, wind, sea, and rain have eroded them, and continue to do so, a reason to leave these cliffs undeveloped. The Indians understood these natural forces and used more stable inland elk trails for their travel.

The beach widens by the time Tolovana Beach is reached in 1.1 miles. Geological wonders are seen in the sea and at the edge of the water: an incredible array of rock formations, called "needles," that makes Cannon Beach one of the most spectacular beach areas of the state. Only 0.9 mile from Tolovana is Haystack Rock, a 235-foot monolith with its surrounding "Marine Garden," a designated sensitive area where all invertebrates are protected—sea stars, barnacles, algae, crabs, chitons, limpets, sculpins,

anemones, nudibranchs, and many more for the curious to find and identify. Sea birds are numerous, with pelagic cormorants, pigeon guillemots,
and tufted puffins nesting in their special habitats. The Haystack Rock
Awareness Program has volunteers that give interpretive information most
summer weekends, especially during low-tide mornings. No climbing on
Haystack Rock is permitted above the high-tide line.

The Oregon Coast Trail goes inland at Third Street. Backpackers doing
the trail will find "unofficial" camps on the south side of Silver Point and
the south side of Austin Point.

ECOLA STATE PARK

Hours/Season: Day use; year-round
Area: 1,304 acres
Facilities: Picnic tables and shelter, restrooms, hike-in camp from Indian
  Creek area, summer day-use fee for vehicles
Attractions: Offshore lighthouse, hiking, photography, wildlife viewing,
  ancient forest, geology, fishing, surfing
Access: Off US 101, 2 miles north of Cannon Beach on park road

When you drive into Ecola State Park and walk to the viewpoint south,
you will no doubt recognize the scene from the many published photographs of it. It is a seascape to savor and file into your memory circuits. Sea
stacks and Haystack Rock punctuate the long sweep of incoming surf moving toward the town of Cannon Beach, backed by the curving peaks of ridge
upon ridge of coastal mountains. The southern end of the park begins just
north of Chapman Point, which pairs with Ecola Point to bracket Crescent
Beach. A dirt path accesses this sandy slice of shoreline, but paved walks
take one to varied headland vistas, all spectacular.

Ecola was developed originally by the CCC, and in the early 1950s a
campground was developed. However, this was abandoned in 1954 as being inappropriate to the setting.

In summer, a road is open to Indian Beach to the north, which also has
day-use facilities and a cove bounded by basaltic Indian Rock to the north
and Bald Point, the toe of an old landslide, on the south. Included in the
park further north is the vast undeveloped whole of 1,200-foot-high
Tillamook Head to road's end in Seaside, for a total of 9 miles of ocean
shore. This volcanic spur of the Coast Range has a large intrusion of basalt
rock sandwiched between layers of mudstone. Tillamook Head exists because the basalt was luckily positioned to resist the pounding surf. Landslides of the softer rock frequently have caused damage in the park.

Over a mile offshore is 100-foot-high Tillamook Rock with its storm-bat-
tered, inactive lighthouse that is now privately owned and used as a
Columbarium, a place to entomb urns of cremated ashes. This offshore
chunk of basalt rock was once part of the mainland.

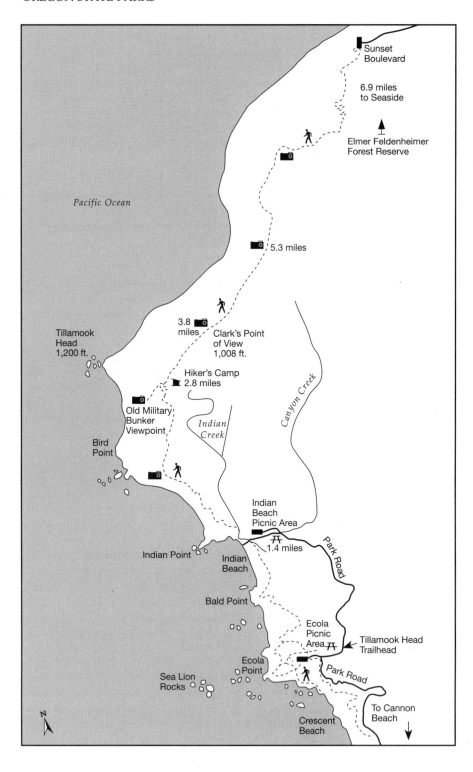

Sunset Boulevard

6.9 miles to Seaside

Elmer Feldenheimer Forest Reserve

Pacific Ocean

5.3 miles

3.8 miles

Clark's Point of View 1,008 ft.

Tillamook Head 1,200 ft.

Hiker's Camp 2.8 miles

Old Military Bunker Viewpoint

Canyon Creek

Bird Point

Indian Creek

Indian Beach Picnic Area

Indian Point

1.4 miles

Park Road

Indian Beach

Bald Point

Ecola Picnic Area

Tillamook Head Trailhead

Sea Lion Rocks

Ecola Point

Park Road

To Cannon Beach

Crescent Beach

N

Grand view south to Cannon Beach, Ecola State Park

The State Park Agency has sought to preserve this fragile headland from wind and storm damage by maintaining a wide swatch of forest. The donation of the Elmer Feldenheimer Forest Reserve, which adjoins the northeast section of the park, has increased the cushion of trees, including old-growth Sitka spruce and western hemlock and habitat for elk and deer. Several offshore wildlife refuges—Bird Rocks, Tillamook Head Rocks, and Sea Lion Rocks—increase the wildlife viewing possibilities. Ecola is also an official whale watching site.

A prehistoric Indian village was located at Indian Beach and several middens have been found in the area.

The name of the park comes from the Indian word for whale, *ekoli*. Lewis and Clark passed this way on January 8, 1806, and saw burial canoes of the Tillamook Indians when they followed an elk trail south from Seaside to Cannon Beach to an Indian village on what is now Elk Creek. They bartered for three hundred pounds of blubber from a beached whale.

Today, hikers can follow roughly the same route that Lewis and Clark took over Tillamook Head. It was dedicated as a National Recreation Trail in 1972, a scenic 6.9-mile hike. It's not a difficult trail, but it is often quite muddy, even in summer, so wear boots.

Although the trail begins at the park entrance, most people start from the north side of the parking lot at the Ecola picnic ground. Good ocean views are seen on the 1.4-mile hike along the marine terrace to Indian Beach. There is a fault zone near Bald Point, where earth layers have slipped out of alignment. Another 1.4 miles of hiking leads to a hikers' camp at the top of Tillamook Head. A fork in the trail at this point leads to an old military bunker viewpoint. Clark's Point of View (1,008-foot elevation), where Clark thought the view was "the grandest and most pleasing," is 1 mile past the camp. The last 3.1 miles of trail includes a couple of good viewpoints on the north side of the headland. At one of these, the view includes the sweeping mouth of the Necanicum River, the town of Seaside, the Clatsop Plains, South Jetty, and Cape Disappointment. This area traverses some good growths of ancient forest.

Those wanting to hike from the north trailhead should follow Sunset Boulevard in Seaside south to the parking area.

SADDLE MOUNTAIN STATE PARK

Hours/Season: Overnight; *campground closed in winter*
Area: 2,911 acres
Facilities: Picnic tables, primitive campground with 10 tent sites, restrooms
Attractions: Hiking, photography, rare plants and wildflowers
Access: From Cannon Beach, 3 miles north on US 101 to US 26, then 10 miles east to park road; it is 7 miles to the developed area

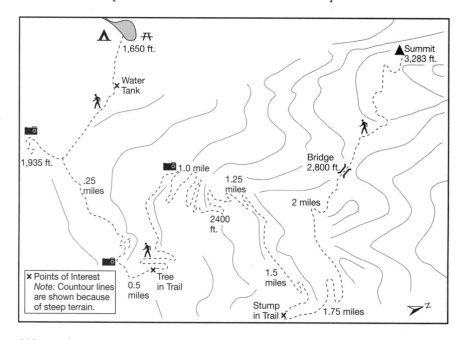

⚑ Saddle Mountain State Park was for a time the largest Oregon state park, and is one of the few located off the main highway system. The entry road and trail were constructed by the CCC. A Registered Natural Heritage Site, this 3,283-foot double peak attracts cautious, experienced hikers and botanists to its wild setting. For some of the 301 identified species of flora, this is their only Coast Range habitat. The mountain top was a refuge for plants from the north during the Ice Age. Saddle Mountain bittercress, Saddle Mountain saxifrage, alpine lily, pink fawn-lily, hairy-stemmed sidalcea, sedge, and trillium grow on the mountain. It is also good habitat for Roosevelt elk and there have been reports of an albino elk.

The saddle of the mountain can be seen from the picnic grounds situated in an alder grove. Its craggy appearance is impressive in late afternoon light. Individual camp sites are for tents, with the only parking in the big paved lot.

Saddle Mountain was a sea-floor volcano that erupted about twenty million years ago, and pillow basalt lava is exposed on the peak. For some thirty-five million years, the Coast Range has been slowly rising from the sea floor.

The modern name of this mountain came from Lt. Charles Wilkes, U.S. Navy, in 1841, obviously because of the shape. According to Indian legend, however, it was called *Swallalhoost*, in honor of a chief who was killed by enemies, became an eagle, and created thunder and lightning on the peak.

Saddle Mountain can be hiked to its summit, an elevation gain of 1,600 feet, but it is a treacherous and hazardous climb above timberline, and people are warned to not attempt it unless they are in good condition and are surefooted. Recent years have seen some erosion of the path and upkeep has not kept pace with its condition, but it is only moderately difficult to hike up to some of the interesting flora.

Toxic Amanita muscaria *mushrooms*

115

The 2.5-mile trail begins by the campsites and first travels through alders, vine maples, mossy trees, Oregon grape, and sword ferns before entering a conifer forest of Douglas fir and hemlock. (Mileage for the trail varies. The state park guide gives it as 2.5 miles, whereas other guides list it as 3 or even 3.4 miles. My comments are based on the 2.5 figure, though the park staff admits it seems more like 3.4 miles.) A side trail at 0.25 mile goes to a steep rocky viewpoint, but there are good views on the main trail shortly before 0.5 mile and 1 mile. Between these two viewpoints, an open trail along a steep vertical face is traversed. Though the surrounding countryside has been logged, there is good regrowth of forest. At 1.5 miles, a small meadow has a rich diversity of wildflowers, many rare or endangered. The path steepens here and narrow rock ledges are traversed. The trail has been worn by storms, elk, and hikers. At 2-plus miles, a bridge spans the saddle and the trail climbs to the higher summit, where a lookout cabin once stood. Those who reach the top tell of the wonderful views of northwest Oregon, southwest Washington, the Pacific Ocean, the Columbia River, and the eastern vista of the Cascade Range. It is not unusual to see surefooted black-tailed deer climb up past the saddle on the steep cliffs.

FORT STEVENS STATE PARK

Hours/Season: Overnight; year-round
Area: 3,763 acres
Facilities: Picnic tables, group picnicking, campground with 213 full hookups, 130 electrical, and 262 tent sites (maximum site is 69 feet), group camping, hiker/biker camp, dumping station, wheelchair-accessible restrooms with showers, boat dock and ramp, exhibit information, historic museum, gift shop, summer day-use fee for vehicles, summer reservations available, phone: (503) 861-1671
Attractions: Hiking and biking trails, beachcombing, windsurfing, wildlife viewing, fishing, freshwater swimming, freshwater lake, guided tours of fort and artillery batteries, *Peter Iredale* shipwreck, photography
Nearby: Fort Clatsop, Astor Column
Access: Follow signs from US 101, with park located 10 miles west of Astoria

▲ Fort Stevens State Park is a flatland park of sand flats, shallow lakes, wetlands, spruce and pine forest, and stabilized dunes fronting the Pacific and the mouth of the Columbia River. It is the third largest of Oregon's state parks and has the most campsites of any of them. Throughout the campground are detailed exhibits on the many habitats of the park and what lives in them.

The largest of the lakes is Coffenbury Lake, a short walk from the campground. A 2-mile trail circles the lake, past pond lilies and fishing spots for numerous trout and perch. A glance at the edge of the water easily spots myriads of tiny fish.

The 1-mile trail from the campground to the beach emerges near the wreck of the *Peter Iredale*, a four-masted, 278-foot British bark that went aground in a heavy southeast wind in late October of 1906, on its way to Portland to load wheat. All hands were rescued. During World War II, the wreck anchored barbed wire which was used as a coastal defense against invasion of Japanese submarines.

Beachcombing is good for sand dollars, with the distinctive design left by scars of their many tube feet. Lucky people might find a glass float after a storm, swept to shore via the "Kuroshia" current. Dune vegetation is varied, with seaside tansy, coast strawberry, beach morning glory, beach pea, and American sea rocket easily discovered. The most extensive sand dune stabilization of the coast occurred here on the Clatsop Plains in the 1930s by the planting of European beach grass, scotch broom, and shore pine. The first two were imported plants.

A viewing tower is located at parking lot "C" at the north end of the park, where it overlooks the south jetty. This is the official whale-watch site. Cape Disappointment is seen just across the Columbia River. Bird and wildlife viewing platforms are located near wetland areas. Ocean fishing for salmon, ling cod, and sea perch is popular on the jetty and fishing spots are found along the mighty Columbia River, which Captain Robert Gray entered and named after his ship over two hundred years ago in 1792. The first sighting of the river was made by Spanish navigator Bruno Heceta in 1775.

The park was named for General Isaac Stevens, the first governor of Washington Territory, who died a hero of the Civil War in 1862.

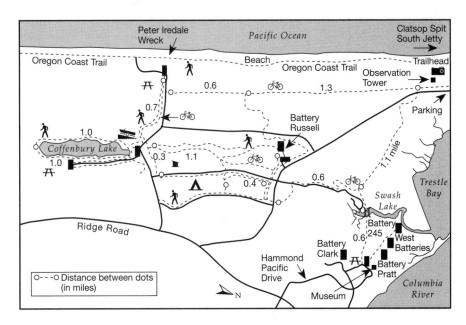

Access to Oregon Coast Trail

An unusual feature of this park is the fort, built in 1864. It was used to protect the mouth of the river from Confederate gun boats during the Civil War, and also as a defense facility through World War II. During the latter, the fort was actually fired upon by a Japanese submarine, but the sub was too far away to cause damage and no fire was returned.

The remains of the fortifications here are extensive and include many abandoned gun batteries and auxiliary buildings. Summer tours in a vintage U.S. Army truck and escorted walking tours are available for a nominal fee, or you can plot your own tour from maps and handout information. The park museum has artifacts and information on the fort's history. A recent addition is a Clatsop Indian long house.

Although one can drive to some of the attractions of this park, the fact that the land is mostly level and open to exploration, added to the availability of 8.5 miles of bicycle paths and 9 miles of walking trails, offers much incentive for self-propelled communication with the natural surroundings.

Fort Stevens has one of the official *Volksmarch* hikes. This 14-kilometer *Volksmarch* includes a section of the beach and passes the wreck of the *Peter Iredale*, the wildlife viewing platform, and the museum and fort area. Detailed maps of the route are available in the park.

The cedar post that marks the northern trailhead of the Oregon Coast Trail is near parking lot C, on the south jetty. This trail was the dream of Samuel N. Dicken, who researched pioneer routes and taught geography at the University of Oregon. With his wife, he explored the proposed route for this hiking trail, and his dream became reality in 1971, when the Oregon Recreation Trails System Act was passed. It is still a priority with the state parks system. About 60 percent of the path is now completed.

After 0.3 miles of hiking along the south jetty, the trail emerges onto the beach and continues along sandy shores for the next 19 miles, except for diversions through the towns of Gearhart and Seaside. It is 3.8 miles total to the *Peter Iredale* wreck in the park.

The area east of the state park has quite a few historical sites. During the winter of 1805–1806, the Lewis and Clark Expedition stayed in Fort Clatsop, which they constructed upon arrival. Though the terminus of their route was on the north side of the Columbia River, the weather, availability of elk

Beach walker and Peter Iredale *wreckage, Fort Stevens State Park*

meat, and salt supply was best on the Oregon side of the river. This spot was found via canoe on what is now the Lewis and Clark River. During that stormy season, they reworked their journals and organized their scientific data. The log stockade on this site is a reconstruction of the original which Clark sketched on the elkhide cover of his fieldbook, and is now a national monument.

The city of Astoria, founded in 1811, was the first permanent settlement in Oregon country and has some good museums and historical buildings. Of special interest is the Astor Column, a monument on Coxcomb Hill decorated with scenes of Indian culture, western settlement, and the Lewis and Clark Expedition. Climb the one hundred sixty-four inside steps to the top of this tower for a panoramic view of Astoria, the shoreline, and the Columbia River with its bridge into Washington.

WILLAMETTE VALLEY

When pioneers moved west on the Oregon Trail, the Willamette Valley was a favored destination. Trappers and frontiersmen "pictured in glowing terms the richness of the soil and the attractions of the climate," and it was true. It was just getting there that was not so easy, yet many succeeded, and historic buildings throughout the valley trace the founding of the oldest settlements.

Named after the Willamette River, which slices through its middle and through the city of Portland, the valley is a broad piece of farmland that stretches south from Portland for two-thirds of the state, with rolling hills, checkered agriculture, and buttes for picturesque touring. Shaped like the thumb side of the right hand, the Columbia River lies north along the curve of the thumb. Two mountain ranges enclose the region on either side, the Coast Range on the west and the snow-peaked Cascade Mountains on the east.

This lowland is the population and commercial center of the state, as several cities arrow south from Portland along Interstate 5. The state's capitol, Salem, is a swift hour below the "user-friendly" city of Portland, voted the nation's most livable city by the U.S. Conference of Mayors in 1988.

Around this population hub is much rural land, crisscrossed by the many rivers that flow out of the mountains—the McKenzie, the Clackamas, the Yamhill, the Tualatin, and the North and South Santiam, to name a few. Ferries were originally used to cross these waterways, and sternwheelers plied the Willamette and some of the larger tributaries.

About sixty covered bridges, built from hand-hewn timber felled near the sites, were constructed over creeks in the valley, to provide transportation for the horse and buggy era and for Model Ts. By covering the bridges, the builders ensured that the trusses and plank decking lasted longer, sheltered from the rainy weather. Since the 1890s, when chain drives and pneu-

Opposite: *Hiking under Lower South Falls, Silver Falls State Park*

matic-tired wheels became fully practical, a popular way to tour these bridges has been by bicycle.

Even before the waterways of the valley became transportation routes, however, they provided habitat for beavers in this once wild land. Therein lies a major reason for the early development of the area: beaver hats became the fashion and approximately half a million skins were handled by the Hudson's Bay Company between 1834 and 1837. Beaver numbers declined sharply and the fashion passed. Fortunately, more recent conservation efforts have increased their population.

Rains are gentler in the valley than on the weather-facing coast, but still come mostly between November and April. The Cascades pull more moisture from the atmosphere as it moves across the state, providing a good snowpack for skiing on the slopes of these mountains. Temperatures are not extreme at lower elevations of the valley, though they are warmer in summer and colder in winter than on the coastal edge.

Optimal growing conditions provide a bounty of good crops of fruits, vegetables, and nuts. Travelers will find many roadside stands and "U-pick" places for picnic fare and snacking. Wineries are found throughout the valley with world-class Chardonnays and Pinot Noirs. Northwest Portland is the hub for breweries and, along with the wineries, features public tours and tasting.

If it gets too hot in the lowland, a jaunt to the mountains lets you select an elevation with the right temperature. In the Coast Range, a drive up 4,097-foot Mary's Peak has views from the Pacific to the Cascades. To get higher, go east to the Cascade Mountains where green forests, clear lakes, and hiking trails are found in the national forests and wilderness areas.

ELIJAH BRISTOW STATE PARK

Hours/Season: Day use; year-round
Area: 847 acres
Facilities: Picnic tables, group picnicking, wheelchair-accessible restrooms, equestrian parking area, horseshoes
Attractions: Hiking, biking, and equestrian trails, fishing
Nearby: Fall Creek National Recreation Trail
Access: Off Oregon Highway 58, 17 miles southeast of Eugene

Elijah Bristow State Park is one of five major state parks developed along the Willamette River Greenway, a 255-mile strip of river frontage that is being acquired for preservation, public access, and long-term recreational use of the Willamette River that includes fishing, hiking, primitive camping, and related activities. Tom McCall and Bob Straub, in particular, supported this plan and the Oregon Legislature endorsed it in 1967 and 1973. The river had become a polluted waterway and a cleanup got underway which has revitalized this major artery of the valley. More development is planned for the future along the Greenway, with some people still holding onto the vision of a continuous bike path.

Located along the middle fork of the river just below Dexter Dam, this park includes open land backed by forested river bottomland with mixed stands of Douglas fir, alder, oak, willow, cottonwood, and maple. Originally called Dexter State Park, it was renamed in 1979 to honor Elijah Bristow (1788–1872), an 1846 pioneer to the valley and one of the first white settlers in Lane County. He founded the community of Pleasant Hill, 10 miles west of the park.

Filbert harvests in the Willamette Valley, Elijah Bristow State Park

Most of the 16 miles of level park trails meander through dense wooded areas like a tangle of intersecting pieces. Some paths are layered with chips; others are muddy after rainfall. Though nearby, the river is not often in view. Lost Creek and Barley Creek traverse the park, bridged for easy crossing. Frogs are heard in the wetlands and creek beds. Bird nesting and other wildlife habitat is here, with lots of intermittent blackberries for summer snacking. One would like to see more trail signs. It might not be difficult to get lost—do take a map with you.

Just east of the park, across the river and east on Fall Creek Road (FS

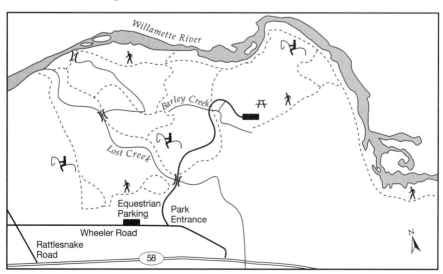

Road No. 18), is the appealing 13-mile Fall Creek National Recreation Trail that closely follows Fall Creek in the Willamette National Forest (*no bicycles*). Several trailheads let you do short day hikes or the entire distance, with an elevation change from 960 feet to 1,385 feet, and there are three campgrounds along the route. Old-growth conifers become more plentiful as one travels east and higher. The scenery includes many deep pools, some fast water, rock formations and outcroppings, and many small streams crossing the trail.

ARMITAGE STATE PARK

Hours/Season: Day use; year-round
Area: 56.94 acres
Facilities: Picnic tables, boat ramp, wheelchair-accessible restrooms, group picnic shelters, summer day-use fee for vehicles, park office, phone: (503) 686-7592
Attractions: Fishing, boating
Access: From Interstate 5, take the Coburg exit; drive just south of town on Coburg Road and cross the McKenzie River to park, 5 miles north of Eugene (there is no sign on Interstate 5)

Sprawled along the south banks of the McKenzie River, Armitage State Park invites picnickers, reunions, and a quick escape from nearby Eugene, especially when summer heat radiates from city cement. The bottomland by the river is a hardwood tract plus conifers that include alder, cottonwood, willow, Douglas fir, western red cedar, aspen, and bigleaf and vine maple. The spacious lawns of this level park are crisscrossed with several walking paths, one along the river's edge.

Though the park once included campground facilities, those are gone, as so often happens with state parks near cities. Nine picnic areas accommodate varying sizes of groups. The lone area reached by a road under Coburg Road to the east end of Armitage has a huge shelter which is rumored to have been an old dance hall that was moved and remodeled. It holds up to two hundred people. Horseshoe pits and volleyball poles are at several places in the park.

BEN AND KAY DORRIS STATE PARK

Hours/Season: Day use; year-round
Area: 92 acres
Facilities: Picnic tables, boat ramp, restrooms
Attractions: Hiking, fishing, boating
Nearby: McKenzie River National Recreation Trail
Access: Off US 126, travel 31 miles east of Eugene

Fishing enthusiasts on rock formations along McKenzie River, Ben and Kay Dorris State Park

This inviting park along the McKenzie River is a popular picnic stop. On a wooded terrace that is 80 to 100 feet above the river, vehicles can be pulled up next to a table, explained by the fact that there was once overnight camping in the park.

Most of the park acreage was a gift of Ben F. and Klysta C. (Kay) Dorris. A paved walkway leads east and downhill from the picnic area to the boat launch, where another picnic table is placed. Fishing enthusiasts scamper atop a huge rock formation, called "Rock House," for good spots to throw a line into the clear blue-green water. It is thought that this overhanging outcropping of rock provided overnight shelter for those using the old wagon road leading through the Cascade Mountains via McKenzie Pass.

A walkway also descends from the west end of the picnic area to the river, going through forest heavily timbered with Douglas fir on the upper section. Bigleaf maple, cedar, and rich undercover dominate the wetland area by the river. This approach has a good view of the Martin Rapids, a definite challenge to boaters, from the sound of them. Fishermen have made a path that lets one follow the river and return to the boat launch area, making a nice loop for exploring.

If you're continuing east on the highway, stop and sample sections of the McKenzie River National Recreation Trail that follows the river for 26.5 miles. The west trailhead is a short distance east of McKenzie Bridge. It continues northeast past Clear Lake to the Old Santiam Wagon Road, passing several campgrounds for overnighting. It is accessed at several locations; a Forest Service brochure will help you decide on portions to hike. The segment south of Clear Lake is particularly scenic, with views of Sahalie Falls and Koosah Falls.

HOWARD J. MORTON STATE PARK

Hours/Season: Day use; year-round
Area: 24.4 acres
Facilities: Picnic tables, chemical toilet, *no water*
Attractions: Fishing, solitude
Nearby: Olallie Trail
Access: Watch milepost markers on Oregon Highway 126 and proceed 0.7
  miles past the 37-mile sign

Finding this park requires close attention to mileage markers. The usual state park sign is not used here; rather, there is a large wooden sign below the grade of the highway on the south side, just before the short entry road turns sharply west to almost parallel the highway.

The sign results from a request by the park donor, Mrs. Winifred K. Morton, for an appropriate, dignified-appearing sign to designate an area left in its natural state in honor of her forester husband, Howard J. Morton. The land was given with the understanding that it would be perpetually set aside for the use and enjoyment of the

Tall Douglas firs along McKenzie River, Howard J. Morton State Park

public. No improvements were to be made and no cutting of trees, except to clear underbrush and to provide a small picnic area.

There are three picnic tables above the river, one with a lovely river vista and a nice grill. A short path leads down to the water for fishing access. Little used, the park is a quiet riverside place for picnicking, contemplation, and relaxation in a nice forest of fir, maple and alder.

Those interested in a nearby hiking trail in a pristine area, where chances of seeing wildlife are good, should stop at the McKenzie Ranger Station, just east of the town of McKenzie Bridge, and ask for the handout for the Olallie Trail. I saw my first wild cougar along this trail, though it quickly disappeared. Located in the Old Cascades, this 10-mile path is mostly gentle, with a side option of the short but fairly steep climb to the top of 5,660-foot-high Horsepasture Mountain. The trail is accessible at three points on Wapiti Road (FS Road No. 1993). Located in the middle of the trail, Olallie Ridge Natural Research Area is of special interest with its variety of plants. Different wildflower species continue to surprise throughout the summer.

CASCADIA STATE PARK

Hours/Season: Overnight; *campground closed in winter*
Area: 254 acres
Facilities: Picnic tables, group picnic shelters, campground with 26 primitive sites (maximum site 35 feet), wheelchair-accessible restrooms, group camping
Attraction: Soda water spring, swimming, fishing, hiking, ancient forest
Nearby: Short Covered Bridge, Menagerie Wilderness, Foster and Green Peter Dams and reservoir
Access: Off US 20, 14 miles east of Sweet Home

Back in 1880, a slave was stalking deer in the area of this park when he discovered a soda springs. People learned of this discovery and came to drink the mineral waters, thought to have medicinal properties, while they hunted, fished, and camped.

It looked like a good piece of real estate, with as many as two hundred tents pitched at one time, so George M. Geisendorfer purchased 300 acres in 1895, including the mineral springs, to develop a health spa and vacation spot. He established a popular resort that included a hotel, post office, camp area, and water system around the soda springs, operating it for about fifty years. In the early 1900s, wagon trains used this well-known watering stop.

In 1941, the State Parks purchased the property from Geisendorfer. Now 254 acres, Cascadia celebrated its fiftieth anniversary on July 24, 1992, at the same time as the opening of a temporary bridge over the South Santiam River, called a bailey bridge, that serves as the entry into the park. When funding is available, a permanent bridge will be constructed, similar to the original wood truss bridge that was built in 1928. After construction starts, the park will be accessed by a detour over Short Covered Bridge (built in 1945), 1.6 miles to the west.

Walkways connect the soda spring fountain area (the old pump was removed recently) with the day-use area and the picnic area by the campground. The separate day-use area is huge, with large meadows. Both the campground and the picnic tables by the entry bridge are situated under a canopy of old-growth Douglas fir and other huge trees. Lichen-covered Pacific yew and lush undergrowth of temperate rain forest are present.

The South Santiam River flows down the western flanks of the Cascade Mountains into the steep-walled canyon of Cascadia. Its waters weave past rocks and ledges, sometimes forming riffles, and offer welcome pools of cool water for summer swimming and a playground of rock jumping. Fishermen can follow along the banks for that good fishing hole. A path accesses the river from the day-use area.

The signed trail to Soda Creek Falls begins along the spur road to the day-use area, but several of the easterly camp sites also have paths that connect with the trail. The path follows the meandering creek moderately steeply uphill for about 1 mile after crossing two bridges. In several places, the trail splits into two paths, which soon rejoin. The first part of the trail was once a self-guided nature trail, but brochures are no longer available. Some of the signposts have names of adjacent vegetation. Ferns abound,

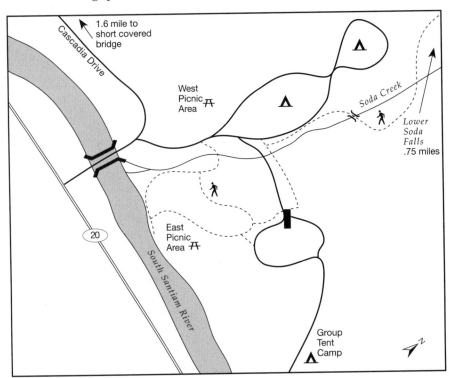

Summer water play along South Santiam River, Cascadia State Park

and trees include firs, hemlock, cedar, alder, cascara, and bigleaf maple. Mosses hang from many of the branches. This is the lowest ancient forest grove left in the South Santiam River drainage. A high delicate waterfall, surrounded by rocky ledges and a pool, is at the terminus of the trail.

A few miles east of Cascadia, on US 20, is a recent addition to the wilderness system. Menagerie Wilderness contains a cluster of rock pinnacles that are resistant lava intrusions left after time and erosion have worked on the old Cascades, ten million years older than the high Cascades of today. Park across the road from the Trout Creek Campground and hike the 2.4-mile Trout Creek Trail through forest to Rooster Rock. The climb to the high point at 3,570 feet ends at an old lookout with a closeup view of Rooster Rock, the wilderness area, and North and Middle Sisters on the Cascade ridge.

West of Cascadia, the waters of the South Santiam River are held back by both the Foster and Green Peter dams. The reservoirs formed are popular with boaters and other water-sport enthusiasts, cool places to paddle, water-ski, fish, or swim on a hot summer day.

DETROIT LAKE STATE PARK

Hours/Season: Overnight; *campground closed in winter*
Area: 104 acres
Facilities: Picnic tables, campground with 107 full hookup, 70 electrical, and 134 tent sites (maximum site is 60 feet), club camping, wheelchair-accessible restrooms with showers, firewood, boat ramps, moorage docks, fishing docks, slide program, campground and boat moorage reservations available in summer, summer day-use fee for vehicles, phone: (503) 854-3406
Attractions: Boating, water-skiing, fishing, swimming
Nearby: Mount Jefferson Wilderness
Access: Off Oregon Highway 22, 2 miles west of Detroit

Reached by good roads and an easy hour or two from most valley population centers, 3,900-acre Detroit Lake attracts many boating and fishing devotees to this canyon location. The campground and separate day-use area of this park sprawl at water's edge on the north shore. Mongold day-use area is 1.5 miles west of the campground section. Across the water, Mount Jefferson is seen rising above smaller peaks of the Cascades.

The lake is the product of the construction of the Detroit Dam on the North Santiam River in the 1950s. The park and lake are named after the nearby town of Detroit, which was settled by several Michigan people. The day-use area is named after the highway construction work camp that was once in the vicinity but is now underwater. The park is within the Willamette National Forest and was originally a Forest Service camp-

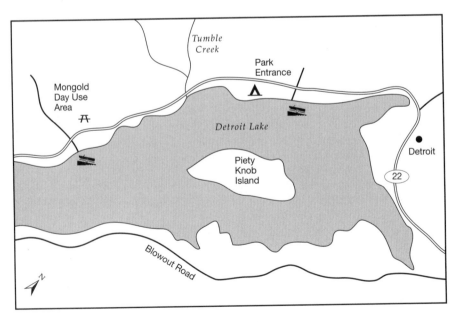

Boat launching at Mongold day-use area, Detroit Lake State Park

ground. The state now leases it. Forested with second-growth Douglas fir, the area was extensively logged before World War II.

In the campground, boat ramps are reached from the "D" and "G" loops, the fishing dock is accessed from the "F" loop, and paths lead from "H" and "F" loops to the floating boat docks. Mongold has widely dispersed picnic tables—lakeshore or forested, in sunshine or shade—a huge paved boat ramp, a courtesy dock, and a special takeoff and landing area for water-skiers, a popular sport here. Check the local regulations for water-skiing. Also in this area, an unsupervised swimming area is marked off by a boom. Though there are no specific trails, it is easy to walk along the lakefront for some distance.

You will notice Piety Knob Island in the center of the lake. If you'd like to boat over and spend the night, there are twelve primitive campsites, pit toilets, but *no water*. The island is not part of the state park.

If you visit during August, check to see if the Detroit Lake Water Festival is being held in town.

Detroit Lake State Park is a good base camp for spending some time hiking and fishing in the Mount Jefferson Wilderness, reached by driving east on Oregon Highway 22 and taking forest roads to trailheads. The hike to Jefferson Park, accessed from Whitewater Road No. 2243, with wildflower alpine meadows and several lakes, is 6 miles one way and probably the most scenic spot in the Oregon Cascades. Unfortunately, the word is out, so weekends particularly are crowded with people. Midsummer has hordes of mosquitos. My overnight trip was on Labor Day, when most people had headed out, the mosquitos were gone, and the wildflowers and the moon rising above the mountain were awesome. This hike would also work as a day hike.

For those wanting a shorter and easier hiking experience, the 2.3-mile hike in to Pamelia Lake, following lovely Pamelia Creek, is a good one, accessed from Pamelia Road No. 2246. Be sure to walk to the south edge of the lake for views of Mount Jefferson. Another good choice is Marion Lake, reached via the Marion Creek Road No. 2255. In 2.5 miles, the hiker ascends to Lake Ann, with its adjacent wetlands, and then to larger Marion Lake, where trails disperse for more exploring. A backpacker camp is found there.

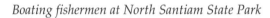

NORTH SANTIAM STATE PARK

Hours/Season: Day use; year-round
Area: 119.5 acres
Facilities: Picnic tables, restrooms
Attractions: Hiking trails, fishing
Access: Off Oregon Highway 22, 4 miles west of Mill City

On the north bank of the North Santiam River, this park has the good feel of some wildness bordering a well-cared-for picnic area on a grassy, open site. Trails wander in various directions toward the river, some leading to secluded picnic tables, others ending at the river's cobble beach, another picnic choice.

This is a pretty section of the river, with rocks, riffles, rapids, and splits in

Boating fishermen at North Santiam State Park

the waterway. The clear green water attracts fishermen. Most of the park is natural, untrimmed and unmanicured, with undergrowth vegetation, heavily wooded with fir, maple, and alder, and moss hanging from trees.

The park and river bear the name of the Santiam Indians, a Calapooyan tribe that lived near the river in the surrounding territory at the time the Euro-Americans arrived.

A trail continues along the river downstream and another goes through the woods. A gravel bar along the river is accessed by a gravel road, and though there is no real boat ramp here, some do put their dories into the water and fishermen cast out lines.

The section of the river between Mill City and Mehama is an intermediate rafting run, rated from class 2 to class 3 depending on the flow of water. A good place to practice surfing, S-turns, and rolls is the play area formed by a small ledge on the right in North Santiam State Park.

SILVER FALLS STATE PARK

Hours/Season: Overnight; *campground closed in winter*
Area: 8,706 acres
Facilities: Picnic tables, group picnic shelters, play areas, campground with 53 electrical and 51 tent sites (maximum site is 60 feet), wheelchair-accessible restrooms with showers, group tent and trailer camp, horse camp with corrals, dumping station, firewood, horseshoes, exhibit information, youth camp, conference center, rustic group lodging, nature lodge (snack bar in summer), summer day-use fee for vehicles, phone: (503) 873-8681
Attractions: Hiking, biking, and equestrian trails, waterfalls, photography, fishing, swimming, wildlife viewing and nature study
Access: Off Oregon Highway 214, 26 miles east of Salem

▲ Silver Falls State Park, Oregon's largest, is a scenic and recreational wonderland that was once considered for national park status. It includes canyons of the North and South Forks of Silver Creek that are ribboned with a clustered series of waterfalls in the forested foothills of the Cascades.

So vast is this park that one needs a map to realize the isolated locations and acreage encompassing Howard Creek Horse Camp, the extensive facilities of the conference center and the youth camp, Upper Smith Creek, and the old and new ranch structures. The latter are set on a meadow area with dormitory-style accommodations and kitchen equipment which can be reserved for family reunions, outdoor schools, and Scout affairs. Upper Smith Creek has eight cabins for a group of twenty to twenty-two people.

The main day-use area is adjacent to South Falls. A hiker/biker trail connects from the campground and passes the play and swimming area of the creek, which even has a sandy beach. The Nature Lodge has a gift shop and information on park history, wildlife, plant life, and geography. A "Friends" group will answer questions and take you on nature walks.

The creeks were perhaps named for James "Silver" Smith, who came to the region in the 1840s with nearly a bushel of silver dollars. In the 1880s, the townsite of Silver Falls City was surveyed and a hotel built at the present location of South Falls. A sawmill was situated along the stream, tracts were cleared for agriculture, and hunting lodges punctuated the forest. Logging was pursued enthusiastically by the Silverton Lumber Company for some time, but by 1929 only one family, that of South Falls owner

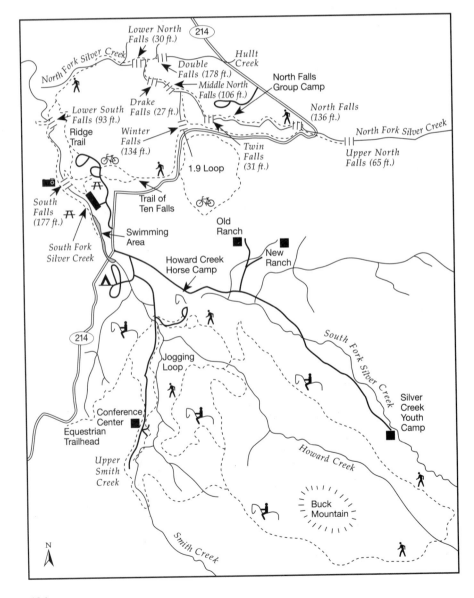

D. E. Geiser, remained in the town. He chose to charge ten cents to see the falls and tried to promote this business by having a man go over the falls in a canvas-covered canoe guided by a wire. That didn't last long—the wire failed, though the man survived. Geiser's next scheme was running old cars over the falls. He charged twenty-five cents for this spectacle.

Fortunately, the state came to the rescue and bought Geiser's property for park purposes. When the surrounding area was considered for national park status in both 1926 and 1935, investigation found it too altered by man. This submarginal agriculture and logged-over forest land, however, was acquired by the federal government during the Depression years and was one of two Recreation Demonstration Areas (RDAs) in the country, with youth camps—YMCA and Girl Scouts—and other recreational facilities. The CCC constructed these camps, the "Trail of Ten Falls," the present Nature Lodge, and South Falls Viewpoint. The latter two places are now on the National Registry of Historic Places. In the late 1940s, the RDA was deeded to the state and added to their piece of parkland.

Enough time has passed that the park has recovered much of its forest and charismatic character. The terrain is rolling to mountainous, elevation from 700 feet in the northwest corner to 3,000 feet in the southeast corner, forested with young timber to 500-year-old Douglas firs, western hemlock, red cedar, a few yew trees, and maple, alder, and cottonwood along stream bottoms.

Geological changes were slower, but profound. Fifteen million years ago, the ancestral Columbia River flowed southwesterly in a broad valley through the old Cascades, into the Salem area, and west to the sea. But then, over a period of two million years, came enormous floods of Columbia River Basalt. At least eight flows of fluid lava poured into this area from fissures to the east and began shoving the river north. Between flows, sediments and forest grew. Since then, erosion has cut deep gorges and a thick soil mantle has sprouted vegetation, but the more resistant rock has formed ledges with waterfalls. Further erosion has cut cave-like formations under both North and South falls.

The exhilarating focus of the park is on the 6.9-mile hiking loop that descends into the canyon from the forest ledge, circles past or near ten impressive waterfalls ranging in height from 27 feet to 178 feet, and follows the two major creeks and their tributaries for a good portion of the trail. Although all the falls and bridge crossings are a joy, it is awesome to walk behind South Falls, Lower South Falls, and North Falls. Remember that spring is best for seeing powerful quantities of water, as well as a multitude of wildflowers. Look for layered lava and sediments, lava casts of trees, vesicles formed by gas bubbles, and fractures in the lava flow.

Access points are at the South Falls Viewpoint, North Falls parking, or Winter Falls parking. Several shorter circuits can be taken. Be sure to have a map of the trail system with you. Most of the trail is not difficult but the alternate 1-mile Ridge Trail is a steep ascent.

For bikers, a 4-mile trail begins at the campground (or at the day-use area), goes along the ledge above the falls, and then makes a loop on the east side of the highway.

Horse trailheads are on the highway on the west side of the park, where there are hitching rails and a loading ramp, and at the horse camp. A 14-mile trail loops into the southeastern higher elevation of the park, circling Buck Mountain. Hikers can also use these trails.

A 3-mile jogging trail is located near the conference center. Hikers wanting to see ancient forest should access the jogging trail from the footbridge crossing Smith Creek between the meeting hall and dining hall of the conference center, and keep left as the horse trail goes right. Old-growth trees can be seen in this section of the park. Though the area was logged, the advantage of selective logging is seen.

Wildlife viewing possibilities are good in the park. It is not unusual to see black-tailed fawns near the campground or beaver at the bottom of the falls. Diligent watchers might spot a bobcat, nutria, dipper, kingfisher, or pileated woodpecker.

SARAH HELMICK STATE PARK

Hours/Season: Day use; year-round
Area: 79 acres
Facilities: Picnic tables, restrooms
Attractions: Fishing
Access: From sign on US 99W, follow spur road short distance to park, 6 miles south of Monmouth

The preservation of the lovely old trees which shade picnic tables along this Luckiamute River park near a highway exemplifies the original concept behind establishment of Oregon's state parks. Something about such mature trees lifts the heart. In the early days of Sarah Helmick State Park, it was a traveling overnight stop on the old route of Pacific Highway 99W.

It is also interesting that this valley park includes the first land given to the Oregon State Highway Commission for park purposes, in 1922, by Sarah Helmick and her son James. The park expanded as others gave more land at later dates. Sarah and her husband Henry came to Oregon in 1845 over the Oregon Trail from Burlington, Iowa, with their oxen-drawn wagon, but it was said that they lost all of their possessions at Cascade Rapids. In 1846 they settled on a 640-acre Donation

Spider webs on Fuller teasel plants

Land Claim on the Luckiamute River. Sarah was known as "Grandma" to all her friends and acquaintances.

The park is along the flood plain of the Luckiamute River with flat to gently sloping land. It is sometimes flooded in winter. The huge trees include Douglas fir, grand fir, maple, ash, cottonwood, willow, and red cedar. Spacious lawns under the trees circle a wild central area with snowberry, salmonberry, and thimbleberry. Paths form diameters to the opposite side of the park. A trail goes down the riverbank for fishing access.

WILLAMETTE MISSION STATE PARK

Hours/Season: Day use; year-round
Area: 1,686 acres
Facilities: Picnic tables, boat ramp, wheelchair-accessible restrooms and fishing piers, exhibit information, summer day-use fee for vehicles
Attractions: Hiking, bicycling, horseback riding, boating, paddling, fishing, wildlife viewing, historical site, world's largest cottonwood tree
Access: From I-5, take Exit 263 and drive 1.75 miles west on Brooklake Road, then turn north on Wheatland Road for 2.5 miles; or travel 12 miles north of West Salem on 221 to Wheatland Road and across the ferry to the park

For Reverend Jason Lee in 1834, this parkland was the fertile valley along the Willamette River at the end of the Oregon Trail. He set up the

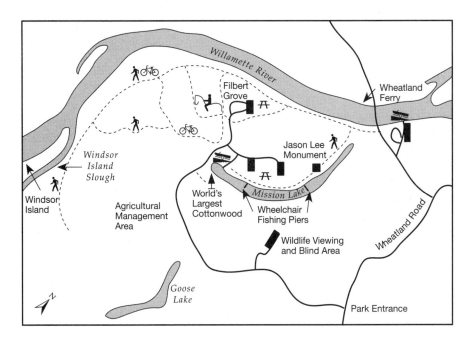

137

Ferry across Willamette River to Willamette Mission State Park

first Indian Methodist mission school in the Willamette Valley, but it was not a successful endeavor.

A more permanent event occurred in 1844 when Daniel Matheny purchased land on the west bank of the river and acquired a ferry built by Lindsay Applegate. In the same year, he operated the first ferry to carry a wagon and team across the Willamette River. A ferry still operates at this site, an interesting way to travel to one of Oregon's state parks.

Willamette Mission is one of the five greenway state parks along the Willamette River. The boat ramp area to the river is separate, just east of the ferry landing on the north side of Matheny Road.

The major day-use area is the East Bank Unit off Wheatland Road, a fertile river bottomland acreage. Soon after entering this area, a spur leads to a nature-viewing platform and wildlife blind.

Mission Lake, a long, narrow strip of water left by an old channel of the river, is bordered by a walnut orchard and fishing piers that are wheelchair-accessible, plus a boat launch. Come in the fall and harvest the good walnuts that have fallen to the ground. A hiking-only trail follows the riparian zone to the Jason Lee Monument, where the mission once was located. Wildlife is abundant, with red-tailed hawks circling, great blue herons fishing, blue jays squawking, and squirrels scampering about. Small fish are easily seen at the edge of the lake.

A short drive northwest takes visitors to the Filbert Grove day-use area, which is along the river. This sizable grove of filbert trees drops a large number of nuts by autumn, but most of them are devoured by some pest (perhaps the filbert worm) that leaves tiny holes drilled in them.

A hiking and bicycling trail circles the filbert grove and then heads off in both directions along the river, one toward the Wheatland Ferry. The latter connects to the monument trail for hikers. The westerly trail loops around for several miles, with a hiking-only spur going to a slough. A 2-mile equestrian trail also begins at the filbert grove.

Don't miss a look at the world's largest black cottonwood tree, which can be viewed from the boat launch on Mission Lake or by hiking the short signed trail from the park road. This wonderful old tree is 155 feet high with a 110-foot spread, 26.25 feet in circumference, and about 260 years old as of 1993.

Besides the grasslands and orchards, about half of the park has a natural forest of maples, cottonwoods, ash, and willows. Ancient broadleaf forest and forested sloughs of the river can be discovered by canoe. Put into the water at the boat ramp by the ferry or at the Spring Valley access, just upriver off Oregon Highway 221. From this access, one can paddle up Windsor Island Slough, along the East Bank Unit. From the parking ramp near the ferry, one can paddle downriver and access a unit of the park reached only by boat. A copy of the *Willamette River Recreation Guide* is helpful.

MAUD WILLIAMSON STATE PARK

Hours/Season: Day use; year-round
Area: 23.9 acres
Facilities: Picnic tables, restrooms
Attractions: Picnicking and rest stop
Access: Off Oregon Highway 221, 12 miles north of Salem

▲ This park is a good example of the initial motivations of the state park system: a good roadside stop and forest preservation along highways. Overnight camping was once available here, but it is now open only for day use. Tall second-growth Douglas fir trees

Farmland adjacent to forest, Maud Williamson State Park

provide lots of cool shade for a rest or lunch stop. A sharp line separates these woods from open, cultivated farmland to the west of the park.

A historic farmhouse still stands on park land, once occupied by the park donor, Maud Williamson, and her brother. She gave the land for park purposes in memory of her mother, Ruby T. Williamson.

BALD PEAK STATE PARK

Hours/Season: Day use; year-round
Area: 26 acres
Facilities: Picnic tables, toilets, *no water*
Attractions: Photography, viewpoint
Access: Travel 4 miles north of Newberg on Oregon Highway 219 to signed road for park, then continue for another 5 miles

Views of the Coast Range through the trees are visible on the paved drive to the summit of Bald Peak. This is the high point of the Chehalem Hills at an elevation of 1,633 feet. From the northeast-facing bald area of the park, good views of the Cascade spine are seen with Mounts Hood, Adams, and Saint Helens in the distance. The foreground view drops down to the agricultural land of the Tualatin Valley and the north part of the Willamette Valley. Unfortunately, some days there is a smog line up to the height of Mount Saint Helens' peak that can wreck any attempt at sharp photography of this splendid view. One hopes that this is not always the case.

The southwest side of the peak is forested, with a meandering path that

Black-tailed deer, Bald Peak State Park

swoops downhill a short distance before it loops back to the grassy summit area.

In 1939 the park was considered for a memorial to the pioneer women of the Oregon country, but when Parks Superintendent Boardman brought an inspection group to the site, it was rejected for various reasons.

CHAMPOEG STATE PARK

Hours/Season: Overnight; year-round
Area: 615 acres
Facilities: Picnic tables, group picnic shelter, campground with 48 electrical and 6 tent sites (maximum site is 35 feet), RV group camp with meeting hall, group tent camp, wheelchair-accessible campsite and restrooms with showers, dumping station, firewood, dock, exhibit information, visitor center, gift shop, summer day-use fee for vehicles, phone: (503) 678-1251
Attractions: Newell House, log cabin museum, monument, historical pageant in July, hiking, boating, bicycling, fishing
Access: From US 99W in Newberg, follow signs 4 miles southeast to park; or from Interstate 5, take Exit 278 and follow signs 5 miles west to park

Champoeg State Park is a park for the imagination, a place for the mind's eye to recreate history along the south bank of the Willamette River. Picture the village Champooick of the Calapooya Indians where they harvested camas roots, fished, and hunted. In 1811, their lives changed when the site was first visited by hunters and fur traders of the Hudson's Bay Company and the company built a warehouse and gristmill in this loca-

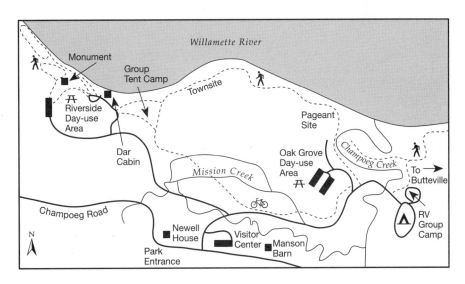

Autumn trees by hiking trails, Champoeg State Park

tion. Retired French Canadian trappers established the first white settlement of Champoeg, taking Indian mates, and sowing wheat and children after fashionable beaver hats had caused much of the beaver population to be trapped out by the 1840s.

The present park site was chosen by the early settlers as a meeting place because of good access by boat or other available transportation of that day. Initial "Wolf Meetings" about area predators developed into government concerns. On May 2, 1843, 102 settlers voted 52–50 to organize a provisional government, the first American government on the Pacific Coast and a spur to orderly settlement.

In 1861 a flood swept away most of the town buildings, and in 1892 the townsite was abandoned. Walk through this mostly flat park with a map of the sites of the old buildings and envision former times when steam whistles announced the arrival of a sternwheeler. A few buildings are reminders of the past—the Manson Barn, the DAR Cabin, and the restored Newell House.

From the westerly Riverside day-use area, the bicycle path traverses the south prairie for 1.5 miles and then hugs the riverbank for another 2.5 miles to Butteville. A hiking-only trail separates from this path near the DAR Cabin and borders the river for 1.5 miles, passing through diverse plant and animal habitat of both prairie and woods before rejoining the bike trail near the Oak Grove day-use area, located under one of the oldest groves of whiteoak trees in Oregon. Side trails lead to the Visitor Center and down Champoeg Creek to the old gristmill site.

The visitor center has a splendid array of information and artifacts of this early settlement area. Exhibits feature Indian culture, Willamette Valley and Pacific Northwest history, the Oregon Trail, archaeological artifacts, pioneer life, sternwheelers, and state park history.

The Sesquicentennial Celebration of the provisional government vote was observed in 1993. Each year in July an outdoor pageant by the river re-creates images of life in old Oregon.

MOLALLA RIVER STATE PARK

Hours/Season: Day use; year-round
Area: 567 acres
Facilities: Picnic tables, boat ramp, restrooms
Attractions: Hiking trail, fishing, boating, water-skiing, great blue heron rookery, RC flying
Access: From the city of Canby, follow signs to ferry for 2 miles north, on North Holly Street

This large park along the wide Molalla River was developed as part of the Willamette River Greenway System authorized by the Oregon Legislature in 1973. It is primarily used as a recreation area by local residents. The acreage includes the confluence of the Molalla with the Pudding River in the southern part, and extends to where these waters join the Willamette River to the north. The road past the park has a ferry that crosses the Willamette River—a short distance southwest of Willamette Falls and locks—though the ferry is not always operating.

The developed part of the park is gently rolling land to level river bottomland and is surrounded by flower and vegetable farms. It is at the easterly edge of the historic French Prairie, where agriculture started in Oregon about 1830. This was part of the rich farmland that lured pioneers to travel the Oregon Trail. The land was originally the ancestral home of the Molalla Indians.

The park is a sunny, warm valley location in summer that urges water sports and fishing in its calm waters. It is not unusual to see motorboats zooming past or water-skiers zigzagging back and forth across the wide water. Some boaters pull young children on huge, brightly colored rubber tubes that emulate the ride of the water-skier.

Water skiers on river, Molalla River State Park

A 0.75-mile flat, graveled hiking path borders the river along the high tree-covered riverbank before it gradually descends, winding through the soft dirt of the woods, to a beach on the river. One can fish from the muddy beach here but there are no picnic tables at this location.

Plenty of picnic tables are available, however, near both of the parking areas. One of these is by an interesting wetland region with good vegetation of that habitat. Paths circle this large area and tables are spread out under the trees. The other picnicking area is close to the river. Between the two areas is a large open field where radio-controlled airplanes are often flown.

Bring your binoculars and see if you can find the great blue heron rookery. These huge birds are most easily seen flying to their nests in tall trees from late spring through July, when they are busy providing food for their young. Watch carefully when you spot a heron trying to catch food in the wetlands or by the river, and follow it with your binoculars when the great blue flies home after a successful fishing expedition.

MILO MCIVER STATE PARK

Hours/Season: Overnight; *campground closed in winter*
Area: 952 acres
Facilities: Picnic tables, group picnic shelters, campground with 45 electrical sites (maximum site is 50 feet), group tent camping, wheelchair-

accessible restrooms with showers, dumping station, firewood, boat ramp, model airplane strip, summer day-use fee for vehicles
Attractions: Equestrian and hiking trails, fishing, rafting, wildlife viewing, RC airplane flying, fish hatchery
Access: From Oregon Highway 211 south of Estacada, take Springwater Road to park, 5 miles northwest of Estacada

This spacious park is mostly gently sloping land on the southwest bank of the Clackamas River that preserves river access and habitat only 20 miles from Portland. Campground sites and most of the park are up and away from the water, offering few river views, though a pond and wetland area is centrally located. Rather, it is a place for social gatherings where picnic and play areas on large lawns can accommodate from twenty-five to one thousand people. An unusual feature is the model airplane strip, where RC clubs and individuals can enjoy good flying and safe landings.

The park and a viewpoint near the entrance are named after Milo K. McIver, a member of the Oregon Highway Commission from 1950 to 1962, and a strong supporter of State Parks activities. From the viewpoint, one sights past the partly forested park across the valley to the foothills of the Cascades and a distant view of Mounts Saint Helens, Adams, and Hood.

In the south region of the park, horseback riders will like the 4.5 miles of trails that have been made through lush vegetation of Oregon grape, sword fern, cedar, maple, and Douglas fir. Wildlife is plentiful in this habitat and viewers can see deer, rabbits, squirrels, songbirds, and osprey. Hikers are welcome along the trail. Intersections, however, are confusing and one would wish for more signs. Hiking-only trails are located near the north day-use area.

A fish hatchery operated by the Oregon Department of Fish and Wildlife

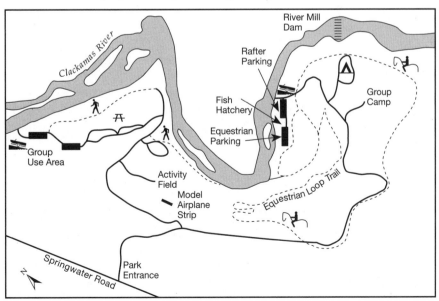

is at the south day-use area. It annually raises and releases more than one million Chinook salmon.

Rafting the river in the park is possible for experienced boaters most of the year, according to the Willamette Kayak and Canoe Club. The put-in is at the boat ramp by the fish hatchery, below River Mill Dam. This 2.5-mile section starts with the first and largest drop, followed by twistings, small rapids, a pass through a rock garden, a play-spot with standing waves and eddies, more bends, and small rapids, to the park take-out at the lowest picnic area. River runners can continue another 5.5 miles to a take-out at Barton Park. This area is rated class 2+, but use caution at the first drop in high water.

BONNIE LURE STATE PARK

Hours/Season: Day use; year-round
Area: 94 acres
Facilities: Picnic tables, chemical toilet, *no water*, river access
Attractions: Fishing, hiking, boating
Access: 6 miles north of Estacada, turn west from Oregon Highway 224 at the Eagle Creek intersection onto Burdett Road and continue to County Road 24028; follow this to park

This park has no sign and is mostly used by local residents who know where it is. You will notice a parking area and picnic tables just past a

Eagle Creek near its confluence with Clackamas River, Bonnie Lure State Park

one-lane bridge across Eagle Creek. The land was purchased from The Nature Conservancy in 1976.

A level trail leads to the easily accessible Clackamas River, and paths wander along the river and into the woods at various spots. It's an interesting lowland forested riparian area to explore, with chatterbox orchids blooming and blackberries growing among a profusion of vegetation.

MARY S. YOUNG STATE PARK

Hours/Season: Day use; year-round
Area: 133 acres
Facilities: Picnic tables, wheelchair-accessible restrooms
Attractions: Hiking, fishing, photography, bicycling
Access: Off Oregon Highway 43, 9 miles south of Portland

Urban dwellers living in nearby subdivisions spend many a pleasant day in this chunk of nature along the southwest bank of the wide Willamette River. Most of the park is level land on a bench above the water. The south side of the park, near the road, is a largely cleared area that once was cultivated for grass and now makes a great play area. This city park was a gift of Thomas E. Young and his wife, Mary S. Young.

A 0.5-mile biking trail and a 2-mile hiking trail are part of the recreational improvements. These trails descend through a forest of Douglas fir, cedar, alder, bigleaf maple, oak, and cottonwood to the river. One can make a

Slough at edge of Willamette River, Mary S. Young State Park

walking loop by going along the river to reconnect with another trail. A wooden-staired alternate path over a creek can be taken from the west paved path up to parking and the bike path.

Although it is quiet enough in areas to see great blue herons at water's edge, the river is a great expanse of activity on good days as kayaks, jet-bikes, and motorboats launch from the opposite side of the water. The waterfront is varied terrain with rocks for fishing spots, undulating water sloughs, and points of land projecting into the Willamette.

Rules are stringent here, with *no fires, no pets, and no beer in kegs* allowed in the park.

TRYON CREEK STATE PARK

Hours/Season: Day use; year-round
Area: 630 acres
Facilities: *No picnic tables or fire rings*, picnic shelter (pack out what you bring), wheelchair-accessible restrooms, nature center, exhibit information, gift shop, phone: (503) 653-3166
Attractions: Hiking, equestrian, bike, and all-abilities barrier-free trails; nature study and wildlife viewing
Access: At 11321 SW Terwilliger Boulevard, 6 miles south of downtown Portland, travel south 2 miles from Exit 297 on Interstate 5; or northwest from Interstate 205 on Oregon Highway 43

Shortly before it joins the waters of the Willamette River, Tryon Creek flows through a shallow, forested canyon bordered on the east by SW Terwilliger Boulevard and on the west by Boones Ferry Road, in the suburbs of Portland. Logged in the past, the forest has reasserted itself and joins with shrub areas, grassy meadows, and marsh to provide the landscape for an extensive trail system complete with a nature center and a shelter.

The park is a legacy of the Carter administration and the concept of urban parks. In the 1960s, when local people realized that this large undeveloped tract would soon be developed by real estate interests, they sought to preserve it as an untouched ecosystem for native plants and animals, and a place for people to enjoy and to study.

Multnomah County began the park process by its purchase of 45 acres in 1969. This spurred the organization of "The Friends of Tryon Creek" in 1969—the first such group—who raised funds for more land and, with tremendous community support, appealed to the state for help, with the result that a state park was established.

The Friends of Tryon Creek helped design and then financed the Nature Center and Jackson Shelter. The group continues to work with the State Parks Agency to maintain the center, assist staff, give educational programs, organize a summer concert series, and host the yearly Trillium Festival and native plant sale. The Nature Center has seasonal exhibits on varied

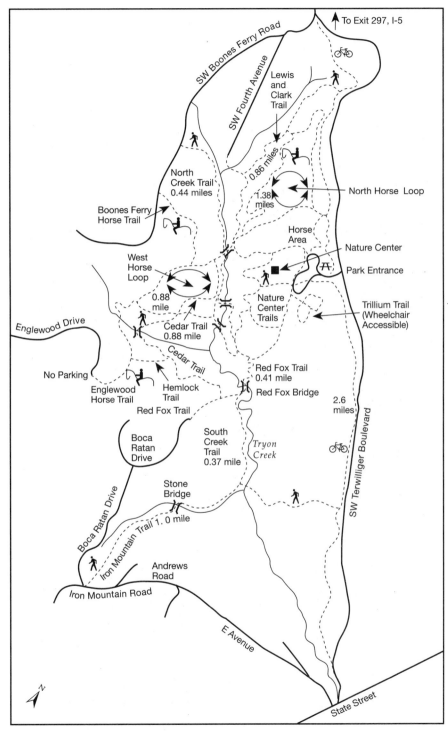

To Exit 297, I-5

SW Boones Ferry Road

SW Fourth Avenue

Lewis
and
Clark
Trail

0.86 miles

1.38
miles

North Horse Loop

North
Creek Trail
0.44 miles

Boones Ferry
Horse Trail

West
Horse
Loop

Horse
Area

Nature Center

Park Entrance

0.88
mile

Cedar Trail
0.88 mile

Nature
Center
Trails

Trillium Trail
(Wheelchair
Accessible)

Englewood Drive

Cedar Trail

No Parking

Englewood
Horse Trail

Hemlock
Trail

Red Fox Trail
0.41 mile

Red Fox Bridge

Red Fox Trail

2.6
miles

Boca
Ratan
Drive

South
Creek
Trail
0.37 mile

Tryon
Creek

Boca Ratan Drive

Stone
Bridge

Iron Mountain Trail 1. 0 mile

Andrews
Road

SW Terwilliger Boulevard

Iron Mountain Road

E Avenue

N

State Street

149

topics and a nature-oriented gift shop. Two other affiliations of the group are the Tryon Creek Photo Club and the Daytrippers Hiking Club, which has weekly hikes in spring, summer, and fall.

Eight miles of hiking trails, 3.5 miles of horse trails, and 3 miles of bike trails offer many route possibilities since, except for the bike path, they intersect often. A map is necessary to see the numerous ways to enter the park by trail, and to keep you on course.

The Trillium Trail is two easy loops totaling 0.35 mile for wheelchair riders. Three short, easy nature trails—Maple Ridge, Center, and Big Fir—are

Family on Cedar Trail, Tryon Creek State Park

0.5-mile loops by the Nature Center that let you view the canyon but do not descend to the creek. Other trails connect and lead to the creek from Maple Ridge and Big Fir loops in about 1 mile. From Tryon Creek, trails continue to Lewis and Clark, to Boones Ferry Road, to surrounding suburban areas, or let you loop around on the west side of the creek and return to the Nature Center.

All of these longer trails are good exercise with their ups and downs of going to the creek, crossing the various bridges, and climbing again to the ridge. Though the trails near the Nature Center are maintained for year-round hiking with barkdust, longer excursions may be muddy and slippery.

Take time to appreciate the natural surroundings. Douglas fir dominates the forest, which includes western red cedar, grand fir, western hemlock, bigleaf and vine maple, red alder, Oregon ash, and black cottonwood. Seasonal finds might be oyster mushrooms, buttercups, waterleaf, false Solomon's seal, yellow violets, wild ginger, and trilliums—the park treasure. If you're unobtrusive, perhaps you'll glimpse beaver, raccoon, skunk, opossum, squirrel, black-tailed deer, jays, woodpeckers, thrushes, hawks, and owls.

Horseback riders can choose from the North Horse Loop or the West Horse Loop, or combine them for a longer ride from the Equestrian Parking Lot. The North Horse Loop round-trip mileage from the parking area is 1.93 miles. From the same starting point, the round-trip mileage using the West Horse Loop is 2.34 miles. These graveled trails are passable even in wet weather. They begin near the ridgeline and travel down to the creek, across it, and back.

The 2.6-mile bicycle trail parallels the eastern edge of the park, near the road. It starts at the Lewis and Clark Law School, just outside the park, and continues to the intersection with Oregon Highway 43, a fine option for transport. In 1975, on the day the park was dedicated, an impromptu bicycle race between the law school and the new visitor center resulted in victory for Highway Commission Chairman Glenn Jackson over David G. Talbot of the State Parks Agency, U.S. Congressman Al Ullman, and Governor Straub.

WILLAMETTE STONE STATE PARK

Hours/Season: Day use; year-round
Area: 1.6 acres
Facilities: *No restrooms or water*
Attractions: Survey monument
Access: 4 miles west of Portland on Skyline Boulevard

Willamette Stone State Park has geographical significance—it preserves, and makes available to the public, a small forested tract of land that contains an important survey stake in a concrete apron. This stake marks the intersection of the Willamette Meridian and the Willamette Baseline, the point from which all lands in Oregon and Washington were sectioned. The townships and ranges on your property description all relate to this initial origin point. In this way, surveyors can accurately locate a piece of land.

This point was established by the first Surveyor General of Oregon, John B. Preston, on June 4, 1851. It was rededicated in 1988. A trail leads from the parking area to the monument.

BANKS/VERNONIA STATE PARK

Hours/Season: Day use; year-round
Facilities: Restrooms, park manager residence at Buxton
Attractions: Hiking, bicycling, horseback riding
Access: Off Oregon Highway 47, between Banks and Vernonia

A 21-mile abandoned railway right-of-way is being converted to a linear rails-to-trails pathway between the towns of Vernonia and Banks that will have several access trailheads. This stretch of land is a quiet rural area of agricultural and forest landscapes with scenery that includes numerous bridges, waterways, two large trestles, and fossil fields.

Thimbleberry blossom

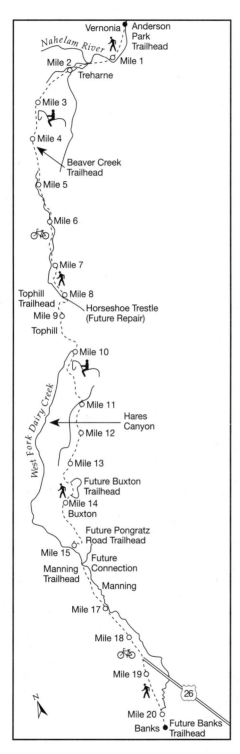

The original railroad between these two towns was developed by the Portland, Astoria, and Pacific Railroad. From 1913 until its abandonment in 1973, it was used for hauling logs, finished lumber, freight, and passengers.

The northern 6.5-mile segment of the trail (with trailheads at Vernonia and Beaver Creek) can already be hiked. There are signs in this vicinity. Opening of the Tophill and Manning trailheads in July 1993 will add another 13.5-mile segment, but the trail will not be continuous. A 1-mile gap between Pongratz Road and Manning is still to be linked, and there are future plans for additional trailheads and upgrades.

Hikers and bicyclists should use the gravel or paved side of the 12-foot-wide trail; horseback riders use the dirt side. No motorized vehicles are allowed on the trail.

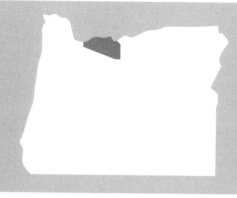

COLUMBIA GORGE

▲ Imagine a scene some twelve thousand years ago when glacier-melting caused catastrophic floods and landslides. Ten times the combined flow of all the rivers of the world sluiced into a slot carved by the Columbia River through the Cascade Mountains. As the river valley was widened by this force, the tangled veins of river tributaries were cut off in midstream and left suspended on high rocky notches. The result was the greatest concentration of high waterfalls in North America. The Oregon side has at least seventy-seven waterfalls. In 1986, this area east of Portland was officially declared the Columbia Gorge National Scenic Area.

The cliffs looming above the mighty river are unique in character. Weathered, mossy, and textured with varied patterns of rocks juxtaposed, this geology, spewed from fiery mountains altered by landslides, is a spectacular collage of natural art forms and colors.

The best way to see the gorge is via the historic Columbia River Scenic Highway that begins near Troutdale. Dedicated in 1916, this was the only road along the Oregon side of this river for thirty-seven years. This engineering marvel climbs from farmland to rain forest and twists like a sidewinder at the edge of lichen-smeared cliffs. Because of his spiritual concern for mankind's relationship to nature, engineer Samuel Lancaster hired Italian stonemasons who "built their souls" into the dry masonry of the moss-covered stone walls and bridges that marry the highway to the rugged terrain.

Moods change on this ascent, depending on the time of day or the season. Morning may bring seductive mists or a rainbow. Evening may splash distant urban lights that fringe a purple river under a cherry sunset.

A web of hiking trails penetrates the forest wilderness and forms connecting links with the waterfalls. One path climbs to the top of Larch

Opposite: *Viewing Latourell Falls, Guy W. Talbot State Park*

Mountain as it passes singing snowmelt creeks, giant sword ferns, and wildflowers.

The Columbia River once contained numerous cascade rapids in the days before it was tamed by dams and locks. The metal "Bridge of the Gods," named after the natural rock bridge of Indian legend once at this location, crosses the river at the town of Cascade Locks, a National Historic Site.

Images change frequently here—both real and imagined—and capture one with their intensity. It is not difficult to conjure up an image of a Chinook Indian poised on a rock near the river, spear over his head, waiting to stab a salmon. And fishermen still try for huge sturgeon that can be over a hundred pounds and a hundred years old.

The summer wind blows strong in this stretch of river. Indians thought it originated from Wind Mountain where the Wind God lived, but more often it blows east from the Pacific Ocean. Windsurfers come long distances to catch a ride on the Columbia River, getting a fringe benefit of gorge vistas.

Rising above the gorge, in the center of this region, is an 11,245-foot composite volcano, Mount Hood. A jog south at the city of Hood River onto State Highway 35 hugs its eastern flanks. It is the highest peak of the Oregon Cascades. Weather swirls violently around its summit, daring mountain climbers to predict when it's safe to climb to the top. Glacier-fed Hood River plunges down its east slope, and side roads take skiers and hikers to Cooper Spur and Mount Hood Meadows. In summer, the meadows are boggy nurseries for wild orchids and elk.

Past Barlow Pass and near Pioneer Woman's Grave, US 26 loops west near the spur road to Timberline Lodge. Built as a project of the Works Progress Administration, this impressive inn is an example of conservation and the creativity of Oregon craftspeople as they recycled local materials into works of art.

Some of the Oregon Trail pioneers circled Mount Hood on the south, though one couldn't say whether that route was better than rafting downriver from The Dalles. It was a boggy trail of roots, snags, and forest. Men and women stretched muscles as they pitched down the mountainside, using ropes tied to trees to lower their wagons on the old Barlow Road. Today's journey is easy, yet the nearby Mount Hood Wilderness has not been tamed and promises much for outdoor wanderers.

LEWIS & CLARK STATE PARK

Hours/Season: Day use; year-round
Area: 56 acres
Facilities: Picnic tables, boat ramp, wheelchair-accessible restrooms, historical exhibits
Attractions: Nature trail, fishing, boating
Access: From Interstate 84, take Exit 18, 16 miles east of Portland

Exhibit about exploration at Lewis & Clark State Park

This state park is situated at the western gateway to the Columbia River Scenic Highway and the Columbia River Gorge National Scenic Area, so it makes a good starting point for explorations in this region.

The Sandy River edges the park and fishermen launch boats or fish from its shores. Depending on the season, salmon, steelhead, or shad might grab a hook. In early spring, a short smelt run occurs when the silvery fish come up from the Columbia River to spawn. Nets fastened to long poles are dipped into the water to snare these small, good eating fish.

A campground was once part of the park, but proximity to urban areas and the attendant vandalism resulted in the park being open for day use only. Signs caution against the use of alcohol and unsupervised swimming.

The first white men in this area were a boat crew from the HMS *Chatham*. When they sighted Mount Hood near where the Sandy River empties into the Columbia on October 30, 1792, Lieutenant William Broughton, a British naval officer under the command of George Vancouver, named the peak in honor of Vice Admiral Samuel Lord Hood. They also named the present Sandy River the Barings River, but that appellation did not stick.

The state park, however, is named in honor of Expedition Captains Lewis and Clark, who arrived at the mouth of this river on November 3, 1805. Though the water was only a few inches in depth, "a very bad quicksand" prevented them from wading across the river. Because of this, they called this stream the Quicksand River, later shortened to the Sandy River.

The river upstream was explored at that time for about 1.5 miles, approximately the site of this park, where they found the river to be "a very considerable stream." They returned to camp near the Columbia and shared a "sumptuous supper" with Indians.

On their homeward trip in April of 1806, Lewis and Clark stayed six days at a "handsome prairie" opposite the Sandy River to hunt for food, examine the river, and obtain canoes. They had hoped the Sandy might be a major navigable river, but Sergeant Pryor's scouting found it could only be canoed 6 miles upstream before encountering rapids and waterfalls as it flowed from the slopes of Mount Hood. The Indians confirmed this, but Lewis and Clark discovered that they had missed the major river that watered what is now the Willamette Valley. Clark, seven men, and an Indian guide backtracked to explore what the Indians called the Multnomah, now named the Willamette River.

It seems appropriate to have a nature trail in the park named after these explorers, considering the wealth of information they acquired about the flora and fauna of the area. The Lewis & Clark Nature Trail circles the edge of the grassy lawn of the park and weaves through trees at the edge of a woods where an unstable rock and dirt bluff rises above the trees and vultures circle. *(Don't try to climb this.)*

There are lovely old trees in the picnic area. In particular, huge apple and pear trees, loaded with fruit in late summer, are numerous, along with various conifers and hardwoods.

Lewis and Clark became well acquainted with *wapato* (from the Indian *wappatoo*) or duck potato (*Sagittaria latifolia*), common in wet places in the area. It comes up each spring from a starchy tuber with three small white petals and large arrowhead-shaped blades, and is about 40 to 50 centimeters tall. The abundant bulb was an important food source of the Indians and a principal article of trade. Lewis and Clark wrote that it was the most valuable of Indian roots.

Management of the resources of the Columbia River Gorge was the subject of much political discussion for many years. No other sea-level river flows through the Cascade Mountains. Besides its unique natural and recreational features, the area is a transportation corridor that contributes to the economy of the Pacific Northwest. The goal is to safeguard these qualities.

Dew on rain forest maidenhair fern

On November 17, 1986, President Ronald Reagan finally signed into law the act of Congress that created the 292,000-acre Columbia River Gorge National Scenic Area. This landscape is managed in partnership by the states of Oregon and Washington, the U.S. Forest Service, the U.S. Department of Agriculture, and six local counties. The goal is to "protect and enhance scenic, cultural, recreational, and natural resources of the Gorge while encouraging compatible economic growth and development."

DABNEY STATE PARK

Hours/Season: Day use; year-round
Area: 135 acres
Facilities: Picnic tables, wheelchair-accessible restrooms, summer day-use fee for vehicles
Attractions: Hiking, fishing
Access: On the Columbia River Scenic Highway, 3.5 miles east of Exit 18 on Interstate 84

Dabney sprawls for a considerable distance along the wooded north bank of the Sandy River. A 1.5-mile round-trip hiking path follows the flow of the water and offers a fine walk. Since the current and water height of the river vary with upstream water control, visitors are cautioned to stay

Pond, waterfowl, and woods in Dabney State Park

on the banks of the river. Marshy wetland areas with bigleaf maple trees border the river and invasive ivy climbs the tall Douglas fir trees of this natural area.

Trails branch off from the main path to the three parking areas, adjacent to picnicking locations. These picnic spots are spaced far apart on rolling terrain of treed lawns. The farthest one has a shelter.

Not far from this last picnicking spot are two wetland areas with ponds. I surprised a great blue heron at one, side by side at the edge with a flock of Canada geese. Chipmunks scampered across the grass. Chatterbox orchids flowered nearby and mimosa trees were in full bloom. I watched them spray, so don't eat the berries near the parking areas.

No dogs (even on leash) or alcohol are allowed in the park.

PORTLAND WOMEN'S FORUM STATE PARK

Hours/Season: Day use; year-round
Area: 7.26 acres
Facilities: Exhibit information, parking, *no restrooms*
Attractions: Exceptional panoramic viewpoint, photography
Nearby: Larch Mountain
Access: Travel 9 miles east of Exit 18 on Interstate 84 on the Columbia River Scenic Highway; or take Exit 22 to Corbett east for 1.5 miles

This is the quintessential viewpoint of this area, the place where so many photos of Vista House and the surrounding Columbia River Gorge landscape have been taken. Known as Chanticleer Lookout, at an elevation of 850 feet, the geological landslide amphitheater in the foreground was sculpted by the catastrophic floods at the end of the Ice Age 12,800 to 15,000 years ago.

If one uses the Vista House as a compass point at 12 o'clock, 850-foot Beacon Rock is directly above. Rooster Rock, a landslide block of Yakima Basalt, is 0.8 miles away at 11 o'clock. The Larch Mountain shield volcano is at 8.5 miles and 1 o'clock. Two Boring Lava cinder cones, Mount Pleasant and Mount Zion, are across the river at 10:45 o'clock and 11:15 o'clock, respectively.

Chanticleer Inn once occupied this site, the place where Sam Hill, Sam Lancaster, John B. Yeon, Simon Benson, and others met in 1913 to plan construction of the scenic highway. After the inn burned in the 1930s, the area became a state park.

The original 3.71 acres of the park was a gift from the Portland Women's Forum, a group made up of representatives of the principal women's organizations of Portland. This group was active for many years in the preservation of the natural beauty of the gorge, under the leadership of Mrs. Gertrude Jensen. It was responsible for appointment of the first Columbia Gorge Commission in the 1950s.

View of Columbia River Gorge and Crown's Point, Portland Women's Forum State Park

At the entrance to the parking area, several historical bronze plaques are mounted on a fifty-ton granite boulder. Sam Hill, Road Builder, and Lewis and Clark are honored with plaques. Another is titled "Aboriginal's Paradise," complete with Indians and their tepees, salmon drying, and dugout canoes against the geological backdrop of the Columbia Gorge. Yet another illustrates "Columbia River Navigation," with sternwheelers, steamboats, and sailing ships.

To view the area from Larch Mountain, take the turnoff from the scenic highway to Larch Mountain Road just 0.4 mile east of this park. The glaciated summit and picnic area are reached by a good paved road in 13 miles. This is the terminus of the 7-mile Larch Mountain Trail that climbs up the mountainside from the Multnomah Falls Lodge and passes several waterfalls (or it is the beginning of a downhill trail, if you prefer). (See map for Ainsworth State Park.)

A 0.3-mile trail leads to Sherrard Point, a lookout with a view of five major Cascade peaks. This is a great place to watch sunsets.

It is interesting that the mountain was so named because early lumbermen thought the noble fir growing there was larch. There are no western larch trees on the mountain.

CROWN POINT STATE PARK

Hours/Season: Day use; year-round
Area: 307 acres
Facilities: Vista House, gift shop, restrooms, information center, exhibits
Attractions: Views of Columbia River Gorge, monument to early pioneers, photography
Access: From the west, take Exit 18 from Interstate 84 and proceed on the Columbia River Scenic Highway for 10 miles; or travel west for 12 miles from the eastern access at Exit 35

Crown Point State Park has awesome views of geological happenings, is a cogent joining of human engineering with the shapes of nature, and is a National Natural Landmark.

A 720-foot promontory along the Columbia River, Crown Point was scoured by the formative Bretz floods. It was here that the dedication of the newly completed Columbia River Scenic Highway took place on June 6, 1916.

Samuel Lancaster, chief engineer of the highway, proposed this as an ideal site for "an observatory from which the view both up and down the Columbia could be viewed in silent communion with the infinite." He wanted to inspire travelers, give them a rest stop, and share his wonder of the gorge. The name "Vista House" was his suggestion.

Vista House, Crown Point State Park

Construction of Vista House began in 1916, under the direction of John B. Yeon, Multnomah County roadmaster. Portland architect Edgar M. Lazarus decided on a nonhistoric design reflecting modern German architecture. The plans for interior decoration were furnished by Lancaster. It was built at a total cost of approximately $100,000 and officially dedicated as a monument to early pioneers of Oregon on May 5, 1918.

Vista House is a rotunda 44 feet in diameter and 55 feet high with interior floors, stairs, and basement wainscoting of Tokeen Alaskan marble. Most of the interior rotunda is Kasota limestone, including a hand-carved drinking fountain. The dome exterior was originally matte-glazed green tiles, but it is now copper-crowned. As a tribute to the early settlers, eight carved panels line the interior of the dome, each with a different design: chestnut, acorn, pinecone, grape, apple, wheat, Oregon grape, ginkgo, and pioneer tools and utensils.

Vista House and the original 1.71 acres were donated to the park system in 1938. It was registered as a National Historic Landmark in 1974. In 1982, after the scope was expanded to include an interpretive center, a group of local Corbett residents began the Vista House Project as a way to become involved with the future of the landmark, to share in its preservation and restoration, and to inform the public. This group became the "Friends of Vista House" in 1987.

The main floor has historical photos and exhibits, an information center, and a three-dimensional table map of the gorge area. Lovely posters, photographs, serigraphs, paintings, and plaques of early explorers decorate the walls. A good collection of both fresh and dried flowers is included as an aid to native plant identification.

The basement floor has more wall displays and a gift shop that specializes in handcrafted artworks. A world map pinpoints the diverse origin of visitors to Vista House.

For gorge observation, ascend to the upper outdoor level for a wonderful panoramic view.

Volunteers man the information counter from May 1 through October 15. They also coordinate Folk Art Programs on weekends: demonstrations of different handcrafted artwork—spinning wool, weaving, calligraphy, woodcarving, making baskets, and more. Profits from the gift store are used for interpretive programs and to maintain and staff Vista House.

GUY W. TALBOT STATE PARK

Hours/Season: Day use; year-round
Area: 378 acres
Facilities: Picnic tables, restrooms
Attractions: Waterfall, hiking, photography
Access: On Columbia River Scenic Highway, 12 miles east of Interstate 84 Exit 18

▲ Traveling east on the highway, a mile past Crown Point, one enters the
⊥ "Figure Eight Loops," an engineering marvel of road building with
maximum 5 percent grades and curve radii of not less than 100 feet. This
design accomplishes a 600-foot drop in elevation and parallels itself five
times. At the same time, a good example of western Oregon rain forest is
viewed—if you are not driving.

Coming out of this design feat, you encounter the first of a series of
spectacular gorge waterfalls in this park. Latourell Falls, named for a pioneer settler, is 249 feet high, second-highest in the Columbia River Gorge.
The land for the park was donated by Guy W. Talbot, a lumber baron.

In Indian legend, the beauty of the wife of the coyote god Speelyai was
preserved for eternity when he transformed her into this waterfall to pre-
vent her from escaping from him.

Parking on the east side of the bridge over Latourell Creek is easy to find,
though it is also available at the separate picnic area west of the bridge,
reached by a short road.

A paved path from the highway parking lot descends in a short distance
to the bottom of the falls. This waterfall, an example of the type called a
"plunge," drops vertically and away from the cliff side, losing contact with
bedrock. It pours over a single flow of brickbat basalt with curved columns

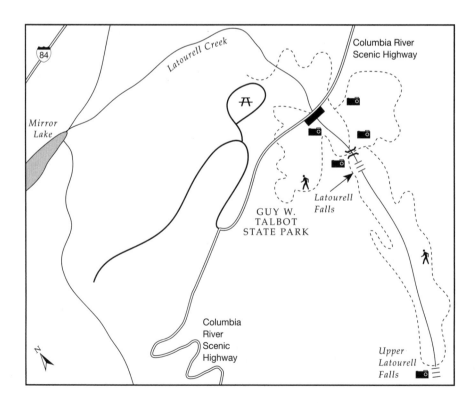

toward the base. Note that the recent notch at the top is only 20 feet deep. The golden smear of lichen on the rock walls adjacent to the water makes for a great photo with the green of trees and gray of rock.

A wooden bridge in front of the falls allows the hiker to cross the creek and connect to another paved trail that goes under the highway bridge to the picnic area. The falls are an easy hike from there also.

Another trail ascends steeply from the highway parking lot. This makes a loop that goes to the top of the falls. The falls are visible on the way up through the trees and a sunny morning will reward hikers with rainbows on the water. Higher up there are good distant views, several benches to rest on, and massive rock formations that poke above tree tops. At the top, the small creek that feeds the falls is easily crossed, but safe viewing of the falls itself is prevented by obstructions. Returning through forest on the west side, you pass an old building falling down among the trees. On reaching the road, cross the bridge to parking.

ROOSTER ROCK STATE PARK

Hours/Season: Day use; year-round
Area: 873 acres
Facilities: Picnic tables, group picnic shelters, wheelchair-accessible restrooms, boat basin, sandy beach, exhibit information, summer day-use fee for vehicles, park office, phone: (503) 695-2261
Attractions: Unusual rock formation, fishing, boating, hiking, windsurfing, birdwatching, swimming, sunbathing privacy
Access: Off Interstate 84, 22 miles east of Portland at Exit 25

The 200-foot columnar basaltic spire that rises amid trees at the west end of this park has been officially named Rooster Rock, though the pioneers used a phallic term to designate this pinnacle, and at one time it also was called Cape Eternity. The rock serves as a guide for boaters, and attracts artists, geologists and rock climbers.

On their way west, Lewis and Clark passed through this area from October 31 to November 2, 1805. They had just brought their boats through what they called the "great chute," a wild place on the Columbia River now drowned by Bonneville Dam. They named another 800-foot volcanic remnant near this water chute "Beacon Rock," a unique and easily identifiable guide mark for travelers. According to Lewis and Clark, "great numbers of sea otters" came up the river this far, and they wrote that Beacon Rock "may be esteemed the head of tidewater." On their return, they camped under Rooster Rock from April 6 to 9, 1806.

Before it became a state park, this land was used in connection with fish seining, and one of the old salmon canneries was located in what is now the boat basin. Because problems arose during times of low water, a channel was dredged to allow boats delivering salmon to get to the cannery dock.

165

Rooster Rock near boat launch, Rooster Rock State Park

Directly above and south of the park, Vista House overlooks the vast array of parking lots and picnic areas that stretch along the 3.5 miles of park frontage on the Columbia River, enough accommodations for scads of people from far and near who are looking for recreation. The park is a registered Natural Heritage Site.

A separate parking area exclusively for boat trailers and boat launching is located at the west end of the park, overlooking the namesake rock. A fee is charged for overnight use, payable at the Park Office. The Columbia River widens here and a channel winds around Rooster Rock and south to form the boat basin.

The eastern half of the park has sandy beaches with good views of the bluffs and cliffs lining the gorge to the east. Several stairways lead to different sections of the beach. The water level of the Columbia River varies according to water usage, controlled by dams and periods of drought. This determines the width of the beaches. Happily, weekends usually bring lower water levels and more beach, since water requests are higher on Mondays.

Wetland areas punctuate the river's edge on this side of the park, rich with vegetation and food that attracts birds. Bring your binoculars.

At the extreme eastern end of the park, a stairway leads to paths meandering through bushy vegetation to secluded beaches where "clothing optional" sunbathing is allowed. Nudity is restricted to an area 100 yards east of this stairway.

Some 3.2 miles of hiking trails weave through the park. You can access some natural areas on the trail at the eastern end of the parking areas. This trail winds along the top of the tree-covered bluff overlooking the Columbia for some distance, through woods and blackberry patches plump with succulent berries. Many plant species and wildflowers might slow you down, including maroon-centered Queen Anne's lace and wild roses. Many trails branch off, some descending to the beach, so you can wander about as you wish and not get lost. Notice Sand Island on the east, bordering the river.

The challenging sport of windsurfing has become increasingly popular in the gorge area of the Columbia River. Weather and the river provide a unique set of conditions. The windsurfer contends with the westward flow of the river and with winds usually coming from the opposite direction, blowing inland from the sea and being funneled through the gorge. This is an ideal situation for windsurfing across the river and back. Winds are often strong here, although they are not assured, and sometimes they are intermittent. Experienced windsurfers have an array of different sails for these varying conditions.

Wind and wave conditions may be stronger and rougher than they appear to the uninitiated. To test your equipment and skill, use short reaches. It is best not to windsurf alone. Sailboards, considered vessels, must follow the rules of the road. Look before jibbing and jumping. Maintain a watch for barges—which travel faster than they appear but cannot make sudden turns or stops—and other vessels.

Topnotch international competitors come to the gorge in the summer to participate in scheduled events. The "Columbia Gorge Pro-Am" is an event for professionals and amateurs which spectators and photographers will enjoy in the second week of July at Hood River. Then in late July, the "Gorge Cities Blowout" features premier races of the windsurfing world

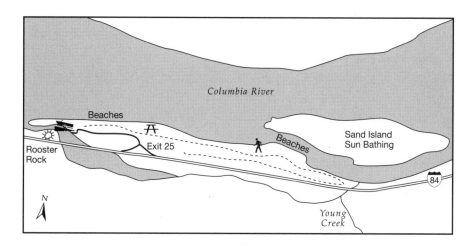

from Cascade Locks to Hood River. Amateurs race to benefit the American Heart Association in the "High Wind Classic," held the last weekend of June at Hood River.

SHEPPERD'S DELL STATE PARK

Hours/Season: Day use; year-round
Area: 519 acres
Facilities: *Limited parking*
Attractions: Short trail to waterfall viewpoint
Access: From Exit 18 on Interstate 84, 13 miles east on Columbia River Scenic Highway

▲ Young's Creek flows into this rocky canyon, forming a succession of small waterfalls. It then cascades under the 100-foot concrete deck arch highway bridge. A short paved trail descends into the fern-covered canyon for a better view of the falls. Though the park is large, it is mostly rugged, rocky, and inaccessible, bordered on the north by the Union Pacific Railroad and bisected by the scenic highway.

The park was a gift of George G. Shepperd, a memorial to his wife. When the land still belonged to his family, and there were no good roads to let them attend church, this dell was a place they used to renew themselves spiritually. It is easy to see how these surroundings would do that.

BRIDAL VEIL FALLS STATE PARK

Hours/Season: Day use; year-round
Area: 15.6 acres
Facilities: Picnic tables, wheelchair-accessible restrooms
Attractions: Hiking trail to waterfalls, all-abilities path to gorge overlook, photography
Nearby: Wahkeena-Perdition Loop Trail
Access: On Columbia River Scenic Highway, 15 miles east of Interstate 84 Exit 18

▲ The Bridal Veil Falls area was once the scene of large-scale commercial logging and a planing mill operation. A book published by the Depression-inspired Writers' Program, *Oregon, End of the Trail*, notes this and remarks: "Formerly Bridal Veil Falls was noted for its beauty but the waters now are confined in a lumberflume." Fortunately, the waterfall has regained its beauty and is now part of this park.

Opposite: *Hike to nearby Multnomah Falls, Bridal Veil Falls State Park*

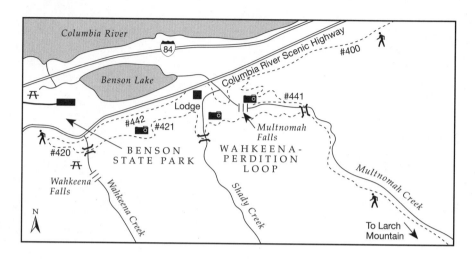

A small picnic area is adjacent to the parking lot. In late summer, several of the trees above the tables are laden with ripening pears and you might want to position yourself carefully, as they frequently fall to the ground.

To view the falls, take the path behind the restrooms to descend to the falls in 0.66 mile. It is a moderately steep dirt and rock trail with some switchbacking, and crosses Bridal Veil Creek just before ascending a stairway to a platform with a good view of the waterfall. This is a multiple falls of two tiers, full of water even in late summer of a drought year. The remains of the old mill and pond can be seen just east of the viewing platform.

Don't miss the all-abilities interpretive trail. This paved 0.5-mile level loop is a pleasant walk adjacent to natural wildflower meadows and camas fields backed by tall trees at the edge of cliffs overlooking the Columbia River. Fuchsia, wild roses, blackberries, fireweed, lupine, penstemons, and native grasses are some of the varied vegetation.

The Indians were well acquainted with the benefits of the camas fields. This wildflower has azure blooms in April and an onion-like bulb. When boiled, the root is palatable and tastes somewhat like potato. The Indian way to prepare it, and probably the best way, is by fermenting it for several days in underground pits filled with hot stones. When removed, the bulbs are a dark brown color and sweet, like molasses. They are made into large cakes that are slightly baked in the sun. Pioneers learned much from Indians about what wild things to eat. One delicacy that resulted was camas pie.

Several viewpoints along this trail have expansive views of the Columbia River Gorge. The round-topped cliffs drop almost vertically here, like massive oblong stones propped on their ends. These cliffs and the guardrails at the viewpoints are seen in good perspective as you drive along Interstate 84. Please stay on the trail in this area and don't destroy the vegetation.

Although there are miles and miles of wonderful hiking trails in the gorge, the nearby Wahkeena–Perdition 3.3-mile loop is particularly fine. Start at the Wahkeena Falls Picnic Grounds, 2 miles east of Bridal Veil State

Park. Hike up along the waterfall on Wahkeena Trail No. 420 and cross Wahkeena Creek on the stone bridge at 0.2 mile. *Wahkeena* is an Indian word meaning "most beautiful" and this impressive 242-foot multiple falls, lined with summer wildflower color, lives up to its name.

Continue to the junction with Perdition Trail No. 421 at 0.4 mile and take this route for 1.2 miles. This trail has many stairs along the way. Short side trails to viewpoints of the gorge occur at 0.5, 0.7, and 0.9 mile and a bridge crosses Shady Creek at 0.8 mile.

The loop continues on Larch Mountain Trail No. 441, crossing Multnomah Creek almost immediately. This is the stream that flows down from Larch Mountain and feeds the 620-foot Multnomah Falls, highest in the gorge, but the stream itself is a special place here before the plunge begins. Few people think of this as a destination for a picnic, but they should. It is a wonderful place of rocks, clear flowing water, green trees, and solitude. The spur to the top of the falls is a short distance further, to the left, and it is one reason this place is missed. Most people coming from the other direction don't come this far.

Follow the Larch Mountain Trail for a total of 1.1 miles as it descends to Multnomah Falls Lodge and the bottom of the falls. A quarter-mile above the lodge, cross the Benson arch bridge over the water after passing a pool under the upper falls, where water sprays from its vast energy and wildflowers blow in the wet breeze. The most visited tourist attraction in Oregon, Multnomah Falls is a spectacular double falls that caused Meriwether Lewis to write how it "fell from a great height over the supendious [*sic*] rocks ... the most remarkable of these cascades falls...." No one is disappointed here. In winter, the fall may freeze into a suspension of giant icicles.

Geology enthusiasts might want to inspect the rocks in the walls of the Lodge. If you know what to look for, you can find Yakima black basalt, Cascade or Boring gray basalt, Troutdale quartzite boulders, and Eagle Creek petrified and opalized wood.

Take Return Trail No. 442, on the west side of the lodge, for 0.6 mile back to the Wahkeena Picnic Grounds.

BENSON STATE PARK

Hours/Season: Day use; *closed November through mid-March*
Area: 272 acres
Facilities: Picnic tables, wheelchair-accessible restrooms, boat ramp on Columbia at Dalton Point *(westbound access only)*, summer day-use fee for vehicles
Attractions: Swimming, boating, fishing
Access: From Interstate 84, *eastbound access only*, 30 miles east of Portland

▲ This park was named in honor of Simon Benson, a principal benefactor of the Columbia River Scenic Highway and a native of Norway. The developed area lies between the freeway and the Union Pacific Railroad, although the acreage includes tracts along the Columbia River Scenic Highway and east of Multnomah Falls. Hiking, biking, and horse trails are slated for the future in these areas.

A good place to cool off on a summer day is the small lake that forms from Multnomah Creek and dominates the park. Picnic before or after a swim, or perhaps rest under cottonwood, alder, and maple trees on the level lawn. On such a day you will find the park busy with swimmers of all ages, some learning to swim, some crossing the lake, some simply on floats in the sunlight. Others hop onto rafts or into canoes and paddle around, avoiding the crowds at the edge of the water. A walk around the circumference will find you a quiet fishing spot.

AINSWORTH STATE PARK

Hours/Season: Overnight; *campground closed in winter*
Area: 156 acres
Facilities: Picnic tables, campground with 45 full hookup sites (maximum site is 60 feet), restrooms with showers, dumping station, firewood
Attractions: Hiking, access to gorge trails and photography
Nearby: Horsetail-Oneonta Loop Trail
Access: On Columbia River Scenic Highway, 21 miles east of Exit 18 from Interstate 84, or 1.2 miles west of Exit 35

Anyone interested in an extended visit in the waterfall area of the gorge should consider using this campground as a base because of its proximity to many of the trails. With over 60 miles of trails in the gorge, it is an aerobic paradise of waterfalls and views. RVers should use smaller vehicles to drive the Columbia River Scenic Highway; it is often narrow and winding.

Those interested in geology will notice that pinnacles of Yakima Basalt are seen in a 3-mile area starting at Ainsworth, some visible from the campground but particularly where meadows are in the foreground near Exit 35. These tall rocky spires are embedded with lichen and trees rooted in cracks of soil. Rising 1,500 feet above the river, Saint Peter's Dome is an erosional remnant of at least six flows of this basalt. A cross-section of one of the Cascade volcanoes, with its vent exposed, can be seen on the upper cliffs of Nesmith Point. The Benson Plateau, the Cascade summit surface, is south of here at elevations of 3,900 to 4,300 feet where numerous small cirques on the east side have been cut by ice.

The day-use area of Ainsworth State Park is along the scenic highway west of the campground. The Ainsworth Loop Trail goes from the corner of the campground through forest to the day-use restroom area in 0.2 mile. From here, one can connect to Gorge Trail No. 400 in 0.1 mile—a low-elevation, east/west path through the entire gorge, although some sections are yet to be constructed. This trail increases loop options. It can also be accessed from the campground.

The picnic area is reached via another 0.2 mile on the Ainsworth Trail, a quiet spot backed by lush forest growth of firs, bigleaf maples, ferns, cedar trees, mosses, and lots of snowberries. A natural spring with elaborate stonework constructed by the CCC provides water.

The 2.7-mile Horsetail-Oneonta Loop Trail starts only 0.5 mile west of the campground, so you can either walk the distance or park at 176-foot-high Horsetail Falls on the scenic highway to begin hiking (as mentioned, Gorge Trail No. 400 connects from the campground). Climb steep Horsetail Falls Trail No. 438, to Upper Horsetail Falls at 0.4 mile. Walk around the ledge behind the free-falling water, edged with ferns. These falls have been nicknamed "Ponytail Falls." The lush vegetation and wildflowers just past the falls provide a fine foreground for photography.

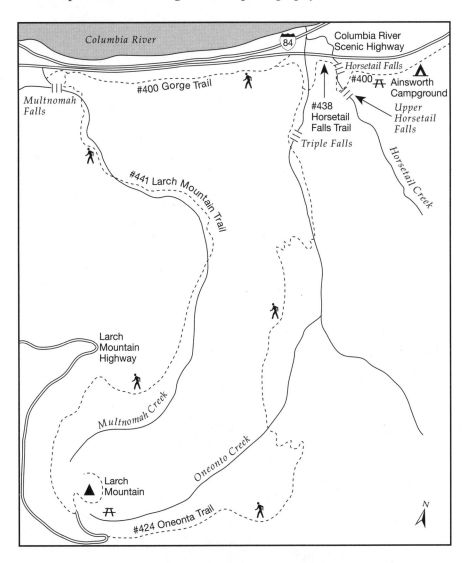

At 0.8 mile, the trail splits and the north one offers a high viewpoint of the Columbia River. At 1.2 miles, cross the bridge over Oneonta Creek and come to a junction with Oneonta Trail No. 424 at 1.3 miles. One has the option here of continuing immediately right on the loop or taking a side trip to Triple Falls, a good rest and picnic spot. This additional trail is 1.6 miles round-trip and would bring the total hike to 4.3 miles.

Hike to Horsetail Falls, Ainsworth State Park

Backtracking, if necessary, to the Oneonta Trail junction, it is 0.9 mile to the scenic highway. A 0.5-mile stroll on this road returns you to Horsetail Falls, almost immediately taking you past the Oneonta Gorge, where a creek flows between a gash in basalt rock. Another side trip is the waterfall that lies 900 feet upstream, reached by wading past rocks and round holes that are tree molds left from scouring by flood. In some of these holes, pieces of opalized, carbonized, or otherwise silicified wood have been left behind. This small gorge has much botanical interest as well.

JOHN B. YEON STATE PARK

Hours/Season: Day use; year-round
Area: 284 acres
Facilities: Exhibit information, parking pullover, *no water or restrooms*
Attractions: Hiking trailheads, photography, waterfalls
Nearby: Eagle Creek Trail, Bonneville Dam
Access: Take Warrendale Exit, 40 miles east of Portland, and turn west to park on the frontage road; or from Ainsworth, continue east on the frontage road for 3 miles

In Mount Hood National Forest, several trails winding through quiet natural sections cut by gulches can be accessed from this trailhead park. It honors John B. Yeon, a Portland citizen who contributed considerable energy, experience, and wealth to the development of the Columbia River Scenic Highway.

Yeon is the trailhead for Elowah Falls, reached by a 0.8-mile hike. Alternately, one can go to Upper McCord Creek Falls in 1.1 mile. These two begin together and are also part of Gorge Trail No. 400. Almost immediately, 4.9-mile Nesmith Ridge Trail No. 428 branches off to the west, which climbs to 3,880-foot-high Nesmith Point. This latter trail also accesses Gorge Trail No. 400 in 0.1 mile, taking one to the Ainsworth Campground in 4.5 miles.

Just across the river from the park is Beacon Rock, a guide point named by Lewis and Clark as they traversed this area. Indian legend says that an Indian chief forbade his daughter's romance and she jumped from this 800-foot pinnacle. When the Chinook winds blow, it is said that she can be heard weeping.

If you opt to go to Elowah Falls, the trail is easy at the beginning and becomes moderately difficult for 0.2 mile to where Upper McCord Creek Falls Trail splits off to the right. Just past this point, a pair of ospreys started squawking as I approached their nest, and I looked up to see one fly to a nest at the top of a tall fir with a fish for their young. This nest would be hard to spot without an osprey flying to it.

Level for a while, the path soon descends in fairly steep switchbacks to the bottom of the falls. From a height of 289 feet, Elowah Falls plunges down and reminds one of Latourell Falls, even with yellow-green lichen on the steep canyon walls. Situated in a stone-rimmed amphitheater, the water bounces off huge boulders, collects in a pretty pool, then meanders down the creek bed under a bridge. The forest is exuberant with the growth of fir, maple, penstemon, pearly everlasting, Queen Anne's lace, and dripping walls with ferns. The trail continues across the bridge as Gorge Trail No. 400.

An excellent base for exploring more good hiking trails is nearby Eagle Creek Forest Camp, the nation's oldest such camp, which is eastbound accessed only (westbound travelers can loop back from the Bonneville Dam Exit). A pair of ospreys call this campground home, with their nest high in a tree, and kingfishers and great blue herons earn their meals from the creek.

The popular Eagle Creek Trail trailhead is just south of the picnic grounds. Overnight backpackers should park near the fish hatchery rather than the trailhead for security reasons. The 13.2-mile trail has been carved into basaltic cliffs above forested Eagle Creek and sometimes descends to the streamside. If you don't want to do the entire trail, there are several worthwhile intermediate destinations.

The first one is at Punchbowl Falls in 2.1 miles. Descend to the creek there and explore, photograph, picnic, or fish. High Bridge crosses a deep gorge at 3.3 miles. Trekkers pass through a 30-foot tunnel blasted from solid rock near 100-foot-high Tunnel Falls in 6 miles. Camping is permitted at High

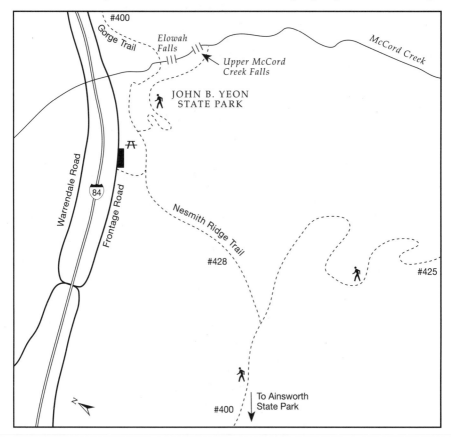

Bridge. Tenas Camp is a major camp at 3.7 miles. For complete details and restrictions (because of heavy use), get a trail guide from the Forest Service.

Other trails accessed from Eagle Point Camp are the moderately steep 0.6-mile Buck Point Trail and the easy 1.8-mile Wauna Trail. Both lead to excellent gorge viewpoints.

Those wanting a challenge—*only experienced hikers, please*—might hike difficult Ruckel Creek Trail No. 405, accessed from the campground via a 0.5-mile walk east on Gorge Trail No. 400. Ruckel Creek Trail climbs steeply to hanging gardens of spring wildflowers and rugged cliffs. Gorge Trail No. 400 continues east to intercept the Pacific Crest Trail at Cascade Locks in 2.5 miles.

For an appreciation of how dams have changed the lives and numbers of salmon coming upriver, it is worthwhile to drive to nearby Bonneville Dam. Here you can visit the fish hatchery, the fish ladder, and the Visitor Center on Bradford Island. Particularly fascinating is fish viewing at the center's lighted underwater windows. Besides seeing a closeup of salmon and steelhead, other curious fish—shad, sturgeon, lamprey, etc.—sometimes move by. There is no doubt that the numbers of salmon are greatly diminished. Some stocks are endangered now.

STARVATION CREEK
STATE PARK

Hours/Season: Day use; year-round
Area: 153 acres
Facilities: Picnic tables, restrooms
Attractions: Short trail to waterfall, photography, trail to Viento Campground
Access: Off Interstate 84, 10 miles west of Hood River, *eastbound access only*

▲ Winter in the Columbia River Gorge is often mild, but occasionally a storm blows in and dumps snow, even freezing some of the waterfalls. This happened in the winter of 1884–1885, and passengers on an Oregon-Washington Railroad & Navigation train were snowbound for several days in 30-foot drifts in the vicinity of this park.

Getting food and keeping warm were priorities. According to newspapers, seats were burned to keep them from freezing. Men from Hood River were employed to carry food using homemade skis. A relief train finally got through from the west. Though no one starved, lack of food did earn the name "Starvation" for the park, creek, and its waterfall.

A short trail leads past the restrooms to the 186-foot Starvation Creek Falls. Picnic tables are placed beside the creek below the falls so you can have lunch in view of the falling water. A 1-mile trail connects to Viento State Park via a section of the old Columbia Gorge Scenic Highway; you can see one of the original concrete milepost markers.

Mount Defiance Trail No. 413 begins west of the park, alongside the entry road. If you want to see more waterfalls, hike the easy beginning of the trail, 1 mile on an old wagon road before it becomes a trail. Cabin Creek Falls is seen at 0.3 mile, followed by the falls on Warren Creek at 0.6 mile—named for a Portland fish packer who died aboard the *Titanic*. Still farther, at 1.3 miles, Lancaster Falls honors the engineering wizard of the Columbia River Scenic Highway.

The trail changes after this easy jaunt. Only the fittest will want to attempt the 7-mile climb to the summit of 4,960-foot Mount Defiance, "The Guardian of the Gorge." This trail has the most elevation gain of any in the gorge, a rugged, challenging climb that is used by local mountain climbers to get in shape for climbing Mount Hood.

Starvation Falls seen through trees from picnic area, Starvation Creek State Park

VIENTO STATE PARK

Hours/Season: Overnight; *campground closed in winter*
Area: 248 acres
Facilities: Picnic tables, campground with 58 electrical sites (maximum site is 60 feet) and 17 tent sites, wheelchair-accessible restrooms with showers
Attractions: Short hike to Viento Lake and Columbia River, windsurfing
Nearby: Sternwheeler at Cascade Locks
Access: Off Interstate 84, 8 miles west of Hood River

The name for this park and the creek that flows through it, *Viento*, means "wind." The name, however, actually arose from that of a nearby railroad station which combined the letters of railroad builder Henry Villard, capitalist William Endicott, and a contractor named Tolman. The CCC built a rustic foot bridge across the creek. The picnic area is a grassy meadow with nice trees adjacent to the camping area.

From the north side of the campground, a 0.25-mile trail leads to Viento Lake. This is a pretty little lake, perhaps a quiet place to meditate, with a wetland area around which nourishes cattails and other water-loving plants.

Another 1-mile paved trail, accessed from across from the entry spur to the park, and on the other side of the freeway, lets campers walk over to see the Starvation Creek Falls, or to access the other trailheads at that park.

Many of those who choose to visit this park are windsurfing enthusiasts. The river here is a good practice area and also a camp for those participating in the many competition events in this windy gorge.

It should be mentioned up front that windsurfing access is across railroad tracks between the park and the Columbia River. This area is private property with a "no trespassing" sign. However, the fence has an open entryway across tracks to connect to well-worn trails through a wooded area to the beach along the river. Since so many windsurfers use this without any problem, it is imperative that those crossing this property are cautious and understand that responsibility is theirs, not the railroad's, for any accidents. A nice view of the windswept gorge is seen from this driftwood-strewn beach.

During your stay at this campground, you might want to get a feel for the past by boarding the *Columbia Gorge*, a 145-foot sternwheeler at the marine park of Cascade Locks National Historic Site, for a two-hour narrated tour of the river to Bonneville Dam and Stevenson, Washington. In your mind's eye, imagine the wilder ride over rapids (now buried by dams) taken by pioneers at the end of the Oregon Trail, following the earlier river journey of Lewis and Clark. Passengers today don't have to furnish their own food and blankets, as some did on early sternwheelers.

The sternwheeler *Harvest Queen* caused some excitement in 1890 when she shot the Cascade Rapids. The diesel-powered *Columbia Gorge* is a reminder of the importance of the steam-driven paddlewheelers of the past, when their arrival was an exciting event, bringing goods, news, a means of travel, and the thrilling entertainment of races among the sternwheelers, with passengers cheering them on.

WYGANT, VINZENZ LAUSMANN, AND SENECA FOUTS STATE PARKS

Hours/Season: Day use, year-round
Area: 919 acres for all three
Facilities: Picnic tables, pit toilets, *no water*
Attractions: 6-mile hiking trail, viewpoints, photography
Access: Exit 58, *eastbound access only*, on Interstate 84, 6 miles west of Hood River; the road goes only to these parks

Exit 58 has a sign for the Mitchell Point Overlook, but there is no mention of the three parks. They flow together at the end of this entry spur, so it is hard to tell where one starts and another begins. Construction of In-

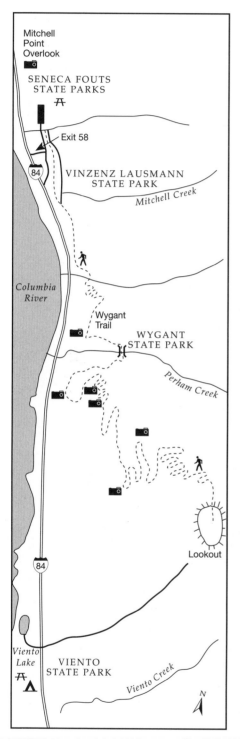

terstate 84 cut off the public access to Wygant State Park, now reached only by a trail. Seneca Fouts State Park is at the eastern end where the gorge overlook is located, adjacent to a vast paved parking space.

The Mitchell Point Tunnel was once located near this overlook, a famous engineering feature of the Columbia River Scenic Highway. Sam Lancaster was inspired by the three-windowed Axenstrasse tunnel, which he viewed with Sam Hill in Switzerland, and he designed a five-window tunnel cut out of solid rock. He thought the view across the Columbia to the Cascade Mountains surpassed the beauty of the Rhine River in Germany. Workers "were lowered on ropes as much as 200 feet where they hung like spiders" while they built this tunnel. Bypassed for safety reasons in 1953, the tunnel was destroyed in 1966. One remaining rock wall fragment rests on a ledge.

A memorial plaque in a circle of trees near the western edge of the parking space locates Vinzenz Lausmann State Park.

The primary attraction, however, is the Wygant Trail, in the third park. This mostly unknown hiking trail is accessed from the old highway that branches off west from the entry road, closed now to vehicular traffic. There is a sign pointing in that direction, plus signs along the way at crucial points. Follow the old pavement for a short distance until it leaves the road to cross Mitchell Creek, and then returns to pavement again. The hiking trail soon takes off to the left through the forest,

High vista point on Wygant Trail, Wygant, Vinzenz Lausmann, and Seneca Fouts State Park

and begins to climb moderately steeply. Just after you see a sign for the Chetwoot Trail, which branches off to the left, there is a spur from the Wygant Trail to the first Columbia River Gorge viewpoint.

Continuing on the main trail, descend to a good bridge across the fast-moving waters of Perham Creek. The trail is fairly easy and level as it switches back toward the Columbia River and the second gorge viewpoint. This could be your destination if you want a short hike with an incredibly panoramic view, perhaps a place to bring a picnic and savor the scenery. Thick, soft moss edges some huge boulders that are perched on the steep edge of the gorge. *Do use caution near this sheer dropoff.*

There are many areas of tanoak woods along the trail, but also sections of tall conifers. The gorge seems to be good habitat for ospreys with these tall trees on cliffs overlooking the river. These birds are easy to spot because they start whistling a frenzied *cheereek!* if you get near a nest. I saw one in this area flying with a fish in its bill, the second such happening in the gorge area in a short period, so they are not difficult to find.

Mushrooms, ferns, and mosses are seen along the trail. There are three more viewpoints before switchbacks climb up to the summit lookout, besides lots of good peeking at water views through the trees. The Washington side of the gorge is laid out like a three-dimensional map as one spots Dog Mountain and the Little White Salmon River flowing out into Drano Lake, and then into the Columbia. Washington Highway 14 and a bridge are situated on the narrow arm of land between the lake and the river.

I could not hike about the last 0.5 mile to the summit because of an enormous downed tree where there was a steep dropoff. I felt it was unsafe to try to crawl over the tree when hiking alone, especially since the trail became quite eroded and appeared little used. By backtracking a short distance to where a sign on a tree points to the downhill Chetwoot ("Black Bear") Loop, this route can be taken back to the highway, though one might prefer to take the easier Wygant Trail downhill. Near the beginning of the Chetwoot, there is a view of the gorge with the snowy peak of Mount Adams protruding above its rim. The path then follows a narrow ledge to the bridge over Perham Creek and then descends through woods to the intersection with the Wygant Trail.

Both trails have a section in the middle where they cross an old road near power poles. This disturbed area hides the trails with heavy bushy vegetation for a short distance, but it is easy to follow. The Wygant Trail goes directly across the road. The Chetwoot Trail jogs slightly to the right.

MEMALOOSE STATE PARK

Hours/Season: Overnight; *campground closed in winter*
Area: 337 acres
Facilities: Picnic tables (highway rest stop), campground has 43 full hookup sites (maximum length 60 feet) and 67 tent sites, wheelchair-

accessible restrooms with showers, dumping station
Attractions: Sacred Indian burial ground on offshore island, windsurfing
Nearby: Deschutes Recreation Area
Access: Off Interstate 84, *westbound access only,* 11 miles west of The Dalles

Situated on a sloping hillside overlooking the Columbia River and the rugged, picturesque bluffs of Washington, the Memaloose Campground narrowly escaped being destroyed by a raging forest fire in July of the extreme drought year of 1992. Black, burnt ground surrounds the sites and ground squirrels poke their heads out of black holes. Although people were evacuated, the campground survived in good shape. Considering the handsome large trees—tanoaks, weeping willows, maples, and more—that still stand today among the campsites, this was indeed fortunate.

Trails weave through the surrounding black area downhill where many windsurfers lug their boards, cross the railroad tracks through the open break in the fence (with the understanding that "no trespass" signs warn of their responsibility), and catch the wind blowing up the river.

The park was named after the Chinookan word *Memaloose,* meaning "island of the dead," since two islands nearby were sacred Indian burial places.

The Columbia River's huge runs of salmon supported vast numbers of Indians in the past. Since all things about the river

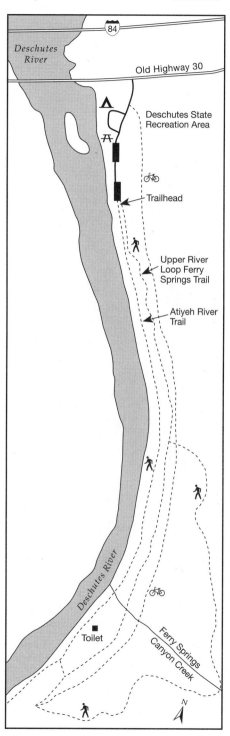

183

were sacred, it is understandable that islands were chosen as burial places. Big Memaloose Island, above The Dalles, is now covered by The Dalles Dam pool. Lower Memaloose Island is seen from the state park, where a white monument marks the burial spot of Victor Trevitt, a pioneer and resident of The Dalles, who wanted his resting place to be "among honest men."

Also buried by The Dalles Dam was Celilo Falls, extraordinary fishing

A walk along the Columbia River, Memaloose State Park

grounds of the Native Americans. When salmon and steelhead trout migrated as far as 1,000 miles upriver to spawn, these falls poured through many cracks and fissures in the basaltic rock obstructions and concentrated the efforts of the fish. The Indians positioned themselves on platforms built on rocks jutting into the water and caught the anadromous fish with nets on long poles.

Because this place was the heart of Indian life, it was called the Tumwater, or Tum Tum, to reflect the sound of a heartbeat. It was a happy place during the good fishing from spring to fall, when spring chinook weighed over seventy pounds and early June steelhead were over thirty pounds. The Indians feasted and offered thanks to the Giver during this time.

Fishing sites were a valued possession, controlled by families and handed down from father to son, or by marrying into the family. When fish canneries sprang up, cable cars were built to let the Indian fishermen have access to otherwise unreachable fishing spots. But then settlers started using fishing wheels which were capable of catching eight tons of salmon per day, lowering the resource drastically until they were outlawed in 1926. For more than ten thousand years, Indians lived and fished on the banks of this river. Some still use these platforms to fish today, but the Columbia River salmonoid fishing has declined 75 to 85 percent since 1910.

It is worth the drive to nearby Deschutes State Recreation Area, 17 miles east of The Dalles, to do the new hiking and/or biking trails. The climate shifts quickly to the warm, dry sunshine of central Oregon where the Deschutes River empties into the Columbia. Go in spring, before the hot summer, to see wildflowers and many Canada geese with their young on the river.

Both the 5.5 miles of hiking trails and the mostly level 16-mile mountain bike trail—an old gravel service road closed to motor vehicles—follow the path of the river. The bike trail begins just north of the campground. The hiking trailhead starts south of the overflow camping area where a sign gives you the choice of following the Atiyeh River Trail or Upper River Loop, Ferry Springs Trail. You should sample at least some, if not all, of both hiking trails since they offer different experiences—one through the wetlands bordering the river, and the other with wonderful panoramic river views from desert sagebrush countryside that crosses a couple of creeks. The Ferry Springs Canyon Loop branches uphill and crosses some private land via fence stiles and ladders before rejoining the Upper River Trail.

Early morning is fine for seeing fishermen in the river, some floating along in innertubes, and for birdwatching. Mergansers rest on rocks in the river, blue herons fly overhead, and chipmunks and lizards scurry before your footsteps. *Do watch for rattlesnakes.* Old homestead buildings are seen at the beginning of the trail and one passes an abandoned waterwheel once used for irrigation on the Lower River Trail.

This is one of the eight Oregon State Park Volkswalks, a 10-kilometer hike rated 4+, with 5 being most difficult. Detailed maps with instructions on how to make the circuit are available from the campground host.

MAYER STATE PARK

Hours/Season: Day use; year-round
Area: 677 acres
Facilities: Picnic tables, restrooms, boat ramp, beach access, summer day-use fee for vehicles
Attractions: Windsurfing, hiking, nature study, birding, swimming, fishing, boating, photography, bicycling, and the outstanding view of eastern Columbia River Gorge from Rowena Crest
Access: Off Interstate 84 at Exit 76, 10 miles west of The Dalles

Mayer State Park is in three different areas. Its varied terrain was valued by the Wasco Indians in times past when they caught fish from the Columbia and went to the Rowena Plateau to gather edible plants.

From the freeway exit, follow the sign to East Mayer on the river. This is essentially a day-use parking area with many spaces for windsurfers; it is a popular place for launching into the strong wind on the river.

To reach West Mayer, from the same freeway exit, backtrack on a parallel road west a short distance to a park sign, before crossing the freeway and then a small wooden bridge (limit six tons, *no trailers or motorhomes*). The park is wetland habitat with lakes, vegetated channels, and small islands at the edge of the Columbia River, with wetlands woven throughout the area and some adjoining woods.

This landscape offers good birding, fishing, and boating, plus a quiet place to spend some time. You might want to don your swimming suit in the warmer summer weather on this eastern side of the Cascades.

The third area of Mayer State Park is reached by following the 9-mile portion of the Columbia River Scenic Highway, from the same exit, that loops uphill to an elevation of 1,000 feet. This will take you to the park's Rowena Crest Overlook. (Please be aware that the park does not include property all along this drive, though you'll certainly want to travel the whole distance.)

This view hints at what an eagle sees as he flies above the land, including the route of the mighty river, the dizzying loops of Lancaster's highway, and the dry eastern vistas. Compare this landscape to that of Crown Crest on the western side of the Cascades.

Rowena Crest is also the site of the Tom McCall Nature Preserve, over 219 acres on the Rowena Plateau dedicated as a memorial to Governor McCall's commitment to preserve the Oregon landscape. The Nature Conservancy owns and manages the preserve to maintain its biodiversity. This place is one of the premier wildflower blooms, occurring from late February through May. State Park Director David G. Talbot wrote that he spent a day there when "the wildflowers were so beautiful, the display knocked my eyes out." The wildlife includes golden eagles, red-tailed hawks, and rattlesnakes (*use caution*). This is also good hiking country as paths wind among the flowers and along cliffs.

Windsurfers on the Columbia River, Mayer State Park

This section of the Columbia River Scenic Highway offers some challenging bicycling, with less traffic than on the road by the waterfalls. It is still a place for caution, particularly with the steep downhills. Have good brakes and wear a helmet. The route can be expanded considerably by including the Seven Mile Hill Road and making a 22-mile loop.

187

CENTRAL OREGON

▲ The heartland of Oregon begins on the pine-clad eastern slopes of the Cascades. The Cascade Lakes Scenic Byway is the best road for getting within yodeling distance of several of these snow-peaked mountains. The road swings southwest from Bend and climbs past a string of clear alpine lakes, ski resorts, hiking trails, osprey nests, and wilderness vistas.

East of the north/south ridge of the Cascades, the violence of volcanic action has left imprints of lava flows, cinder cones, and lava caves for spelunking. Two lakes, Paulina Lake and East Lake, nestle in the Newberry Crater, once a massive fire mountain of some 12,000 feet. This area attracts cross-country skiers and snowmobilers in winter, hikers and bikers in summer.

With all the geological upheaval, rockhounds come to the many public lands to look for thundereggs (the state rock), agates, petrified wood, obsidian, or even a rare opal or amethyst. Rock climbers, both novice and expert, find the kind of towering pinnacles that challenge them.

Most of central Oregon is a high, dry desert plateau with the pungent, distinctive aroma of sagebrush and juniper. There is little rain and temperatures are in the eighties or nineties in summer, though nights are crisp and cool with the low humidity. Winter climate varies greatly, and depends upon whether you are in mountains or valleys.

Two rivers dominate the landscape, the Deschutes and the John Day, both designated "Scenic Waterways." A wild, churning river much of the time, the Deschutes attracts whitewater rafters who have the best view of the rugged canyons along the river's route to the Columbia. The Crooked River also does its share of carving canyons. Several reservoirs—Lakes Billy Chinook, Ochoco and Prineville—are focal points for outdoor recreation that attracts boaters, fishermen, and expert water-skiers.

Recreation at Warm Springs Indian Reservation is enhanced by a merg-

Opposite: *Rock climbers, Smith Rock State Park*

189

ing with cultural aspects of Native Americans. Ka-Nee-Ta, a multimillion-dollar vacation resort, has been developed, where visitors can sleep in a te-pee, soak in a pool fed by hot springs, or attend tribal celebrations.

Ghost towns make another window into the past, full of interest for the history buff. Shaniko and Richmond are worth a visit. An abandoned one-room schoolhouse is seen near Clarno. Life has not been easy on the wind-swept prairie where the feel of the "Old West" still resides. Grasslands near Prineville whisper of a cowboy heritage that is not yet gone. Rodeos—social events in a land of much open space and isolation—let expert horse people show off their techniques for the public.

Coyotes welcome the dawn at the Painted Hills of John Day National Monument as light washes volcanic ash which has hardened into shale. Fossil remains at this site, and at the Clarno Unit of the monument, hint of a once warm, moist climate when crocodiles, primitive horses, and large swamp-dwelling rhinos flourished.

E. R. CORBETT STATE PARK

Hours/Season: Day use; year-round
Area: 63 acres
Facilities: Undeveloped
Attractions: Hiking, mountain biking, horseback riding, fishing, and solitude
Nearby: Suttle Lake, Pacific Crest Trail
Access: At the Corbett Sno-Park, 14 miles west of Sisters, and just east of the Santiam Pass on US 20, take the gravel road for 0.75 mile to the trailhead, then 2 miles to the park

Corbett is a different experience from most state parks. It is completely undeveloped and a long hike in, at least 2 miles, not the 0.5 mile mentioned in the official state park guide.

This park was donated by Henry L. and Gretchen Corbett in memory of their son, Elliott Corbett II, who was lost in action during World War II. They wanted it preserved as a wilderness area, as it has been. The park includes the southern portion of Blue Lake at an elevation of 3,453 feet. Its environs are the only easily accessible part of the park.

The old wagon trail over the Cascades once passed through the park and the meadow was a good stopping place to spend the night, especially with the small creek on the south side of it.

To take the trail to the park, look for the blue signs—one to Blue Lake Trail, which is the same route—on a tree at the trailhead. The signs are easily seen from the road, but the "E. R. Corbett" sign has been uprooted and lies on the ground, at least when I was there. A sign on the entrance gate to FS Road No. 200 warns that the road is now to be used only for foot, horse, and mountain bike use—*no motorized vehicles*—to protect the wildlife habitat. This logged-over land is not part of the state park.

Several roads branch off from FS Road No. 200, but stay on this main graveled road. You will probably follow deer tracks. Only one small Corbett Trail sign is seen some distance along the way.

It is downhill to the park, through a logged forest that offers mountain, woods, and Suttle Lake views in the distance as the trail curves and switchbacks past rolling hills dotted with wildflowers blooming in the open sun.

Early morning is a good time to take this walk or ride, with the sounds and activities of a number of birds—juncos, woodpeckers, and vultures above.

When the road ends—and you are now into wilderness forest with lodgepole and ponderosa pine plus glimpses of deer—a loop trail branches off in two directions. There are no signs. Since this is the outside curve of a loop, take left spurs if you proceed to the right, and right spurs if you proceed left. This loop is part of the Blue Lake Rim Trail and you will see signs at certain intersections. A sign designating E. R. Corbett State Park is seen just west of the expansive meadow. Proceed west of this sign to one indicating the route to the lake, which is part of this loop and the park. Horse trails also branch off from this loop. In winter, cross-country skiers use the area. Be prepared for this trail-finding experience by having emergency equipment, time, and energy.

There is an alternate route to the park that is accessed from the Blue Lake Resort, private property

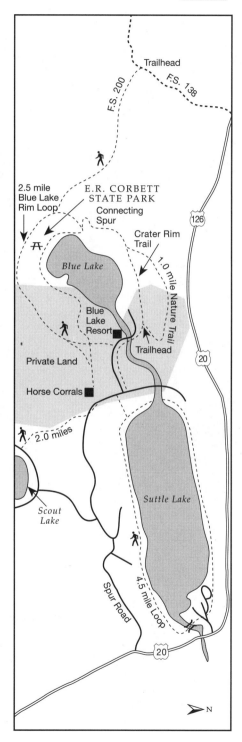

Hiking trail views of Suttle Lake and Cascade Mountains, E. R. Corbett State Park

reached via the Suttle Lake turnoff on US 20. The attendant at the information booth will give you a day pass to park and take the Blue Lake Crater
Rim Trail. Ask for a map. The trail begins along a self-guided nature walk
and then connects to the rim trail on the steep slopes above the lake. Horses
are available for rental at the resort.

While in the area, adjacent Suttle Lake is a popular destination with
windsurfing, fishing, swimming, and Forest Service Campgrounds in the
Cascade Mountains. A 4.5-mile trail circles the lake and connects trails to
Scout Lake and Blue Lake.

Or one might wish to do a portion of the Pacific Crest Trail, since it's so
close. This national recreation trail is accessed at Santiam Pass on US 20,

approximately 2 miles west of the access road to Corbett, where there is trail parking. Hiking north, the Mount Jefferson Wilderness is only a short distance, and a wealth of trails and lakes abound. Get a map of the wilderness area at a ranger station and plan a hike that fits your needs. Three Fingered Jack (7,841 feet) is passed first on the Pacific Crest Trail.

TUMALO STATE PARK

Hours/Season: Overnight; *campground closed in winter*
Area: 330 acres
Facilities: Picnic tables, campground with 21 full hookups and 68 tent sites (maximum length 44 feet), restrooms with solar showers, group picnic shelter, group tenting, hiker/biker camp, firewood, summer day-use fee for vehicles, phone: (503) 388-6055
Attractions: Fishing, swimming
Nearby: High Desert Museum, Lava Lands Visitor Center, Cascade Lakes Highway
Access: From US 20, 5 miles northwest of Bend; follow signs to park

Along a scenic section of the Deschutes River, Tumalo State Park is a pleasant stopping place, and a quick trip for Bend residents who know about the swimming hole at a bend in the river. Basalt rock formations form a backdrop for the scenic river view. The smells are of pungent high desert plants.

The day-use area is a huge expanse of spacious lawns, paths, and trees— juniper and ponderosa pine, with willow and poplar near the water. Wildlife scurry about the park: golden-mantled squirrels and chipmunks dash here and there; rabbits are out in the early morning. Swallows fly in and out of homes in holes in the high rocks. Great blue herons silently stalk at water's edge. The name of the park derives from the Klamath Indian word *temolo*, meaning "wild plum."

Just south of Bend, the outstanding High Desert Museum has 20 acres of nature trails and exhibits that include live birds of prey, river otters, and porcupines in their natural surroundings. The Earle A. Chiles Center on the Spirit of the West has exhibits about the settlement of the West. Various authentic dwellings of the pioneers are outdoors.

Another nearby attraction is the Lava Lands Visitor Center, across the road. The surrounding countryside abounds in remains of the region's vast volcanic happenings and this center will introduce you to them. Then go exploring to see some of them—Lava Butte, Lava River Caves, Lava Island Falls, Arnold Ice Cave, Lava Cast Forest, Hole in the Ground, and many more. Geologists will go wild.

For a spectacular loop close to snow-covered mountains and a string of high-country lakes, take the Cascade Lakes Highway (Century Drive) west from Bend. You can hike, observe wildlife, ski (in winter), or just relax in

Basalt rock formations along Deschutes River, Tumalo State Park

this wonderful atmosphere where canoes slide into lakes in early morning as the mist rises when sunlight warms the water. Miles and miles of trails will take you into the Three Sisters Wilderness, or to the Pacific Crest Trail, or to waterfalls and alpine meadows of wildflowers. Backpackers and mountain climbers access several of the Cascade peaks from this loop.

PILOT BUTTE STATE PARK

Hours/Season: Day use; year-round
Area: 101 acres
Facilities: Viewpoint, *no water or restrooms*
Attractions: Vista of Cascade Mountain peaks, hiking to it, photography
Access: Off US 20, on the east side of Bend

Land for this park atop Pilot Butte was the gift of several donors in 1927. It was dedicated with a plaque in memory of Terrance Hardington Foley, a prominent citizen of Bend. Early pioneers named the butte because it was such a conspicuous landmark as they approached from the east. It enabled them to aim their way to a safe ford among the many canyons along the Deschutes River.

The butte is a lone cinder cone that projects some 500 feet above the surrounding land, at an elevation of 4,136 feet above sea level. Ponderosa pine, juniper, and sagebrush grow on its slopes. A 1-mile steep, narrow, winding road circles around the cone, like the turnings of a spiral, to reach the top, which is flat with a few trees, lava rocks, and some parking space.

Watch out for pedestrians on the drive as hikers like to make the aerobic climb on foot, especially on a Sunday morning, even in the hot desert summers.

In the center of the butte top, an alidade has been mounted on a pedestal with pointers that identify several Cascade Mountains peaks—Hood, Washington, Jefferson, Sisters, Broken Top, and Bachelor. One also gets a good perspective of the city of Bend and the surrounding countryside. Because of the fantastic view, this site was used as an airplane observation post for a year during World War II.

CLINE FALLS STATE PARK

Hours/Season: Day use; *closed in winter*
Area: 9 acres
Facilities: Picnic tables, restrooms
Attractions: Fishing, swimming
Access: On US 126, travel 4 miles west of Redmond

Cline Falls State Park is a narrow strip of frontage along the crystal-clear Deschutes River, a pleasant place to cool off in summer, go fishing, and picnic. The river is calm here with large, many-shaped rocks punctuating the rippling water and green trees (mostly juniper, locust and poplar) bordering it. A much-visited series of boulder-enclosed swimming holes is just across the highway. The falls is a distance north of the park.

A popular swimming hole on the Deschutes River, Cline Falls State Park

THE COVE PALISADES STATE PARK

Hours/Season: Overnight; *campground closed in winter*
Area: 4,130 acres
Facilities: Three day-use areas with picnic tables, two campgrounds with 87 full hookup, 91 electrical, 94 tent sites (maximum length 60 feet), handicapped access, restrooms with showers, dumping station, group camping, slide program, fish-cleaning houses, reservations available, firewood, boat ramps, marina with supplies plus boat and sports equipment rental, summer day-use fee for vehicles, phone: (503) 546-3412
Attractions: Water-skiing, boating, fishing, photography, hiking, swimming, outstanding views and geology
Access: 15 miles southwest of Madras; follow signs from US 97

▲ The first impressive view on arrival at The Cove Palisades State Park is
⊥ of the snowy peak of Mount Jefferson looming over a vast labyrinth of golden canyons filled with blue water. The Cascade peak is soon hidden from view as the road dips into the canyon and twists around the edges of Lake Billy Chinook.

This three-armed lake was formed in 1963 when Round Butte Dam confined the waters of the Metolius, Crooked, and Deschutes rivers as they flowed out of Oregon mountains. It was named for Billy Chinook, a local Indian guide who helped Captain John Fremont in his Oregon explorations.

The original state park site was nearly 900 feet deep, at the bottom of Crooked River Canyon. It had to be moved or it would have been flooded. Today two campgrounds overlook the Deschutes River and Crooked River

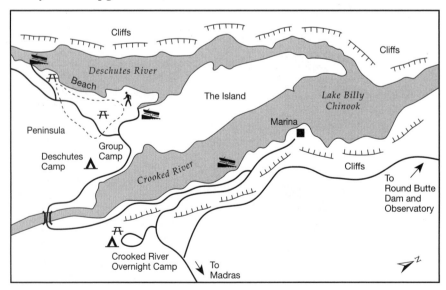

Boating in the Crooked River Canyon, Cove Palisades State Park

arms of the lake, with towering cliffs visible across the waters. A short distance northeast of the Deschutes Camp, Indian petroglyphs are seen on a basalt boulder called "The Ship," moved here from a series of rapids on the Crooked River that were drowned. Across the road from this feature, a high plateau called "The Island" projects a long finger toward the confluence of the two rivers.

One day-use area is on the east edge of the Crooked River arm. Two day-use areas on the Deschutes River shores are reached by hiking trails leading down from the Deschutes Camp. Trails connect the two areas so that a loop can be walked.

This is central Oregon's most visited state park—the second largest in the whole state—so don't come for solitude, particularly with its many motorboats. Although there are 72 miles of shoreline, over half a million visitors come each year and it can get crowded. Even so, deer wander into the campground, orioles flit from tree to tree, and rattlesnakes live in the surrounding territory. Water-skiing is popular with both participants and observers.

Be aware of rules and regulations, especially for boaters. The lake is surrounded by both public and private land. The land on the north side of the Metolius River arm is the Warm Springs Indian Reservation. *Do not trespass on these private lands.*

Visitors to Round Butte Dam can follow a scenic road on the east rim of the canyon past four viewpoints to an overlook with observatory and museum at the dam.

197

The fascinating geology of the area tells us that as long ago as ten to twelve million years, in the Pliocene Epoch, lava flowed from shield-type volcanoes as the base of the Cascade Mountains formed, causing the land to sink in this region. In the process, the westward flow of the Deschutes River and its tributaries was rerouted, forced into moving in north/south courses.

These ancient rivers deposited sediment—ash, cinders, and thin beds of lava—and built a layer more than 1,000 feet thick, called the Dalles Formation, along their waterways. Finally, between two and three million years ago, volcanic eruptions put a basaltic cap—the rim rock—on top of the palisades around Lake Billy Chinook.

As the Cascade Mountains developed, a general uplift of this land occurred, causing the Deschutes, Metolius, and Crooked Rivers to flow more swiftly and gouge canyons through the soft land. Recent lava flows entered the upper Crooked River Canyon and were then cut through by the mighty power of flowing water. Remnants of this basalt coat the canyon walls, fused to the light, soft rocks.

SMITH ROCK STATE PARK

Hours/Season: Day use; year-round
Area: 623 acres
Facilities: Picnic tables, bivouac area for tents, showers, restrooms, *drinking water only in picnic area*, summer day-use fee for vehicles
Attractions: Unusual rock formations, access for experienced rock climbers, 7 miles of hiking trails, freshwater fishing, river swimming, photography, nature study
Nearby: Crooked River National Grassland
Access: 3 miles east, via a well-signed country road, from US 97 at Terrebonne (6 miles north of Redmond)

▲ The meandering Crooked River flows through a spectacular canyon of
⊥ multicolored rock pinnacles and crags, geological features that were reasons for preserving this park for the public.

This area was called "Monument Canyon" in the U.S. Geological Survey of 1905. The name "Smith Rock" seems to have resulted from the time a soldier named Smith fell to his death after climbing on an unstable rock to see the view.

The scenic attractions of this park have lured movie and television companies to use it as a location. *Rooster Cogburn,* starring John Wayne, was shot here.

Summer weather is quite hot at Smith Rock and it is not the best season for hiking and climbing, so try to visit in spring or fall when the air is more invigorating and conducive to exploring.

Expert rock climbers from around the world are attracted to the sheer vertical rock walls of the gorge carved by the Crooked River. The routes are shorter than the major big-wall climbs of Yosemite, but the climbs are as difficult as any in the United States. Some magazines have called these the "most challenging free climbs in North America." More than two hundred eighty routes go up rock faces, with names such as "Morning Glory Wall," "The Crack of Infinity," and "The Young and the Restless."

Climbers are asked to protect the fragile environment of the canyon by using existing trails to access climbs. The use of "clean" climbing equipment (chocks, nuts, Friends, etc.) and techniques is encouraged. This is not possible on some routes, with inadequate cracks or other natural depressions, and permanent anchors have been placed. Climbers should test these fixed bolts for safety and then use them. Avoid placing additional permanent anchors so further damage to the easily scarred rock doesn't occur. No additional fixed protection is needed for any of the routes listed in *Oregon Rock, A Climbers' Guide*, by Jeff Thomas.

Hikers will enjoy several signed dirt trails, a total of 7 miles, that can be

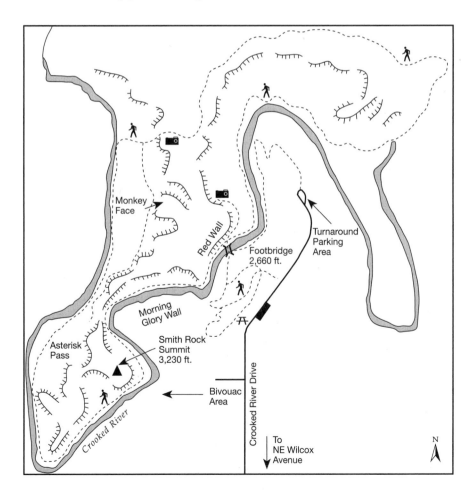

hiked in the park. These are accessed from the bluff overlooking the river near the picnic area, the turnaround parking area at road's end, or the bivouac area, and descend into the canyon. From the river elevation, a tangle of paths weaves through the vegetation and skirts the water on this southeast side of the river. A footbridge (elevation 2,660 feet) crosses the river to connect with the major trails.

Turn left after crossing the bridge (0.6 mile from the picnic area) and travel 2.8 miles (elevation gain, 250 feet) to the base of Monkey Face, a landmark formation, where you can watch climbers. As you round the single rock named Smith (tallest peak at 3,230 feet), and head north, enjoy the good views of the snow-peaked Cascade Mountains to the west, an interesting contrast to the orange and gold tints of the park.

A right turn at the bridge proceeds more strenuously, in 3.6 miles (elevation gain, 880 feet), to a viewpoint across from Monkey Face.

A shorter, and newer, hike branches off north immediately after crossing the footbridge and edges the Red Wall via a series of steps switchbacking steeply up to a viewpoint. Other stairstep trails on the steep talus slopes of the north riverbank are spurs along the beginning of the Monkey Face Trail and are primarily access routes for rock climbers to Morning Glory Wall, the Dihedrals, Asterisk Pass, and so on.

Exploring early in the day, before too many visitors and higher temperatures arrive, rewards you with good wildlife viewing. Birds sing at 4:00 A.M. in May. Geese that have nested by the river in spring swim with their young following them. Ledges and overhangs high on the rocks house a variety of birds that include swallows and birds of prey. (*All hikers and climbers are asked to keep their distance from nests inhabited by birds of prey. Do not disturb the young or adults.*) Magpies fly among the tall pines along the south bank and kingfishers dive into the water. *Watch for rattlesnakes in summer.*

Scents of juniper and sage are in the air. To see wildflowers, come in early spring, though a few bloom later. The bronze-colored cliffs are reflected in the river in the early morning and late afternoon for good photography shots. After exploring, enjoy a huckleberry ice cream cone at the store near the entrance to the park.

Though the sign at the Terrebonne turn-off says "Day Use Only," a walk-in bivouac area offers rock climbers and other visitors a chance to enjoy the evening and early morning hours in the park. Tent sites are chosen in an area of juniper trees. The fee for camping and shower facilities is nominal, but no sleeping in vehicles is permitted. Trails edge the bluff near tenting, and go into the gorge past a wetland area complete with cattails and water dripping downhill over rocks.

If you like grasslands, the vast area located north of Smith Rock and spreading past Madras is designated the Crooked River National Grassland. Part of the National Forest System, this is a good example of this particular habitat, a rolling grassland of sagebrush-juniper, often referred to as "high desert." It supports a small herd of antelope, numerous mule deer, quail, and chukars. Haystack Reservoir and a viewpoint plus trail at Rimrock Springs are good places to visit.

OCHOCO LAKE STATE PARK

Hours/Season: Overnight; *campground closed in winter*
Area: 9.8 acres
Facilities: Picnic tables, campground with 22 primitive sites (maximum length is 30 feet), hiker/biker camp, boat ramp
Attractions: Fishing, boating, hiking, rockhounding, bird watching, photography
Nearby: Steins Pillar
Access: On US 26, 7 miles east of Prineville

▲Both the separate day-use area and the campground are situated on a craggy bluff overlooking the northern shore of the Ochoco Reservoir. Primarily constructed for irrigation and flood control, the 125-foot-high Ochoco Dam impounded water of Ochoco Creek, a tributary of the Crooked River, in the early 1920s.

Ochoco is a Paiute Indian word for "willow," a tree ubiquitous in the region. On the dry, rocky edge abutting the facilities of the park, however, Western junipers and ponderosa pine grab the photographer's attention with their exposed roots and picturesque shapes.

Paths lead from the picnic and campground areas down into flat grassland surrounding the water that is edged with several rock formations. The trails meander and entice you to various points along the reservoir. This is high desert country with a warm, dry climate and open spaces. The Ochoco Mountains and Ochoco National Forest rim the view to the northeast.

Not a particularly large reservoir, Ochoco is suitable for rowboats, and the trout fishing is reputably good. Water levels in

Tree edging Ochoco Lake, Ochoco Lake State Park

summer are variable, and a long triangular strip of land with vivid red vegetation is often exposed. My second visit, during a bad drought year, revealed more exposed central islands with channels of water flowing between them. The land sloping into the water was striated with vegetation, a layering of colors of orange, gold, green, and brown pleasing to the eye.

The scene was enhanced by the activities of a large number of Canada geese and many ducks, who found this habitat to their liking, no doubt drawn to the aquatic plants which they eat.

A side trip to Steins Pillar is worthwhile. Located 11 miles north of the state park on Mill Creek Road in Ochoco National Forest, Steins Pillar is an impressive 300-foot-high monolith surrounded by similar, less impressive formations. View it from the road or you can hike to it, a good photography subject at the edge of daylight.

Wildlife in this national forest includes antelope, a herd of wild horses, an occasional wildcat, and (rarely) a cougar. Golden and bald eagles are commonly sighted in spring.

Good rockhounding is found in this area and adjacent to Ochoco Lake across the highway to the northwest. (See the write-up on Prineville Reservoir for more information on this activity.)

PRINEVILLE RESERVOIR STATE PARK

Hours/Season: Overnight; *campground closed in winter*
Area: 365 acres
Facilities: Picnic tables, bathhouse, campground with 22 full hookups (maximum length 40 feet) and 48 tent sites, restrooms with showers, firewood, group camping available, slide program, boat ramp, fish cleaning station, summer reservations available, phone: (503) 447-4363
Attractions: Boating, water-skiing, fishing, swimming, rockhounding
Access: From US 26 just east of Prineville, watch for a sign for the state park, then travel 17 miles southeast

Prineville Reservoir is a large body of water, some 12 miles long and 1 mile at its widest point, in the midst of sagebrush, desert buttes, mesas, canyons, and alkali flats. It sprawls out over the desert plateau with many coves and turnings, water appropriated from the Crooked River by 245-foot-high Bowman Dam, west of the park. Bowman was constructed in 1961 for irrigation and flood control, and for years had the only elevator in Crook County.

The reservoir attracts fishermen year-round, with good catches of largemouth bass, trout, and catfish. Its large size makes it a good place for water-skiing and boating.

Several good rockhounding spots edge the reservoir at different places. If you're a rockhound, this is the place to get out your tools, whether you

Beach and distant skiff on reservoir, Prineville Reservoir State Park

prefer shovels, picks, mattocks, rock hammers, crowbars, or long-handled chisels. Crook County's many thousand acres of public lands offer good digging sites for a wide variety of semiprecious quartz-family stones.

Thundereggs can be found north and west of US 26. These spherical masses, the official state rock of Oregon, sometimes have marvelous cores ranging from five-pointed stars to miniature landscapes.

Agate is the most common gemstone. The best rocks have swirled grain such as the "angel wing," or impurities that might look like miniature trees inside the stone. Sagenite, green jasper, jasper interlaced with agate, limb casts, obsidian, and petrified wood are some of the discoveries you can make, and a rare opal or amethyst is not an impossibility.

Digging is a dirty, rugged hobby, but offers enjoyment for many. You'll find lots of fellow enthusiasts at the Prineville Rockhound Pow Wow in June.

The excellent *Central Oregon Rockhound Guide*—complete with map, rock photos, and geology information—is put out by the combined efforts of the Forest Service, the BLM, and the Prineville–Crook County Chamber of Commerce. It points out areas that are set aside for rock collectors.

History buffs might be interested to know that in 1845 Stephen Meek led a large group of Oregon Trail pioneers (estimated between 1,000–1,500) across an untried Oregon route that split off near Farewell Bend on the

Snake River, passed through the Prineville area, and then wandered north-west, past the Smith Rock area, to reconnect with others at The Dalles. Called the Meek Cutoff, the journey was one of near disaster, of getting lost, of insufficient supplies, of sickness and deaths beyond the average, and of trouble finding water. Many of the members of Meek's group became influential residents of the Williamette Valley, so the trip was not without some measure of accomplishment.

Along the way, while groups were out scouting for water, one of them dug into the moist gravel and found gold nuggets in the bed of an almost dry creek. Legend says that a blue bucket was filled and carried back to camp, where some tested the metal for malleability. This was possibly the first gold mine discovered west of the Rocky Mountains, three years before the California find. One of the most likely areas for the gold location lies between the South Fork of the Crooked River and the Deschutes River, two days' journey east of Pilot Butte. For many years, miners searched for this lost gold mine without success. Today, questions about its location are treated with a good deal of skepticism and are considered symptomatic of just plain craziness.

SHELTON STATE WAYSIDE

Hours/Season: Overnight; *campground closed in winter*
Area: 180 acres
Facilities: Picnic tables, campground with 36 primitive sites (maximum site is 50 feet), pit toilets, firewood
Attractions: Hiking, peaceful camping
Access: Off US 19, 11 miles southeast of Fossil

Flowering violets of moist wooded area, Shelton State Wayside

While traveling the lonely, quiet roads of this section of central Oregon, where one is even a distance from national forests and their camps, it is good to know that there is a pleasant state park campground tucked away in the forest along Service Creek. Just south of Butte Creek Summit Pass at 3,948 feet, summers are hot in the sun along the highway, but the sites are cooler near the creek that runs through the length of the park. This gently sloping canyon area is on a southern slope of a ridge of the Blue Mountains between the John Day River and Lone Rock Creek.

In the middle of the park a 2-mile nature trail crosses a meadow and enters the woods. Wildflowers bloom in several places.

The land originally belonged to the Kinzua Lumber Company, who gave a small gift of land before the remainder was purchased by the park agency. Kinzua requested that a plaque honor L. D. W. Shelton, an Oregon pioneer of 1847 who lived in this area, a soldier and surveyor. The park preserves evergreen trees of old ponderosa pine, Douglas fir, and juniper.

J. S. BURRES STATE PARK

Hours/Season: Day use; year-round
Area: 7 acres
Facilities: Picnic tables, pit toilets, *no water*
Attractions: Fishing, scenic waterway rafting
Access: On State Highway 206, travel 25 miles northwest of Condon

This is an isolated section along the John Day River Scenic Waterway that is preserved as a state park. It offers good public fishing access and a scenic view of the river. It is basically a huge gravel parking area for some serious fishermen, with peace and quiet in an area of huge farms, golden wheat fields, and canyons. Pheasant and quail wander across lonely roads. The wagons on the Oregon Trail crossed the John Day River just a few miles northeast of here. Bass fishermen are asked to be on the lookout for tagged fish, and to report them.

The park is also one of the few haul-out points for those who want to float the John Day River. The river is a designated Scenic Waterway for 147 miles from the Service Creek Bridge to Tumwater Falls on its way to the Columbia River. It is a 70-mile trip (class 2 and 3 rapids) from the Clarno launch point to Cottonwood Bridge in Burres State Park. River runners see magnificent canyons in a landscape seldom touched by man. Day float trips can be arranged in Fossil. If you do put your raft, canoe, or kayak into the river at John Day River Wayside at Clarno, take the time to explore the adjacent John Day Fossil Beds National Monument, Clarno Unit, where you can hike among rocks with fossilized leaf impressions and see dramatic palisades formed by eroded ancient mudslides.

Fishing from a boat on Lost Creek Reservoir, Joseph P. Stewart State Park

SOUTHERN
OREGON

Oregon's only national park lies in southern Oregon—Crater Lake National Park. It is a blue jewel set in a stunning circle of jagged peaks, but a fine supporting cast of scenic treasures and cultural opportunities is found in this region.

A little north of Crater Lake, Mount Thielsen reflects its unique shape onto the surface of Diamond Lake, a popular recreation center. To the south, Oregon's largest lake, Upper Klamath, is ringed by wildlife refuges with abundant bald eagles and white pelicans.

The magnificent Rogue River is a major waterway of the area as it flows from its source in Crater Lake National Park. It is edged by the long-distance Upper Rogue River Trail as the river churns its way over lava flows, through basalt gorges, and into Lost Creek Reservoir before it becomes a calm valley river. The river changes again west of Grants Pass, becoming a wild, raging affair through the Klamath Mountains.

Travel a short distance north of Grants Pass on Interstate 5 and you can stop to eat at Wolf Creek Tavern, an old stagecoach stop, where famous people have often stayed. Jack London did some writing in those surroundings.

For famous animal touring, drive through Wildlife Safari near Winston. Hundreds of wild animals roam free (for the most part) as you drive through, caged in your vehicle. This park has bred more than one hundred cheetahs to maintain a gene pool for this endangered animal species.

Cross the freeway east of Winston to follow another of this region's major rivers, the North Umpqua. A fine touring road leads to Diamond Lake, with many possible stops at excellent waterfalls, hiking trails, and picnic sites. Zane Grey gave up the Rogue, after it got too much publicity, "to camp and fish and dream and rest beside the green-rushing, singing Umpqua." Both summer and winter steelhead are plentiful and restricted to fly-fishing only on the 30-mile stretch from Rock Creek to the Soda Springs Power Plant. Rafting and kayaking are also popular on the North Umpqua.

For some cultural entertainment, go south to Ashland's Shakespearean Festival, which attracts people from all over the country because of its excellence. Many also go to nearby Jacksonville, a National Historic Landmark town in the pastoral Applegate Valley, to delight in its charming restorations and echoes of the gold rush. The renowned Peter Britt Music Festival has concerts for all tastes in summer.

The Oregon Caves National Monument, in the extreme southwest of the region, is an underground cavern that was called the "Marble Halls of Oregon" by poet Joaquin Miller.

The eastern half of this region is a place of cloudless skies, alkaline lakes, and open spaces—a high desert plateau of several thousand feet elevation. Fort Rock is a remnant of an ancient volcano that rises above a desert lake bed, where Indians camped more than ten thousand years ago and made sandals out of sagebrush.

A few of the pioneer wagon trains traversed this southern land. One of these crossed where Goose Lake usually straddles the Oregon–California border, but it had no knowledge of doing so. The lake was dry during that summer, a rarity. Years later, the lake evaporated again and wagon ruts were seen entering the lake and exiting on the opposite side.

In the more isolated area to the northeast of Goose Lake, the Hart Mountain National Antelope Refuge is a massive volcanic ridge that is habitat for pronghorn antelope, mule deer, bighorn sheep, and upland birds.

ILLINOIS RIVER STATE PARK

Hours/Season: Day use; year-round
Area: 368 acres
Facilities: Picnic tables, restrooms
Attractions: Fishing
Access: Off US 199, less than 1 mile south of Cave Junction

▲ This is a pleasant, well-maintained river park, a good rest or lunch stop by the Illinois River. Easy access to the river entices some visitors to cool off in the water on a hot day, splashing among the rocks. The confluence of the East and West Forks of the river is just beyond the picnic area. Old roads through this wilder area of the park let you explore a bit. The river was so named because the Althouse brothers of Illinois emigrated from that state and found gold in the river in 1849.

The climate is drier on this side of the Siskiyou National Forest, which begins at the western edge of the park. A sparse stand of pine, fir, and oak is found in the park. The portion of the Illinois River that winds its way through the Kalmiopsis Wilderness is designated a Scenic Waterway.

VALLEY OF THE ROGUE STATE PARK

Hours/Season: Overnight; year-round
Area: 277 acres
Facilities: Individual and group picnicking with shelter, boat ramp, campground with 97 full hookups (maximum site is 75 feet), 55 electrical, 21 tent sites, wheelchair-accessible restrooms with showers, dumping station, firewood, group camping, meeting hall, phone: (503) 582-1118
Attractions: Boating, fishing
Nearby: Wild and scenic Rogue River
Access: Off Interstate 5, 12 miles east of Grants Pass

According to the former owner of this parkland, it has a history of being used temporarily as a reservation by Takelma Indians. Indian artifacts and graves are rumored to have been found in the area and a fort was formerly located across the river.

Located on the legendary Rogue River, and the only campground along Interstate 5, Valley of the Rogue State Park attracts more campers than any other Oregon park, except for those along the coast. It serves as a good base camp for exploring Rogue River Valley attractions. Its day-use area is a rest stop for freeway travelers with 1,355,900 visitors for the 1990–1991 year.

Sheltered by fir, oaks, madrone, pine, and planted trees—following early park directives—over green lawns, the park sprawls out for about 2 miles of riverfront and highway frontage on a flat-to-sloping bench above the

Rafting on scenic Rogue River near Valley of the Rogue State Park

Rogue. Across the river to the southwest are the Siskiyou Mountains and National Forest.

River access for boats is near the picnic area, the one place where the high bank is breached. Though one can find a picnic table with a view of the river, the camping sites are a short distance from the water and have no river views.

Surrounding the park is the sedate valley section of the Rogue River along its 215-mile journey to the Pacific, with hot, dry, sunny summers and a number of vineyards that are producing respectable wines. This is a scenic, placid area of this river, in transition between two wild sections.

The character of the river begins to change gradually and dramatically some miles west of Grants Pass, the largest city along the Rogue River. At Hellgate Canyon, its waters pass through a narrow slot between 250-foot-high vertical rock formations. Jet-boat excursions out of Grants Pass will take you through this canyon, or you can kayak or raft there and continue on to follow the river as it begins to spawn riffles.

Good roads take you to the Grave Creek Bridge, the eastern trailhead for the famed 40-mile Rogue River Trail which traverses the roadless section of the "wild and scenic" river. This is also the entry point for rafters and kayakers to float the challenging water downstream to Agness. Permits are required for this, and must be obtained well in advance. Several commercial operators will help you do the trip.

The river and its environment will not disappoint you. Towering cliffs, rocky chutes, timbered slopes, waterfalls, rapids, wildlife, wildflowers, and geology move past your vision. Take time to enjoy what you see. *Do be alert for rattlesnakes.* Backpackers and boaters will find several primitive camps along the route, plus a few commercial lodges. Make plans for the wild section of the Rogue early.

TOU VELLE STATE PARK

Hours/Season: Day use; year-round
Area: 54 acres
Facilities: Individual and group picnicking (reservations), restrooms, horseshoes, boat ramp, summer day-use fee for vehicles
Attractions: Wildlife viewing, hiking, fishing
Nearby: Applegate Valley, Jacksonville
Access: From Interstate 5 at Central Point, take Exit 32 north and go right to first light at Table Rock Road, then turn left 5 miles to park

Tou Velle State Park is a place for Sunday picnics, wildlife observations, and avid fishermen. Many come for all three reasons. The park lies on both sides of the Rogue River by the Bybee Bridge. The take-out for boats is under the bridge on the north side of the river. A number of poplar trees and shapely oaks are found in the park. Hybrid roses add color. Several pic-

Flyfishing on Tou Velle State Park section of the Rogue River

nic areas are along the park road (one with a large stone fireplace). *No alcohol is allowed in the park.*

Follow the paved path to the east end of the picnic area, cross the bridge over a watery draw, and you will access a path along a quiet area of the river. Prime steelhead and salmon fishing is found here as the river jogs north and you see a few riffles. To the east is Mount McLoughlin.

This eastern area is part of a wildlife refuge and can also be accessed by a loop trail that begins on the upland past the last restroom of the park. This path weaves past wetland expanses and through meadows before going to the riverfront and returning along the water to the picnic area. Wildlife signs alert one to owls and fish. Bring your binoculars. Hawks fly overhead. Great blue heron are often seen and wading birds frequent the gravel bar in the middle of the river.

Only a few miles away, the town of Jacksonville traces its beginnings to the discovery of gold in 1851. Unlike so many such towns, however, it has stayed a viable city by preserving its lovely Victorian homes and historic businesses, and is now a National Historic Landmark. Saunter through town and learn about its early days. Spring is a good time, when lawns are splashed with the colors of flowering shrubs and trees.

Today, Jacksonville is renowned throughout the country for its summer Peter Britt Music Festivals, named after the photographer who came here with his bulky photography gear via the Oregon Trail in 1852. Picnic on the hillside above the lights of the town while you listen to a concert under the stars. Choices include jazz, classical, folk, country, pop, dance, and musical theater.

A few miles southwest of Jacksonville, a paved road branches off Oregon Highway 238 at Ruch and leads south along the Applegate River. This road gradually ascends through rolling countryside to the Applegate Dam and the headwaters to the river. This is in the Rogue River National Forest with several inviting campgrounds available, many hiking trails, from easy to difficult, and from short to long backpack trips. Stop at the Star Ranger Station just before you enter the national forest for maps and hiking information. Applegate Lake is photogenic, particularly with the peaks of the Red Buttes Wilderness in the background, another area with an extensive trail system.

After skirting the lake, the road makes a loop near the California border, letting you see more scenery and return to the town of Applegate. There are several good swimming holes in the river along this tour.

CASEY STATE PARK

Hours/Season: Day use; year-round
Area: 80.6 acres
Facilities: Picnic tables, boat ramp, restrooms
Attractions: Hiking, boating, fishing
Access: Off Oregon Highway 62, 29 miles northeast of Medford

Escaping from impoundment behind the Lost Creek Dam, the Rogue River recaptures some of its wild spirit as it flows through Casey State Park. A frequent stop for picnickers where they lunch under ponderosa pine, Douglas fir, and oaks, the park is situated in the midst of excellent salmon fishing during spawning migration upriver, when the waterway is often lined with fishermen.

Boats of several varieties frequently take to the water here, sometimes combining fishing with riding the whitewater. This sport varies depending on water release from the reservoir upstream, but there are usually some riffles to negotiate. Rafts sometimes launch from just below the fish hatchery and come floating past Casey.

The park was named after a squatter, J. A. Casey, who had a restaurant and other buildings on the property before the federal government transferred the land to the state.

At the eastern edge of the park, you will find a sign for the Rogue River Trail (see map with Joseph P. Stewart State Park). This is the beginning of the 75-mile upper river section that follows the north bank of the river to its

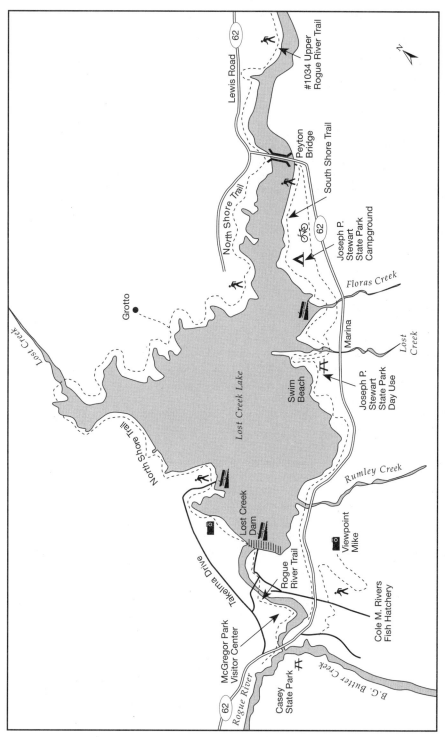

Lewis Road

62

#1034 Upper Rogue River Trail

Peyton Bridge

South Shore Trail

North Shore Trail

62

Joseph P. Stewart State Park Campground

Floras Creek

Grotto

Marina

Lost Creek

Lost Creek Lake

Swim Beach

Joseph P. Stewart State Park Day Use

Lost Creek

North Shore Trail

Rumley Creek

Lost Creek Dam

Rogue River Trail

Viewpoint Mike

McGregor Park Visitor Center

Takelma Drive

Cole M. Rivers Fish Hatchery

Casey State Park

B.G. Butler Creek

62

Rogue River

213

Father and son fishing on Rogue River, Casey State Park

headwaters in Crater Lake National Park. Follow this paved trail to the first junction, which is quite soon, and take the right fork which passes under McLeod Bridge. The path follows the river for 0.4 mile to McGregor Park Visitor Center, which has displays about dam construction, natural history, Native American history, and early settlement of the Rogue Valley. The center also can be reached by road.

The level 0.5-mile stroll along the river in McGregor Park is peppered with secluded picnic tables that are especially attractive, many overlooking the river, so you might want to pack a lunch—perhaps some alder-smoked salmon and crackers—for your hike. This is wetland habitat along the Rogue with Oregon grape, blackberry, ferns, mock orange, and ocean spray growing beneath overhead branches of cottonwoods, California hazel, alder, dogwood, and bigleaf maple. Some spots have horsetail that are three feet tall. Beaver, muskrat, western gray squirrels, skunk, porcupine, chipmunk, and rabbit are at home in this ecosystem. Merganser ducks frequently are seen resting atop individual small rocks that project above the river's surface.

At the spur road to the Cole M. Rivers Fish Hatchery, follow the painted paw prints on the pavement for 0.3 mile as you pass the driftboat ramp and then cross the fish diversion dam. This is the third-largest salmon and steelhead hatchery in the country.

The trail now crosses an open field (often hot) planted with millet to provide nutritious seeds for visiting birds. Besides ospreys, herons, kingfishers, and other birds who fish this quiet spot on the river above the hatchery dam, human fishermen practice catch-and-release fly-casting.

The powerhouse to the Lost Creek Dam is reached in 0.7 mile from the hatchery. One of the main functions of this reservoir is flood control, with low water often in summers, particularly in a drought year. The temperature of released water is controlled to provide the best temperature for fish downstream.

For the long-distance hiker and backpacker, this North Shore Trail continues along Lost Creek Lake for a total of 18.3 miles to the Peyton Bridge. Several camps and side trails are reached along the path. This canyoned side of the lake is reached only by energetic hikers and boaters, since there are no roads.

JOSEPH P. STEWART STATE PARK

Hours/Season: Overnight; *campground closed in winter*
Area: 910 acres
Facilities: Picnic tables, electric kitchen shelters, wheelchair-accessible restrooms with showers, campground with 151 electrical sites (maximum site is 80 feet), 50 tent sites, group camping, firewood, dumping station, boat ramp and docks, fish-cleaning areas, marina, store, cafe, phone: (503) 560-3334
Attractions: Hiking trails (with connections to other trails), bicycle trails, swimming, fishing, water-skiing, boating, photography
Nearby: Upper Rogue River Trail
Access: On Oregon Highway 62, 35 miles northeast of Medford

Lost Creek Lake is a huge expanse of blue water encircled by canyon walls on the western edge of the Cascade Mountains. It is a place of summer warmth, open spaces, cooling water, and several choices of recreation. The park land was once a pear orchard, established by A. J. Weeks. He was the son-in-law of Joseph H. Stewart, one of this country's foremost horticulturists who introduced the commercial orchard to this region and who is honored by this state park.

The campground is on the upper end of the lake, with some view sites overlooking the water. Trees grow along the cliffs but there is much open, sunny space in the campground.

The day-use area and marina are about 0.5 mile further west off Oregon Highway 62 with several picnic areas among the many pines and conifers which accommodate both small and large groups. The swimming area is adjacent to the day-use area, separated from the rest of the lake by buoys and floats, but there is no lifeguard. Open to anglers year-round, the lake has excellent fishing and is stocked with trout and bass. Water-skiers have lots of room to maneuver.

In late summer of bad drought years, the lake can get quite low and activities on the water may be diminished; the swimming area may even be dry. The park is situated on land along the lake's south bank which is leased from the Corps of Engineering.

A paved lane signed with a bicycle design lets bicyclers travel between the day-use area and the campground and east to Peyton Bridge—3 miles of trail through forests and fields. The path is away from views of the lake and runs closer to the highway.

A picturesque hiking path borders the lake atop the cliffs near the campground, accessed easily from any point. One can walk east to Peyton Bridge and then connect to the upstream Rogue River Trail. This path passes viewpoints and goes through shady woods of madrone, pine, red cedar, oaks, evergreen huckleberry, and fir as it crosses creeks with bridges. It then traverses a large open meadow with lovely grasses, California poppies, and huge salsify heads of intricate design. A few steps on Oregon Highway 62, a walk across Peyton Bridge, and you can continue upstream on the Upper Rogue River Trail or jog west to take the North Shore Trail around Lost Creek Lake.

Traveling west on the trail from the campground, one passes a pond, several viewpoints, the marina, and the swimming beach. From there, the South Shore Trail continues on to Casey State Park. The distance between Peyton Bridge and Casey is 8 miles; almost 4 miles of this hiking trail are within Stewart State Park.

Striped coral root, self-heal, Oregon grape, smilacina, wild rose, thimble-berry, vetch, fireweed, mullein, and chicory are just a few of the flora easily discovered along the trails. Butterflies are numerous, monarchs and swallowtails particularly. Habitats for frogs, toads, salamanders, and a variety of reptiles are along the trail.

The park's trails are one of the Oregon State Park Volkswalks. This one is 10 kilometers.

Though Upper Rogue River Trail No. 1034 follows the Rogue from Casey State Park to the river's headwaters, the 48 miles of trail east from Prospect to the headwaters at Boundary Springs, with connections to the Pacific Crest Trail, are the most fascinating.

The river in this area alternates between sections of wild, raging rapids and quiet pools. It is untamed here and no kayak or raft could follow its course because of the huge trees that have fallen into the water. Yet it is a mostly undiscovered hiking trail, with charms that are unsuspected from driving Oregon Highway 62. It can be accessed from several side roads near a string of campgrounds and picnic areas, so it can be hiked in day hike sections or by backpacking.

One can walk and study exciting geology. Lava flows from the Cascades were slowly cut by the Rogue, the "River of Flowing Rock," forming a varied landscape, though the river still seeks an easier route, shown by abandoned oxbows, peninsulas and forested islands. At Takelma Gorge, the river twists and churns through a deep gorge fringed with colorful flowers. The water is diverted into an underground maze of intact lava tubes at Natural Bridge, and emerges in a violent, dangerous release. A collapsed lava tube leaves a long, narrow chute that forces the raging river through it at the Rogue Gorge. In the Winding River Canyon, 250-foot vertical cliffs of pumice have been gashed by the Rogue. Spinning rocks have left potholes. Waterfalls plunge over resistant basalt.

The flora and fauna are also impressive. One sees an ancient forest of Douglas fir and mixed conifers—including massive sugar pines that Douglas searched for and found—as well as alder, yew, vine maple, ferns, and cow parsnip. Wildflowers grow in cracks in swirls of basalt lava and in the wetland and grassy meadow areas. Mossy growth on lava rocks makes for slippery walking in a few places. Chiseled stumps indicate beaver activity. Log jams form pools for cutthroat trout.

Maps and detailed descriptions of these hikes are available at the Forest Ranger Station at Prospect.

JACKSON F. KIMBALL STATE PARK

Hours/Season: Overnight; *campground closed in winter*
Area: 19.4 acres
Facilities: Picnic tables, campground with six primitive sites (maximum site is 45 feet), pit toilets, *no water*
Attractions: Fishing, hiking
Nearby: Sky Lakes Wilderness
Access: Off Oregon Highway 62, 3 miles north of Fort Klamath, accessed from highway from both north and south on a scenic loop road; follow signs to park

A quick jog off the main route to Crater Lake takes you to this quiet park. The primitive camp and picnic tables are nestled under pines and firs along the Wood River, another possibility for overnighting near Crater Lake. Forest birds flit among the trees.

A short trail follows the river and crosses a bridge for a view of the springs that form the headwaters to the river. I startled a grouse there in the brush.

The river widens quickly from its beginnings over rocks in a small pool, and in the short distance to the edge of the campsites it widens into a lake-

Tree reflections on the placid beginnings of the Wood River, Jackson F. Kimball State Park

like affair before it flows onward. The wonderful thing about this shallow lake is its color, a soft green that reflects the tall trees. Sighting downstream, one sees a Cascade peak. Swampy wetlands edge the water. Cows sometimes graze in the pasture across the water, but even so, the sensations are of a wilderness experience.

To the west of Kimball State Park, more than two hundred shallow lakes are scattered on the timbered high plateau that lies on the crest of the Cascades in the Sky Lake Wilderness. Numerous scenic trails zigzag between the lakes, and the Pacific Crest Trail bisects the area as it aims north for Crater Lake. This country is usually free of snow from July through October.

COLLIER MEMORIAL STATE PARK

Hours/Season: Overnight; *campground closed in winter*
Area: 856 acres
Facilities: Two day-use areas with picnic tables, one with a children's play area. Campground has 50 trailer sites with full hookups (maximum site is 60 feet), 18 tent sites, restrooms with showers, firewood, dump station, slide program, phone: (503) 783-2471
Attractions: Open-air logging museum, exhibits, pioneer log cabin, village, 1.5-mile hiking trail, day-use horse rest and exercise area, fishing, gift shop
Nearby: Crater Lake National Park, Klamath Basin National Wildlife Refuges
Access: On US 97, 30 miles north of Klamath Falls

Back in 1826, Peter Skene Ogden, chief trader for the Hudson's Bay Company, passed through this area, no doubt enjoying the attractive scenery. Though many come today to Collier Memorial State Park to see the logging exhibits, outdoor recreation makes them linger.

Day-use areas are located on both sides of the highway. The campground area is on the east side of the highway, a short distance north. The sites are across the Williamson River from the day-use area with easy access to fishing from that side.

As a memorial to their parents, 146 acres of this park were donated in 1945 by Alfred and Andrew Collier, who then began to establish a logging museum. Hundreds of pieces of equipment, from the early days of oxen-powered logging to present time, were gathered and donated by the Collier brothers. It is recognized as one of the finest collections of logging equipment in the country.

Wander through this outdoor logging museum on the west side of the highway to see skidding equipment, steam tractors, loggers' "cats," road graders, trucks, wagons, mighty circular saws, steam-powered Dolbeer donkey engines used to skid logs to landings, and the last boat to haul log rafts across Klamath Lake. Railroad equipment includes a narrow-gauge locomotive, a one-person handcart, a stiff-boom loader, a log buncher, a swing-boom loader, and a track-laying car, all exhibited on railroad track. The steam-generating plant produced enough electricity to run an entire sawmill. A plaque commemorates the breed of men who wore "loggers' boots."

You will see huge sections of sugar pine and Douglas fir trees. One fir—the largest to be cut in Oregon—was a seedling when Marco Polo began his travels, two hundred years before Columbus discovered America. It was toppled in one of the Oregon coast's wild winter storms in 1962, near Seaside, when it was 702 years old, 15.5 feet in diameter, and 200.5 feet tall, even with a broken top. It contained 100,000 board feet, enough wood for ten two-bedroom homes.

Begin or end your logging equipment tour at the authentic logger's homestead, now an information center and gift shop manned by volunteers from the "Friends of Collier Memorial State Park." At first glance, the huge, stuffed Alaskan timber wolf in the loft looks like a bear. Other artifacts and hand tools catch your attention: felling axes, kerosene lamps, a tobacco plug cutter, a drafting table and instruments, a barbed wire display, levers with hinged hooks for rolling logs, and the saddle of Pete French, the cattle baron of Harney County.

Behind this homestead is a blacksmith shed, complete with forge, anvil, bellows, drill press, a collection of harnesses and yokes, and a sling for shoeing draft animals.

Walk north of the museum for a look at a past way of life in a pioneer village. Relocated here are authentic log cabins that include a doctor's of-

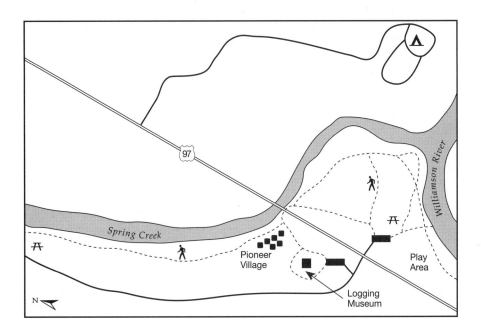

Loggers Homestead and Visitor Center, Collier Memorial State Park

fice, store, sheepherder's wagon, outhouse, explorer's cabin, and one unfinished cabin where the builder was killed before completion. These vary in construction and amenities, from fire pits to cast-iron stoves, from dirt to wooden floors, from dark, crude shelters to glass-windowed homes that let you glimpse a slice of family furnishings inside. As you walk along the paths, notice the signs that identify the various species of native vegetation.

The log cabins are at the edge of lovely, wild Spring Creek. A 1.5-mile trail follows the creek to picnic areas at both ends, passing under the highway bridge. The eastern day-use area is at the confluence of Spring Creek with the Williamson River; both waterways are excellent trout-fishing streams. The river is a mystical sight in early morning when the sun first hits the water and hazy steam rises as the water is warmed. Great blue herons and ducks are silent stalkers along the waterfront.

Collier Memorial State Park is just a few miles southeast of the boundary to Crater Lake National Park, a one-of-a-kind, more-than-a-mile-high, breathtaking blue lake formed in the caldera of a collapsed volcano. Campgrounds in the park are often full during the tourist season so Collier Campground might be a good base.

A 2.5-mile hike to the top of 8,929-foot-high Mount Scott starts from the rim drive at Crater Lake. It will reward you with a bird's-eye view of the landscape around Collier Memorial State Park, as well as an incredible one of the lake and surrounding mountains. The hike is a charmer, though you might want to acclimate to the elevation first. Watch for glacier lilies and pasque flowers if your timing is right.

During fall and spring migrations, birders would be wise to travel to several wildlife refuges in the Klamath Basin. Upper Klamath, Lower Klamath, Tule Lake, and Klamath Forest are all national wildlife refuges that are important stops on the Pacific Flyway. The numbers and varieties of birds are outstanding.

EASTERN OREGON

⚑ Many people never get to the northeastern corner of Oregon, yet it is a place of superlatives. The deepest gorge of our country, Hell's Canyon, edges the Snake River along the state's boundary. The Wallowa Mountains dominate the terrain just to the west of the gorge, magnificent forested peaks that loom above Lake Wallowa. The area has been nicknamed "Little Switzerland" and was once the summer home of the Nez Perce Indians. The winters are extremely cold.

Another mountain range, the Blue Mountains, towers to the west. These steep and rocky mountains were a trial to the pioneers on the Oregon Trail. Today the freeway follows their old route northwest to the Columbia River. Along the way, several of their camp sites are part of the state park system.

The John Day River drains the western slopes of the Blue Mountains and has cut its way through basalt cliffs at Picture Gorge near Dayville, a place to pull out the camera.

Southeastern Oregon is a sprawling high-desert plateau punctuated with rugged canyons, huge ranches, green meadows, craters, and mountains. Temperatures in summer are often downright hot. This is the lonely corner of the state, a place where all is not yet documented. A few good roads exist and many more are strictly for four-wheel-drive vehicles.

An interesting tour goes through historic Blitzen Valley, south of the Strawberry Mountains and the city of Burns, where your senses are flooded with nature's input and your brain with human history. Cattle baron Peter French came to Blitzen Valley in 1872. His round barn and P Ranch headquarters are here, and the Frenchglen Hotel is still signing in guests. Malheur National Wildlife Refuge is along the way, with its marshes, alkaline lakes, and grasslands that attract more than 280 species of birds, including an excellent example of sandhill crane nesting habitat. Oregon's highest

Opposite: *Scenic view along Camas Creek, Ukiah-Dale Forest State Park*

road loops up into Steens Mountain, a massive fault block with splendid valleys, wildflowers, creeks, and trails.

Owyhee country, near the Idaho border, is full of lava beds, river gorges, and sheer walls and pinnacles splashed with colors from pink to chocolate brown—good rockhunting land. Lake Owyhee is downstream of the Scenic Waterway of the Owyhee River. The "Walls of Rome"—eroded cliffs of sedimentary rock capped by lava—are seen in a dry side canyon near where US 95 crosses the river. Colors here are a contrast to the greens and blues of western Oregon—more like the warm-tone canyons of the southwest. Geology buffs will love the area.

HAT ROCK STATE PARK

Hours/Season: Day use; year-round
Area: 756 acres
Facilities: Picnic tables, boat ramp, restrooms, phone: (503)567-5032
Attractions: Unusual rock formation, hiking, swimming, fishing, boating
Nearby: Umatilla Wildlife Refuge
Access: Off US 730, 9 miles east of Umatilla

Hat Rock was the first distinctive Oregon landmark passed by Lewis and Clark on their outbound journey. Clark recorded the sighting in his journal entry for October 19, 1805. The name "Hat Rock" is quite appropriate, as it does resemble a man's silk top hat. The rock has not changed a great deal but the state park would certainly have surprised the explorers with its uncharacteristic well-watered lushness. It is located on the south shore of an arm of a lake formed by McNary Dam on the Columbia River.

A boat dock provides access to the Columbia. The arm of the lake provides a sheltered area for swimming and fishing. A large natural spring on the southern tip of the arm of the lake forms a large pond.

This large pond is a highlight of the park, with its varied wetland associations and cool comfort. Trees and grass shade the walkways that border the pond, cross bridges, pass a water fountain, and access the wooded picnic areas. A multitude of resident ducks and geese are quite friendly. Not so easily approached are the great blue herons, although I saw one heron that was so harassed by a crow punching its rump repeatedly (why, I have no idea) that he might not have noticed me. Kingfishers dive into the water and goldfinches sing in the trees.

This countryside was originally a rolling sagebrush area sloping to the south bank of the river. That type of habitat still surrounds the developed area of the park with Hat Rock looming above, an exposed remnant of a 12-million-year-old basalt flow now speckled with lichen colors. Several foot paths leave the green area from various locations and weave haphazardly up to circle Hat Rock, where I spotted several deer—three does and three bucks with forked antlers—in mid-July.

Hat Rock, namesake of Hat Rock State Park

To the west of the boat ramp, an undeveloped landscape invites exploration as it meanders on bluffs above the river. Summers are hot and dry here with temperatures often over one hundred degrees for several weeks. For those who want to stay in the area longer, a private campground with swimming pool is located across from the park.

Nature enthusiasts might want to visit the nearby Umatilla Wildlife Refuge. From Hat Rock State Park, drive west on Oregon Highway 730 through Umatilla and just past the town of Irrigon to Peterson Ferry Road, where you'll see a sign for this wildlife refuge. This is the unit on McCormack Slough.

When the John Day Dam destroyed critical wildlife habitat, other wetlands were created. These are managed extensively to support bird populations. Local farmers have an agreement to leave part of their crops in the field for the wildlife. McCormack is one of the areas along this 8-mile refuge with public access and space to roam to view wildlife. An informative area map is seen immediately upon entering the refuge, with both roads and hiking trails designated, with hiking also permitted in all open areas. Canoeing is a good way to quietly approach wildlife and enjoy the wetland surroundings with the various plants.

More than 180 species of birds have been recorded in the refuge. The most numerous waterfowl are mallards and Canada geese, especially during spring and fall migrations. Bald eagles, long-billed curlews, and burrowing owls are often seen. Animals include mule deer, coyote, beaver, muskrat, raccoon, porcupine, and an infrequent rattlesnake. For more information, contact the Umatilla Wildlife Refuge Headquarters, U.S. Post Office Building, 6th & "I" Streets, Box 239, Umatilla, Oregon 97882-0239; phone (503) 922-3232.

UKIAH-DALE FOREST STATE PARK

Hours/Season: Overnight; *campground closed in winter*
Area: 2,987 acres
Facilities: Campground with 25 primitive sites (maximum site is 40 feet), restrooms
Attractions: Fishing, nature study
Nearby: Blue Mountain Scenic Byway
Access: Off US 395, 3 miles southwest of Ukiah between Mileposts 50 and 64

The only developed area of this huge, protected forest acreage is at the north end of Unity-Dale Forest, a nice peaceful setting on Camas Creek where you can park by the water and get out your fishing rod. The aroma of wild roses fills the summer air by the rocky-beached water where many tiny fish and crawfish are seen. The steep, narrow canyon of the creek with its grass-covered banks is flanked by forested hillsides that attract many species of wildlife. Ponderosa pine and Douglas fir are found in the lower areas, with larch or tamarack on higher slopes.

The park continues south along the road for 11 miles past the crossing of the North Fork of the John Day River just before ending at Dale. The headquarters of a logging camp once occupied this area. A number of tracts for the park were purchased with grazing reservations, and the U.S. government has reserved the mineral rights in portions.

This park is only a couple of miles from the 130-mile Blue Mountain Scenic Byway, which jogs southeast from Ukiah on Umatilla Forest Road 52, skirts the North Fork John Day Wilderness, and crosses the Wild and Scenic North Fork John Day River before ending at Granite. The route has an abundance of wildlife, recreational options, and historical interest for mining buffs. One might wish to access this park by following the byway from its beginning at the Heppner Junction on Interstate 84 and then continuing on past Ukiah to Granite, where travelers can connect to the Elkhorn Drive.

Rolling wheat fields and an Oregon Trail crossing at Willow Creek are seen enroute to Heppner. From there, Umatilla Forest Road 53 offers panoramic views of the Potamus Canyon before reaching Ukiah-Dale State Park. For information on the byway, contact Umatilla National Forest, 2517 SW Hailey Avenue, Pendleton Oregon 97801, phone (503) 276-3811; or stop at the ranger stations in Heppner or near Ukiah.

RED BRIDGE STATE PARK

Hours/Season: Day use; year-round
Area: 37 acres
Facilities: Picnic tables, wheelchair-accessible restrooms
Attractions: Fishing
Access: Off Oregon Highway 244, 16 miles southwest of La Grande

Just a few miles west of Hilgard Junction, Red Bridge State Park is another shady stop along the Grande Ronde River on the Starkey Highway. The accessible side of the water is generally flat land that faces a steep canyoned wall across the river. Trees are predominately ponderosa pine, but there is also an abundance of cottonwood, poplar, and willows near the stream. The park was once developed for overnight use, but no longer (nearby Hilgard Junction has overnight sites, however). In the past, the old highway bridge over the river was maintained in red paint by Union county, but the new bridge is quite unobtrusive.

View of once-red bridge over Grande Ronde River, Red Bridge State Park

227

HILGARD JUNCTION STATE PARK

Hours/Season: Overnight: year-round
Area: 232.5 acres
Facilities: Picnic tables, campground with 18 primitive sites (maximum site is 30 feet), wheelchair-accessible restrooms, dumping station
Attractions: River rafting access point, Oregon Trail exhibit, fishing
Access: Off Interstate 84, 8 miles west of La Grande

The Grande Ronde River begins in the high elevations of the Blue Mountains southwest of Hilgard Junction State Park, and enters a fairly quiet stretch here in the valley before it continues northeast to its junction with the Snake River just north of the Oregon border. It is an easy place to put a raft into the water and popular with river floaters.

This is along the Oregon Trail route, a place to water and rest before challenging the summit to the northwest. An Oregon Trail exhibit tells about the experiences of these long-distance travelers. A walk along the road west of the park shows good views of the type of landscape traveled by the pioneers in this area.

The park takes its name from a nearby junction of the Union Pacific Railroad line that was named after E. W. Hilgard, former Dean of the College of Agriculture at the University of California. A logging railroad of the Mount Emily Lumber Company once passed through the park area before connecting with the Union Pacific enroute to La Grande.

The picnic and camping areas are quite appealing and relaxing as they sprawl on the bottomland by this fine slow-flowing stream bordered with cottonwoods, willow, and some ponderosa pine. Children fish and play in the shallow river while hip-booted fly fishermen cast long lines into the green water of morning. Swallows glide over the water surface to catch insects, and deer come to drink in the early morning quiet.

EMIGRANT SPRINGS STATE PARK

Hours/Season: Overnight; *campground closed in winter*
Area: 23 acres
Facilities: Picnic tables, group picnic shelter, campground with 18 full hookups (maximum site is 60 feet) and 33 tent sites, Totem Bunk House, restrooms with showers, group tenting, meeting hall, play area, slide program area, firewood, phone: (503) 983-2277
Attractions: Oregon Trail exhibit, nature trail
Nearby: Pendleton Round-Up
Access: On Interstate 84, 26 miles southeast of Pendleton

Modern travelers can pull into Emigrant Springs and camp or picnic under the canopy of yellow, ponderosa, and lodgepole pine trees. Extensive day-use development projects were completed by the CCC in the 1930s, and an overnight camp was added in the 1950s. Oregon Trail information is seen on the north spur from the entry road. The south spur road leads past a covered wagon display to the overnight camp. The Totem Bunk House has two units, each with bunk beds, that can be rented. It is wise to reserve ahead for this or check with the Camp Host.

The plants of the area are identified on a self-guided nature trail that begins near the registration booth and circles through the woods and around the play area to end at the junction of the A and B units of the campground. Be alert for the wildlife that is plentiful in the Blue Mountain area and includes elk, deer, bear, ducks, geese, pheasants, chukar, and a variety of birds.

In January of 1812, trappers and traders of the Astor Overland Expedition, under the leadership of Wilson Price Hunt, crossed the Blue Mountains in this vicinity, afoot in waist-deep snow, and established the route later used by Oregon Trail emigrants. Thousands of pioneers later traveled this way and it was the first forest of evergreen trees seen on their westward trek. These travelers tried to leave in spring so that transit through the mountains was between late August and early October, in order to avoid heavy snowfall. These rugged mountains, blue in the distance, were difficult enough to cross in good weather.

Routes established by horseback were another matter for wagons burdened with heavy loads. To cross the forbidding Blue Mountains, wagons were lifted with ropes and pulleys, and sheer muscle power was needed to slow their descent and keep them from being smashed to pieces.

The park is named for the spring to the west and the fact that emigrants often camped in this area north of the 4,193-foot summit. Besides taking time to refill their water barrels, they easily found firewood in this pine forest watered by mountain rainfall. Wild berries, edible plants, and good hunting made it even more attractive, a welcome change after the arid

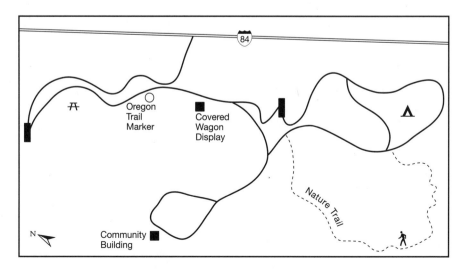

Replica covered wagon exhibit, Emigrant Springs State Park

western stretches of trail. To honor these brave pioneer travelers, a monument was erected at this location and dedicated by President Warren G. Harding on July 3, 1923.

In the 1880s, the trail was replaced by the Oregon Railway and Navigation Company (now the Union Pacific) railroad. During interstate highway construction in the 1950s, trail artifacts were still found in the gulch south of the park.

If you're looking for excitement in mid-September, attend the nearby Pendleton Round-Up, a major western rodeo that attracts some of the best cowboys in the country. After a cowboy breakfast in Stillman Park, visitors can watch rodeo riders compete in calf roping, saddle-bronc riding, bull-dogging, bareback riding, steer roping, and Brahma bull riding. In addition, the local Indian tribes set up tepees and present tribal ceremonial dancing and the Happy Canyon Pageant.

CATHERINE CREEK STATE PARK

Hours/Season: Overnight; *campground closed in winter*
Area: 168 acres
Facilities: Picnic tables, horseshoes, restrooms, campground with 18 primitive sites, firewood
Attractions: Fishing
Access: On Oregon Highway 208, 8 miles southeast of Union

▲ Tenters and RVers who believe in self-sufficiency will find Catherine Creek State Park a place to pull up on the grass beside a clear-flowing mountain stream edged by forest land and enjoy peaceful relaxation or fishing. It's quiet, with considerable charm, and can be reached by a drive with views of the foothills of the Wallowa Mountains. Early mornings are often punctuated with splintered sunlight, shining through the trees onto south-facing slopes covered with sunflowers as wisps of clouds move slowly over fuzzy slopes and rocky projections.

Located near the western fringe of the Wallowa-Whitman National Forest—almost within shouting distance of the Eagle Cap Wilderness—the park is bisected by the creek and extends high on timbered slopes of pine, larch, and cottonwood.

The park focuses on creek accessibility, with two picnic areas strung out along its edge to the southeast of the camping area. The lower one is directly adjacent to these sites; the upper is a short distance further up the road with its own parking area and restroom, but easily walked to from the campground, where I heard kids say, "Let's go to the bridge." A path crosses an arched wooden bridge over the water and continues along the creek for a bit. Horseshoes can be played under the trees as Steller's jays and kingfishers are busy going about their lives. Lichen-smeared rocks jut out of the earth on the hillside across the road in the foreground of the forest.

Entering or leaving the park, the mountain-rimmed valley to the west is a pastoral feast for the eyes as one drives north or south on Oregon Highway 237 from Union. Notice the historic homes in that town as you drive through.

WALLOWA LAKE STATE PARK

Hours/Season: Overnight; *campground closed in winter*
Area: 166 acres
Facilities: Picnic tables, group picnicking, boat ramp, campground with 121 full hookups (maximum site is 90 feet) and 89 tent sites, group club and tent camping, wheelchair-accessible restrooms with showers, dumping station, slide program, firewood, summer reservations available, summer day-use fee for vehicles, concessionaire with water sports rental equipment
Attractions: Hiking, fishing, swimming, boating, photography, wildlife viewing
Nearby: Howard Mountain, Hells Canyon
Access: Off Oregon Highway 82, 6 miles south of Joseph

▲ Among Oregon parks, Wallowa Lake is unchallenged in its combination of uniqueness and charisma. *National Geographic* chose it as one of six outstanding state parks in the far west, and that included Alaska and Hawaii. As visitors drive along the lake to the park, past the burial site of old Chief Joseph of the Nez Perce Indians, they are soon dazzled by the setting of this hidden valley. Called "Little Switzerland of America" and "The Alps of Oregon," the snow-peaked Wallowa Mountains rise to 9,000 and 10,000 feet and hug the southern end of the 4-mile glacial lake at the edge of the Wallowa-Whitman National Forest.

Glaciation occurred here during the late Pleistocene Age, about one mil-

Tree skeletons in Wallowa Lake, Wallowa Lake State Park

lion years ago. The great mass of ice dug deep into sediments below and pushed up lateral moraines to the east and west of the lake, with a terminal moraine to the north. The lake formed in the large, deep hole when the ice receded.

The Wallowa Mountains contain tropical fossil corals, mollusks, algae, and sponges that are identical to those found in the European Alps. One theory suggests that they may have common origins and that continental drift caused ancient groups of tropical islands in the middle of the Pacific Ocean—displaced terranes—to attach to coastlines.

The name of the lake and park, *Wallowa*, is a Nez Perce Indian word for a fish trap for trout and salmon. Tripods of stakes were set on opposite sides of a stream to support a network of sticks in the water that trapped the fish, which the Indians then caught by hand.

Wallowa was the cherished summer home of the Nez Perce Indians where they fished, hunted, and raised pinto ponies in the "land of winding waters." They thought the Treaty of 1855, which reserved the Wallowa country for their tribe, would protect their land, so they were friendly with the first white settlers. Confusion arose in 1877 from other Nez Perce agreements and uprisings, however, and caused young Chief Joseph to try to flee with his tribe to Canada. This long, arduous, thousand-mile journey was only a short distance from success when he was forced to surrender in a snowstorm in Montana.

The park is in two units. The campground and one day-use area are on the lake with a swimming area; the second day-use area is another 1 mile south on the swift-flowing Wallowa River that feeds into the lake.

Deer and golden-mantled squirrels wander among the campsites and the surrounding cottonwood, spruce, western larch, ponderosa pine, and grand and Douglas fir trees. A checklist for the many birds of Wallowa Lake is available in the park. Summer weather is often perfect, though a thunderstorm may blow in.

Canoe paddlers will want to launch into the lake and weave among the picturesque white tree skeletons that have drowned with their roots in the water in the tangle of river inlets. The lake invites a variety of water sports and many fishermen use bait and hook (instead of *wallowa* techniques) to catch Kokanee (landlocked salmon) and several varieties of trout.

Nature trails weave through the park area by the lake and the river. One of the Oregon State Park Volkswalks is located here, 10 kilometers with a 3 rating (5 being the most difficult). Ask for a map at the park.

Two longer trails begin by the south day-use area. One goes up the side of Chief Joseph Mountain for 7 miles, but good lake views are seen by hiking 2.2 miles, with an elevation gain of 600 feet. The West Fork Wallowa River Trail leads into the Eagle Cap Wilderness and an area of alpine lakes—Lake Basin—in 9 miles, but daytrippers can sample segments of this scenic terrain. The Ice Lake Trail that branches off from this trail is one possibility. This is horse country and nearby facilities will rent you a mount and guide you for extended pack trips. Obtain trail information at the ranger's station in Joseph.

A wonderful hike awaits visitors in spring and summer atop 8,200-foot Mount Howard. A short walk from the park accesses the steepest vertical lift for a four-passenger gondola in North America. Fifteen minutes of scen-

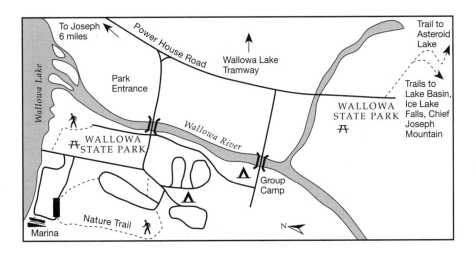

ery later, walk out onto over 2 miles of alpine trails that loop around the summit in the crisp mountain air. Views stretch into four states as you pinpoint a row of peaks that includes Eagle Cap, Chief Joseph, Matterhorn, and Bonneville. Wallowa Lake is like a blue jewel in the western distance, backed by colorful squares of valley farmland.

A short distance east of Wallowa Lake, Hell's Canyon National Recreation Area preserves Snake River country that includes North America's deepest gorge. Most of this area is rugged, undeveloped, varied landscapes. River floaters with permits can choose the 31.5-mile "Wild" section north from the Hell's Canyon Dam to Pittsburg Landing, or the 36-mile "Scenic" section from Pittsburg Landing north to the Wallowa-Whitman National Forest boundary. Nearly 1,000 miles of trails of various difficulty challenge the hiker. About a third of the acreage is designated wilderness and this edges much of the gorge area, but those unwilling or unable to penetrate these undeveloped regions will find much to be recommended in the drives, campgrounds, and hikes of the Imnaha River area west of the gorge.

Good roads access shoreline views of the Snake River north from Oxbow Crossing to Hell's Canyon Dam. One seasonal road leads 54 miles northeast from Wallowa Lake to a precipitous viewpoint of the gorge at Hat Point. Do check on current road conditions for these seasonal roads. Headquarters for the Hell's Canyon National Recreation Area is Box 490, Enterprise, OR 97828; phone (503) 426-4978.

FAREWELL BEND STATE PARK

Hours/Season: Overnight; year-round
Area: 72 acres
Facilities: Picnic tables, boat ramp, fish-cleaning house, campground with 53 electrical (maximum site is 56 feet) and separate area with 43 primitive sites, group tent camping, restrooms with showers in hookup area, dumping station, firewood, summer day-use fee for vehicles, phone: (503) 869-2365
Attractions: Oregon Trail exhibit, birdwatching, swimming, water-skiing, fishing, boating
Nearby: National Historic Oregon Trail Interpretive Center
Access: Off Interstate 84, 4 miles southeast of Huntington

Farewell Bend, between the Snake River and Interstate 84, is the place where one diarist on the Oregon Trail wrote "bid hur a due forever" of the river that had been their visible route for over 300 miles, a fitting spot for a modern campsite. It was also the site where Captain Bonneville, N. J. Wyeth, John C. Fremont, and Wilson Price Hunt camped over the period from 1811 to 1843. The missionary Marcus Whitman guided the first large wagon train through Farewell Bend in 1836. The remains of an old pioneer wagon is seen at the entrance to the park.

Wetland adjacent to the Snake River, Farewell Bend State Park

A ferry to cross the river from Idaho into Oregon was operated by R. P. Olds from 1862 to 1882. The west landing was located 0.5 mile south of the park. Some emigrants stayed in eastern Oregon when they heard of the gold discoveries in the Blue Mountains in 1862, but the gold rush was not long-term. This precipitated many abandoned homes, though some stayed on to farm or log.

When the park was acquired, the open river bank supported a crop of alfalfa, but that has reverted to sagebrush and tumbleweed except for the watered and landscaped picnicking and camping areas. Steep hills are seen across the river, a prelude to the rugged country to the north. Wildflowers add color in spring and summer, and a diversity of rocks can be found in any season. One can wander in the natural areas of the park along the many paths that lead to the water and edge it for a distance to quiet fishing spots

235

along the river's shore. Some call this the "catfish capital," but bass fishing is also good.

Chipmunks and ground squirrels are abundant in the park and wildlife observers can sometimes glimpse deer, antelope, eagles, chukar, and Hungarian partridge. Canada geese are frequently seen with their young in spring, and during late summer—especially in summers of drought—large numbers of geese and ducks are attracted to the edible vegetation growing along the low, nutrient-rich banks of the water and the wetlands across the road. Killdeer flit among them.

Commemorating the importance of the Oregon Trail in the settling of Oregon, the impressive National Historic Oregon Trail Interpretive Center opened its doors to the public on May 25, 1992, as a celebration of the 150th birthday of the Oregon Trail (which is actually in 1993). Follow the well-signed route from Interstate 84, on the north side of Baker City, to Oregon Highway 86, and drive 5 miles east to the top of Flagstaff Hill. The view is a stunning one and gives the visitor a good perspective of the land traveled in this area by the emigrants, with the lush Powder River Valley backed by the Elkhorn Mountains to the west. For the pioneer traveler, the land began to show its promise for settlement here. By 1869, close to 250,000 Americans had made the journey from Independence, Missouri, to Oregon Territory destinations.

The center stresses six major themes: the Oregon Trail Experience, Mining in the West, Explorers and Fur Traders, Natural History of Northeast Oregon, Native American History, and the General Land Office.

Follow in the footsteps of early pioneers by walking the 4.2 miles of the interpretive trail system as it passes an encampment of covered wagons, drops into the valley to a rutted campsite, and passes a lode mine.

The Interpretive Center is open year-round except for Christmas and New Year's Day. For information contact: National Historic Oregon Trail Interpretive Center, Bureau of Land Management, Box 987, Baker City, Oregon 97814; phone (503) 523-1843.

ONTARIO STATE PARK

Hours/Season: Day use; year-round
Area: 35 acres
Facilities: Picnic tables, boat ramp, wheelchair-accessible restrooms
Attractions: Fishing, boating
Access: Off Interstate 84, 1 mile north of Ontario

The attraction at Ontario, just across the Idaho border, is the mile of river frontage on the Snake River which includes Johnson Island with its lush green vegetation and trees. The riverbank is generally level and easily accessed, making boating especially appealing in the hot climate of this area.

The Washoe Ferry crossed near here in the 1860s, north of the mouth of

Johnson Island in the Snake River, Ontario State Park

Malheur River where it flows into the Snake. With six oarsmen to power the ferry, sometimes fees of one thousand dollars a day were earned.

LAKE OWYHEE STATE PARK

Hours/Season: Overnight; *campground closed in winter*
Area: 730 acres
Facilities: Picnic tables, boat ramp and dock, campground with 10 electrical sites (maximum site is 55 feet) and 30 tent sites, restrooms with showers, dumping station, fish-cleaning station
Attractions: Photography, fishing, water-skiing, boating
Nearby: Keeney Pass, Snively Hot Springs, Walls of Rome and Owyhee Scenic Waterway
Access: Proceed a few miles south from Nyssa on Oregon Highway 201 to a signed road for the park, which is 33 miles south of Nyssa

Plan your trip to Lake Owyhee to allow time to enjoy the drive in. The road passes beside the wonders of sculptured rock bordering Owyhee River and through a one-lane rock tunnel, particularly colorful in the early morning or evening hours. Watch for blue herons, cormorants, and fawns drinking in the river. Once past the dam at the northern end of 52-mile-long Owyhee Reservoir, however, concentrate on driving the winding, narrow edges of the canyon for about 4 miles to the park. It's a bit tricky with RVs and boat trailers, but people do it.

A major tributary of the Snake, the river became known as the Owyhee after two Hawaiians, on a fur-trapping expedition for the Hudson's Bay Company in 1819, were attacked and killed by Snake Indians. The spelling is a variation of Hawaii used in that era.

The Gordon Gulch picnic area is separate and about 1 mile north of the camping area, which is on a point jutting out into the lake at Cherry Creek. Weather will determine campsite choices. The lower sites have green shade trees and watered lawns; the upper ones have incredible views, but are scorchers on a hot day. The terrain in the park is rough, steep, and arid, with sagebrush, but the canyon vistas are inspiring with their beautiful colors of purple, brown, gold, rose, tan, and red. One can roam on foot over the hills and into coves on the beach. Rockhounds may find agate and jasper in nearby canyons. A nearby resort to the south has boat rentals.

Boaters and water-skiers merge into a video simulation against the rainbow towers, colorful side canyons, and promontories of the opposing canyon walls. Fishermen throw out lines for trophy bass, trout, and crappie. With binoculars, search the surroundings for deer, antelope, bighorn sheep, pheasant, chukar, quail, and hawks circling above.

This southeastern sliver of Oregon adjacent to the Idaho border is the oldest land area of the state, and probably was the coastal edge about two hundred million years ago. Oregon's most active volcanic period helped structure Eastern Oregon, fourteen million to twenty-eight million years ago, as enormous flows of basalt lava covered most of Oregon east of the Cascades. Later, the runoff from the glacial period and concurrent heavy precipitation accelerated erosion. The Owyhee River was one of the major rivers that sliced through lava plains, creating the large valleys, canyons, and gorges we see today.

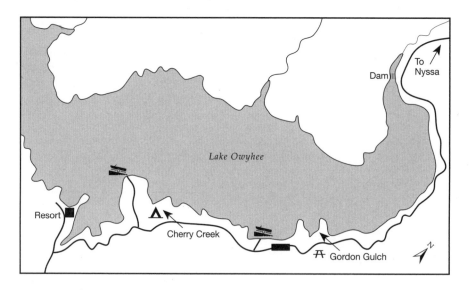

Preparing for water sports, Lake Owyee State Park

A fault, or perhaps a major earth fracture, may have determined the channel of this scenic river, which has cut one of the deepest canyons in the west in a rhyolite flow. Today the Owyhee carries a sizable amount of water only during the spring runoff, yet it is an erosive river at the bottom of a massive granite gorge.

During a short season in most springs—usually April and May—when there is sufficient snowmelt to make the Owyhee River navigable, whitewater rafters can run this most remote of Oregon rivers, with its spectacular canyon walls, abundant birds and wildlife, desert flowers, riverside hot springs, and Indian petroglyphs. Most floaters put boats into the water near Rome, west of Jordan Valley on US 95, and end at Leslie Gulch near Lake Owyhee, about 63 miles and five days later (class 4 rapids).

Anyone in that area should make it a point to head 3 miles north of Rome on an unpaved road to see the Walls of Rome, located on a dry side canyon of the Owyhee. Walk about 100 yards to the base of mile-long cliffs of eroded lake sediments capped by lava.

On the way to Owyhee State Park, visitors pass the Snively Hot Springs, on BLM land, where the road crosses the Owyhee River, about 15 miles north of the park on the east side of the road. A short dirt road leads to this unmarked site where one can fish or soak in riverside hot springs near a cottonwood grove and volcanic cliffs.

Travel north from the park and follow the signs to Vale to arrive at an interpretive site and historic marker on the west side of Lytle Boulevard, a short distance south of Vale. Oregon Trail wagon trains followed this route over Keeney Pass shortly after crossing into what is now the state of Oregon. Though sagebrush has regrown over the ruts left by their wheels, some 4 miles of the original trail can still be walked south of the exhibit.

UNITY LAKE STATE PARK

Hours/Season: Overnight; *campground closed in winter*
Area: 39 acres
Facilities: Picnic tables, boat ramp, campground with 21 electrical sites (maximum site is 60 feet), hiker/biker camp, firewood, dumping station, restrooms with showers
Attractions: Fishing, water sports, swimming, boating
Nearby: Elkhorn Drive
Access: Off Oregon Highway 245, 53 miles east of John Day

A dam was constructed on the Burnt River to provide agricultural irrigation water. On a peninsula on the south shore of the lake that was formed, Unity Lake State Park was created to provide public access to the lake for anglers, boaters, and vacationers. At an elevation of around 4,000 feet, this reservoir is a mini-oasis surrounded by a fairly barren landscape with mountains to the north. Trees have been planted to enhance the park area, and these have grown to a good size and hold several bird houses. Unity Lake State Park is used primarily by people who live in the area, a good gathering place for reunions under the shady trees at water's edge.

Sunflowers at the edge of the Great Basin, Unity Lake State Park

While in this area, don't miss exploring some of the 106-mile scenic byway, Elkhorn Drive. From the park, travel east on Oregon Highway 245 and then north to intersect with Oregon Highway 7. Turn west to take this loop as it borders the Powder River and then enters the Wallowa-Whitman National Forest. You will pass picnic spots, campgrounds, wetlands, and wildlife viewing areas on Phillips Lake before two detours lead to recreational gold panning at the Deer Creek Campground and a ride on a narrow-gauge train. At the Sumpter junction, go north on Oregon State Highway 410 past many reminders of the earlier gold rush and logging days to views of the Elkhorn Mountains. The loop turns east onto FS Road No. 73, past a series of hiking trailheads to the Elkhorn Summit at 7,392 feet. This is prime recreational country and includes the Anthony Lakes ski area and more trailheads before it drops downhill to Baker. For more information, contact the Wallowa-Whitman National Forest, Box 907, Baker, Oregon 97814; phone (503) 523-6391.

CLYDE HOLLIDAY STATE PARK

Hours/Season: Overnight; *campground closed in winter*
Area: 20 acres
Facilities: Picnic tables, campground with 30 electrical sites (maximum site is 60 feet), restrooms with showers, dumping station, firewood, hiker/biker camp, horseshoes, phone: (503) 575-2773
Attractions: Fishing, geology
Nearby: Kam Wah Chung Museum, John Day Fossil Beds/Sheep Rock
Access: On US 26, 7 miles west of John Day

Clyde Holliday State Park is smack in the middle of Grant County's gold and cattle country. The discovery of gold in nearby Canyon Creek in 1862 resulted in $26 million in gold being mined in the John Day/Canyon City area. Cattle ranching started about the same time and is still a mainstay of the local economy. If you're in the area when cattle are being moved between winter and summer pastures, you might see them along the highways and even moving through main streets of local communities.

This park is along a tree-shaded section of the John Day River with well-watered lawns—the park has its own water source for this. The day-use area has a short river access trail that goes east from the restroom. Picnic tables and restful benches for contemplation overlook the river and its riparian vegetation. The Strawberry Mountains are in the background to the south.

Camp sites are near the river but have no views of it. A wetland separates the two parts of the park and birdwatchers will no doubt find several species easily. Lovely shade trees include huge cottonwoods and willows, with several of the species labeled. The campground has a recycling center and the horseshoe pits are found in the hiker/biker camp area.

To get a feel for the geology of the area, look north across the highway to 4,000-foot Mount Vernon Butte, whose southern slopes are eroded on Picture Gorge basalt flows, which slope southwest. The low hill in the foreground, which slopes northwest, is rudely bedded volcanic breccias of the Clarno Formation. The difference in angles is caused by fault movements.

A much larger fault, the John Day Fault, is believed to be buried under

Day-use area along the John Day River, Clyde Holliday State Park

river gravel just south of the day-use area and runs 50 miles east to west along the north foot of the Strawberry Range and along the John Day Valley near Dayville. The principal movement here was eight to ten million years ago, long before the river eroded this wide valley. The movement raised older rock more than 1,000 feet, so the two faults have stairstepped the rocks.

For more area geology, visit the Sheep Rock section of the John Day Fossil Beds, located 31 miles west of Clyde Holliday State Park and just north of Picture Gorge on Oregon Highway 19. This section of the national monument has the Cant Ranch Visitor Center with picnicking and exhibits on geology and local ranching history. Visitors can watch scientists prepare fossils for display. A short trail leads to Sheep Rock Overlook and two other trails lead to Turtle Cove and interesting rock formations. A short distance further on Highway 19 will take you to Cathedral Rock and exhibits at the Foree Deposits, a series of basalt lava flows left by the once active volcanoes of this area.

For a look at some human history, visit the Kam Wah Chung Museum in the city of John Day. This building preserves a structure that served Chinese miners as a general store, trading post, bank and assay office, cultural center, and dispensary of herbal medicines. It was built about 1866 when a large Chinese population was engaged in gold mining—the Grant County census for 1879 shows 2,468 Chinese miners and only 960 Caucasians. The museum is maintained for the park system by a lease arrangement with the city of John Day and is only open during business hours, May to October.

BATTLE MOUNTAIN STATE PARK

Hours/Season: Day use; *closed in winter due to snow*
Area: 420 acres
Facilities: Picnic tables, restrooms
Attractions: Historic site
Access: On US 395, 9 miles north of Ukiah

A stop at this 4,270-foot summit, along a highway less traveled, often finds visitors alone in Battle Mountain State Park. As you read the plaque about the battle fought in this vicinity on July 8, 1878, it is not difficult to go back in the mind's eye to that time and feel the presence of Indians among the rolling golden-green fields that drop to the valley below. Surely there are still artifacts here beneath the soil of the decisive battle of the Bannock War, a war reputed to be the last major uprising of Indians in the Pacific Northwest. The war was started by the Bannock Indians as a protest against white encroachment, but Egan, a Piute, inherited command and led the Bannock, Piute, and Snake Tribes on a wide sweep out of Idaho and through Eastern Oregon into the Blue Mountains to this site, where troops under General Oliver O. Howard defeated him.

The picnic facilities lie on a ridge at the edge of a spur of the Blue Mountains with a view of rolling terrain, a deep canyon to the north, and smaller gulches at the south end of the park. This huge acreage includes a preserve of forest land that is primarily ponderosa pine, larch, Douglas fir, and spruce on both sides of the highway, which was the reason for establishing the park. Scattered wildflowers are those of the high desert. Though there are no established trails, it is easy to do some wandering and not get lost.

In 1935, CCC workers constructed tables, stoves, and a water system. One large outdoor stone fireplace attracts group use during summer when this forested elevation is a good place for a gathering of relatives and friends.

Huge outdoor fireplace built by CCC, Battle Mountain State Park

APPENDIX

WHALE WATCHING

Gray whales migrate yearly from the Arctic to lagoons in southern Baja, California, where they breed and give birth. Their passage off the Oregon coast is south in winter and north in spring, though some linger during the summer along the coast. For those who have never seen them, and for those who want to learn more about these fascinating marine animals, a program is sponsored through the Hatfield Marine Science Center (HMSC) and co-operating agencies during the last week of the year and the week of college spring vacation. During these two weeks, signs pop up at many sites along the Oregon coast that say "Whale Watching Spoken Here." Volunteers are present to help you spot whales and answer questions. Thousands of visitors from throughout the world stop each year to participate in these migration events. Films on gray whales are shown at HMSC.

SITES WITH VOLUNTEERS (NORTH TO SOUTH)

Fort Stevens (parking lot C)
Ecola State Park
Neahkahnie Mountain (historic marker turnout)*
Cape Meares State Park
Cape Lookout
"D" River Wayside*
Inn at Spanish Head (Lobby on 10th floor)
Boiler Bay State Wayside*
Depoe Bay Sea Wall (north end)*
Rocky Creek State Wayside*
Cape Foulweather*
Devil's Rock Punch Bowl*
Pacific Shores RV Park*
Yaquina Head Lighthouse*
Yaquina Bay State Park*
Devil's Churn
Cape Perpetua Overlook
Cape Perpetua Visitor Center*
Cook's Chasm (turnout)*
Sea Lion Caves (turnout just south of tunnel)*
Umpqua Lighthouse*
Shore Acres State Park
Cape Blanco State Park (near lighthouse)*

Battle Rock City Park*
Cape Ferrelo*
Harris Beach State Park*

* *Wheelchair-accessible*

WILD BERRIES

Travelers, and especially hikers, can experience the delectable satisfaction of eating wild berries from June through November as they explore outdoor Oregon. The first of the season, in early June, are the salmonberries, named because their color is like that of the meat of their namesake fish. Their flowers are magenta or light purple. Ripeness of the berries is crucial, and the reason many find these berries not to their taste. Look for plump, deep orange-red specimens that slip easily from the vine. These are found in damp areas.

The picturesque white blossoms of thimbleberries produce bright red berries in sunny locations. When ripe and sweet, this fruit literally squashes in your hand as it detaches, unless you are very gentle. Again, you won't care for them unless they are fully mature. One well-known cook of the Pacific Northwest did a taste test with all the local berries in small pie tarts and found thimbleberries the best.

Both salmonberry and thimbleberry are members of the raspberry family. Blackcap raspberries also grow wild, but they aren't as numerous. Their vines sprawl on the ground and their small black berries are delicious.

Another early berry is the wild strawberry that spreads across foredune areas and hummocks near the beach. Their vines spread horizontally on the sand with red berries following the white flowers. They are very tiny, and you need several to get a good taste of them, but the ripe ones are sweet.

The native blackberry, the dewberry, is a small black fruit from vines that hug the ground with many prickly stickers. It ripens much earlier than the imported blackberries.

Salal berries seem to be everywhere in summer. This purplish black fruit is edible, though not very juicy. Don't eat too many, however, as they seem to have a laxative effect. The Indians used them often, as did David Douglas.

Late in the season, October and November, huckleberries are profuse on their evergreen branches. Small and shiny black, they are good to eat and make great pies, though picking enough is slow. Edible blueberries are often nearby. The deciduous red huckleberry grows in moist coniferous woods. They are too sour to become a favorite. A fool's huckleberry is very similar to the red huckleberry, but it has dry fruit.

Blue elderberries ripen in late August or September and are good for cooking and eating. Red elderberries, however, should be avoided.

The most ubiquitous berries are the Himalaya and evergreen blackberries, large, plump berries that quickly fill containers and are wonderful to eat and use in breads, cobblers, pies, and jams. These ripen in late August in most places.

The purplish blue berries of the state flower, Oregon grape, look tempting, but they are too sour even for animals. One should always be sure of berry identification before indulging, but most of the mentioned ones are easy to distinguish.

GROUP PICNICKING

Armitage State Park
Cascadia State Park
Champoeg State Park
Ecola State Park
Elijah Bristow State Park
Emigrant Springs State Park
Fort Stevens State Park
Jessie M. Honeyman State Park

Milo McIver State Park
Rooster Rock State Park
Silver Falls State Park
Tou Velle State Park
Tumalo State Park
Valley of the Rogue State Park
Wallowa Lake State Park
Willamette Mission State Park

GROUP CAMPING

Beverly Beach State Park
Cape Lookout State Park
Champoeg State Park
Emigrant Springs State Park
Farewell Bend State Park
Fort Stevens State Park
Jessie M. Honeyman State Park

Joseph P. Stewart State Park
Milo McIver State Park
Silver Falls State Park
The Cove Palisades State Park
Tumalo State Park
Valley of the Rogue State Park
Wallowa Lake State Park

HIKER/BIKER CAMPS

Beverly Beach State Park
Bullards Beach State Park
Cape Blanco State Park
Cape Lookout State Park
Carl G. Washburne State Park
Clyde Holliday State Park
Devil's Lake State Park
Ecola State Park
Fort Stevens State Park
Harris Beach State Park
Humbug Mountain State Park

Jessie M. Honeyman State Park
Loeb State Park
Nehalem State Park
Ochoco Lake State Park
Oswald West State Park
Saddle Mountain State Park
Smith Rock State Park
South Beach State Park
Tumalo State Park
Unity Lake State Park
William M. Tugman State Park

HORSE CAMPS

Bullards Beach State Park
Cape Blanco State Park

Nehalem Bay State Park
Silver Falls State Park

YEAR-ROUND CAMPGROUNDS

Beachside State Park
Beverly Beach State Park
Bullards Beach State Park
Cape Lookout State Park
Carl G. Washburne State Park
Champoeg State Park
Farewell Bend State Park
Fort Stevens State Park
Harris Beach State Park

Hilgard Junction State Park
Jessie M. Honeyman State Park
Loeb State Park
Milo McIver State Park
Nehalem Bay State Park
South Beach State Park
Sunset Bay State Park
Valley of the Rogue State Park

RESERVATION CAMPGROUNDS

Beachside State Park: Box 693, Waldport, OR 97394; (503) 563-3220
Beverly Beach State Park: 198 NE 123rd Street, Newport, OR 97365; (503) 265-9278
Cape Lookout State Park: 13000 Whiskey Creek Road W., Tillamook, OR 97141; (503) 842-4981
Detroit Lake State Park: Box 549, Detroit, OR 97342; (503) 854-3346
Devil's Lake State Park: 1452 NE 6th, Lincoln City, OR 97367; (503) 994-2002
Fort Stevens State Park: Hammond, OR 97121; (503) 861-1671
Harris Beach State Park: 1655 Highway 101, Brookings, OR 97415; (503) 469-2021
Jessie M. Honeyman State Park: 84505 Highway 101 South, Florence, OR 97439; (503) 997-3641
Prineville Reservoir State Park; 916777 Parkland Drive, Prineville, OR 97754; (503) 447-4363
South Beach State Park: 5580 S. Coast Highway, South Beach, OR 97366; (503) 867-4715
Sunset Bay State Park: 10965 Cape Arago Highway, Coos Bay, OR 97420; (503) 888-4902
The Coves Palisades State Park: Rt. 1, Box 60 CP, Culver, OR 97734; (503) 546-3412
Wallowa Lake State Park: 72214 Marina Lane, Joseph, OR 97846; (503) 432-4185

CAMPGROUND INFORMATION CENTER

Phone: 1-800-452-5687; Portland and out-of-state: (503) 238-7488. (Service available March through August.) 1-503-731-3411

STATE PARK OFFICES

Salem: State Parks and Recreation Department, 525 Trade Street SE, Salem, OR 97310; (503) 378-6305
Portland: 3554 SE 82nd Avenue, Portland, OR 97266; (503) 731-3293

Tillamook: 3600 E. Third Street, Tillamook, OR 97141; (503) 842-5501
Coos Bay: 365 N. 4th Street, Suite A, Coos Bay, OR 97420; (503) 269-9410
La Grande: 3012 Island Avenue, La Grande, OR 97850; (503) 963-6444
    Oregon Coast Trail Guides, Oregon State Park Volkswalks, Willamette
River Recreation Guides, *Mountain Bike Guide to Oregon* (for a fee), and park
brochures are available from these offices. Write or call for this information.

OTHER INFORMATION SOURCES

Bikeway Program Manager: Oregon Department of Transportation, Room
    200, Transportation Building, Salem, OR 97310; (503) 378-3432 (Oregon
    Coast Bike Route plus Oregon Bicycling Guide maps available)
Bureau of Land Management (BLM): Box 2965, 1300 NE 44th, Portland, OR
    97208; (503) 280-7001
Columbia Gorge Wind Report: call (503) 695-2220 for recorded information
    from April 1 to November 1
National Park Service, Pacific Northwest Region: 83 S. King Street, Suite
    212, Seattle, WA 98104; (206) 553-0170
Oregon Tourism Division: 775 Summer Street NE, Salem, OR 97310; (503)
    378-3451 or 1-800-547-7842
Oregon Trail State *Volkssport* Association: Box 437, Newberg, OR 97132;
    (503) 538-7462, evenings
Oregon Department of Fish and Wildlife: Box 59, Portland, OR 97207; (503)
    229-5403
U.S. Fish & Wildlife Service: 911 NE 11th Avenue, Portland, OR 97232-4181;
    (503) 231-6828
U.S. Forest Service: Box 3623, Portland, OR 97208; (503) 326-2877

PARTIAL SOURCES

Nature

Kozloff, N. Eugene. *Plants and Animals of the Pacific Northwest*. University of
    Washington Press, 1978.
McKenny, Margaret. *The Savory Wild Mushroom*. University of Washington
    Press, 1971.
Niehaus, Theodore F. *A Field Guide to Pacific States Wildflowers*. Houghton
    Mifflin Company, 1976.
Peterson, Roger Tory. *A Field Guide to Western Birds*. Houghton Mifflin
    Company, 1961.
Ricketts, Edward F. and Calvin, Jack. *Between Pacific Tides* (4th ed.). Stanford
    University Press, 1968.
Wiedemann, Dennis, and Smith. *Plants of the Oregon Coastal Dunes*. O. S. U.
    Book Stores, Inc., 1982.

Outdoor Guides

Jones, Phillip N., Editor. *Columbia River Gorge, A Complete Guide.* The Mountaineers Books, 1992.

Plumb, Gregory. *A Waterfall Lover's Guide to the Pacific Northwest.* The Mountaineers Books, 1983.

Thomas, Jeff. *Oregon Rock, A Climbers' Guide.* The Mountaineers Books, 1983.

Willamette Kayak and Canoe Club. *Soggy Sneakers, Guide to Oregon Rivers* (2d ed.). Corvallis, OR, 1986.

Wood, Wendell. *A Walking Guide to Oregon's Ancient Forests.* Oregon Natural Resources Council, 1991.

Geology

Allen, John Eliot. *The Magnificent Gateway.* Timber Press, 1984.

Alt, David D., and Hyndman, Donald W. *Roadside Geology of Oregon.* Mountain Press Publishing Co., 1978.

History

Armstrong, Chester H. *The History of the Oregon State Parks, 1917–1963.* Oregon Highway Department, 1965.

Corning, Howard McKinley, Editor. *Dictionary of Oregon History.* Binfords & Mort, 1956.

Dicken, Samuel N. *Pioneer Trails of the Oregon Coast.* Oregon Historical Society Press, 1971.

Hosmer, James K. *Expedition of Captains Lewis and Clark,* Vol. 2. The Dial Press, 1924.

Lavender, David. *The Way to the Western Sea.* Harper & Row, 1988.

Merriam, Lawrence C., Jr. *Oregon's Highway Park System.* Oregon Parks and Recreation Department, 1992.

O'Donnell, Terence. *That Balance So Rare, The Story of Oregon.* Oregon Historical Society Press, 1988.

Schlissel, Lillian. *Women's Diaries of the Westward Journey.* Schocken Books, 1982.

Sherman, Marty. *Columbia River Gorge.* Frank Amato Publications, 1984.

Williams, Chuck. *Bridge of the Gods, Mountains of Fire: A Return to the Gorge.* Friends of the Earth, 1980.

Writer's Program. *Oregon, End of the Trail.* Binfords & Mort, 1972.

INDEX

ABOUT THE AUTHOR

Jan Bannan grew up amongst the flat cornfields of southern Illinois but felt she had come home when she moved West and found the Oregon Coast. Though she loved biochemical research (but not windowless labs), exploring the outdoors where nature nourishes persuaded her to become a writer/photographer. Now living in Newport, Oregon, Jan has explored the diverse terrain of that state for 15 years. And with her camera she has wandered alone through Baja, taken a Kenya safari, and explored all over the West, taking roads less traveled and hiking many miles into beloved mountains and canyons to make her own discoveries.

Credits include *The New York Times, Oregon Coast Magazine, Wilderness Magazine, The Oregonian, Westways, The Seattle Times,* and a children's book, *Sand Dunes.*

THE MOUNTAINEERS, founded in 1906, is a nonprofit outdoor activity and conservation club, whose mission is "to explore, study, preserve, and enjoy the natural beauty of the outdoors...." Based in Seattle, Washington, the club is now the third-largest such organization in the United States, with 14,000 members and four branches throughout Washington State.

The Mountaineers sponsors both classes and year-round outdoor activities in the Pacific Northwest, which include hiking, mountain climbing, ski-touring, snowshoeing, bicycling, camping, kayaking and canoeing, nature study, sailing, and adventure travel. The club's conservation division supports environmental causes through educational activities, sponsoring legislation, and presenting informational programs. All club activities are led by skilled, experienced volunteers, who are dedicated to promoting safe and responsible enjoyment and preservation of the outdoors.

The Mountaineers Books, an active, nonprofit publishing program of the club, produces guidebooks, instructional texts, historical works, natural history guides, and works on environmental conservation. All books produced by The Mountaineers are aimed at fulfilling the club's mission.

If you would like to participate in these organized outdoor activities or the club's programs, consider a membership in The Mountaineers. For information and an application, write or call The Mountaineers, Club Headquarters, 300 Third Avenue West, Seattle, Washington 98119; (206) 284-6310.

Send or call for our catalog of more than 200 outdoor books:
The Mountaineers Books
1011 SW Klickitat Way, Suite 107
Seattle, WA 98134
1-800-553-4453